# THE GUINNESS BOOK OF
# MONEY

## Leslie Dunkling & Adrian Room

GUINNESS PUBLISHING

*Editor*: Beatrice Frei
*Design and Layout*: Eric Drewery

© Leslie Dunkling and Adrian Room, 1990

Published in Great Britain by Guinness Publishing Ltd,
33 London Road, Enfield, Middlesex

Typeset in Goudy Old Style and Rockwell Light
by Ace Filmsetting Ltd, Frome, Somerset
Printed and bound in Great Britain by
The Bath Press, Bath, Avon

'Guinness' is a registered trade mark of
Guinness Superlatives Ltd

British Library Cataloguing in Publication Data
Dunkling, Leslie, 1935–
    The Guinness book of money.
    1. Money, history
    I. Title    II. Room, Adrian
    332.4'9

ISBN 0–85112–399–6

# THE GUINNESS BOOK OF
# MONEY

# CONTENTS

# MONEY

## ORIGIN OF THE WORD

The word 'money' derives from the name of a Roman goddess, Juno Moneta, wife of Jupiter and model of dignified womanhood. There was a festival known as the Matronalia which women celebrated in her honour on 1 March each year. Juno's title 'Moneta' was explained by the third century BC Roman poet Livius Andronicus as a translation of the Greek name Mnemosyne, 'memory'. Others have seen it as a reference either to Juno's role as an adviser to women or as a reminder to Romans of favours granted them in the past. Whatever the true explanation, Moneta is clearly linked with the Latin *monere* 'to warn, remind'.

From the time of Camillus (d. 365 BC) Roman coins were made in a building adjoining Juno Moneta's temple, which stood on the northern summit of the Capitoline Hill. 'Moneta' was used at first to describe this particular *mint*, and later any place where *money* was made. Both words derive from Moneta via the French *monnaie*.

Curiously enough, Juno Moneta was not the Roman goddess of money. The antiquarian William Camden commented: 'And albeit money had no temple erected to it at Rome for a long time, yet it was as much honoured as either Peace, Faith, Victory, Virtue. Afterward, when all God's gifts were by pagans made gods and goddesses, Money was also enshrined by the name of *Dea Pecunia*, in the figure of a woman holding a pair of balances in one hand and cornucopia in another: unto whom I doubt not but as many commit idolatry now as then.' (*Remains Concerning Britain* (1605))

## DEFINITION OF 'MONEY'

H. G. Wells once pointed out that money 'means in a thousand minds a thousand subtly different, roughly similar, systems of images, associations, suggestions and impulses'. Nevertheless, a working definition would be *anything which is generally acceptable as a means of settling debt*. In sophisticated economies this usually means notes and coins, which represent claims on banks and the government. It could otherwise be anything which possesses intrinsic value, such as pieces of gold, cattle, etc.

More individual definitions are possible: 'Money—a substance known in America as "the poor man's credit card" and in Russia as "the element that makes stupidity shine".' (*Money Talks*, William Davis)

**"**

### THE PHILANTHROPISTS

'Nah! Nah! Nah! You got it all wrong! It's not money that I'm after! No publisher is! If I was after money I wouldn't be in this business. My dear boy . . . You got it all wrong! Publishers don't make money! Nah! Nah! Nah! . . . I thought you knew that.'

Thomas Wolfe *The Web and the Rock*

**"**

# PREFACE

There is a famous scene in *Dombey and Son*, by Charles Dickens, where the five-year-old Paul suddenly asks his father, 'Papa! what's money?' 'What is money, Paul?' replies the father, disconcerted. 'Money?' 'Yes,' says the child, looking his father in the eye, 'what is money?'

That is the question we set out to answer in this book. Dickens tells us that Mr Dombey would like to have given his son 'some explanation involving the terms circulating-medium, currency, depreciation of currency, paper, bullion, rates of exchange, value of precious metals in the market, and so forth,' but realising that this might not be appropriate for a five-year-old, he contents himself by answering, 'Gold, and silver, and copper. Guineas, shillings, half-pence.'

We have provided a rather more elaborate answer to Paul's question along those lines, with chapters on the history of coins and paper money, mints, banks and the like, together with an account of how money circulates. We also quote many a Mr Dombey, who believes that 'money can do anything', that this 'very potent spirit' causes those who have it 'to be honoured, feared, respected, courted, and admired'. Money, Mr Dombey tells his son, makes a person 'powerful and glorious in the eyes of all men'.

To Mr Dombey's amazement, Paul is not very impressed by such statements. If money can do anything, he remarks, why didn't it save his mother's life? Why is it that he himself is not strong and well? Money isn't cruel, is it? he continues.

Others have asked such philosophical questions, and we have quoted many of their thoughts. Dickens himself constantly returns to the subject of money in his novels, exploring the effect it has on those who worship it, on the misery as well as the happiness that it can bring about. Our greatest writers have had much to say on such matters. Whatever their individual ideas about a need for wealth, all have seen that money is indeed 'a very potent spirit' which cannot be ignored.

This book, then, is not a guide to investments, a text-book in economics or a list of money-making ideas. It does not promise its readers that they will increase their personal wealth as a result of reading it. Its main premises are that everyone should give some thought to the development of the modern monetary system, since everyone must live within it; and that our attitude to money is almost as important as money itself.

In the present work, Adrian Room has made himself mainly responsible for the historical and factual aspects of the subject; Leslie Dunkling has been more concerned with the literary and philosophical parts. We hope that the combination of these two approaches will interest and entertain those readers who may have paused to ask, like young Paul Dombey: 'what is money?'

> ## A CRANK SHAFT
>
> *'Monetary questions crop up so constantly in the newspapers, form so large a part of the substance of political and economic controversy, and above all, attract so many cranks that it has become indispensable for intelligent people to know something about them.'*
>
> G. D. H. Cole, *What Everybody Wants To Know About Money* (1933)

# 1
# THE CREATION OF CASH

## ORIGIN OF MONEY

In ancient times, money was closely linked to religion and worship. The very word 'money' originates from Moneta, the title of the Roman goddess Juno, meaning 'she who warns', and the mint (which word also comes from her name) was the workshop that stood by her temple. (See also p. 6)

The Bible is full of references to the corrupting power of money. Jesus, who threw the money-lenders out of the temple, himself said that it was easier for a camel to go through the eye of a needle than for a rich man to enter into the kingdom of God. St Paul gave us the famous quotation: 'the love of money is the root of all evil'.

Gold, too, as a tangible form of money, has similarly featured as a corrupting force in many myths and legends. All that King Midas touched turned to gold—so that his very food was transmuted and he could not eat. In the Bible, again, the Israelites who turned away from God to worship the Golden Calf had their idol melted down and pulverized by Moses as a punishment for their apostasy.

In world literature, some of the most memorable characters are misers. One is Volpone, who in Ben Jonson's play of the same name, announces:

> Good morning to the day; and next, my gold:
> Open the shrine, that I may see my saint.
> Hail the world's soul, and mine.

A match for him is Harpagon, the rich miser who is the main character in Molière's play L'Avare ('The Miser').

Nearer our own day there is the infamous Scrooge, in Dickens's A Christmas Carol: 'a squeezing, wrenching, grasping, scraping, clutching, covetous old sinner', though in the end, of course, Scrooge reformed.

Gold, too, has its positive and favourable associations as well as its negative and unfavourable ones. After all, gold was one of the gifts, symbolizing royalty, that the Three Wise Men brought to the Infant Jesus.

## UNMAPPED TERRITORY

*'Two convenient ways of discussing money present themselves. The first, the traditional, is to treat money as the development of a particular type of portable property and trace its progressive specialization as an intermediary in barter. The second is to consider money as the medium through which the general economic life of mankind is now being conducted and to criticize the laws and conventions determining its use from the point of view of the racial welfare.*

*'There are still imperfectly explored gaps between the current conclusions attained by the one process and those reached by the other. In these still unmapped gaps lie the psychological processes by which money has achieved its present cardinal importance in economic life.'*

H. G. Wells *The Work, Wealth and Happiness of Mankind*

## MONEY AND GOLD

So what actually *is* money, and how did gold come to be equated with it?

We take money for granted today, and think little about the coins and banknotes in our pockets, purses and wallets, except for how much—or how little—they will buy until we get some more from somewhere. Increasingly, too, we have less and less to do with actual money for financial transactions. Coins and notes have to a large extent been replaced by cheques and credit or debit cards, and we are rapidly moving towards a cashless society. The latter makes good sense, after all, and is a simple and logical step. We buy something, and the amount is debited to our bank or building society account. We sell or earn something, and the amount is credited to our account in a similar manner.

Yet even in a cashless society, the amounts themselves are expressed in monetary terms, in pounds and pence, dollars and cents, francs and centimes, or whatever the currency is.

If we stop to think about 'real' money for a moment, as we still know and use it today, we find that it is rather a remarkable thing. What we basically do when we buy something is simply hand over a collection of metal discs or pieces of paper. The person we give them to readily accepts them, without question, despite the fact that those discs and pieces of paper are worth much less than what we get in exchange for them. If we were to try to buy something with similar objects—metal washers, say, or pieces of paper exactly the same size as the banknotes—we should get a very strange (or even angry) look. This would happen even if we engraved a value on the washers, or printed a sum on the pieces of paper.

As children, we soon learn two important things about money. The first is that only *official* money is any good for buying things. We have to use the coins and notes issued by the government, and 'homemade' money, unlike other goods or objects in domestic demand, is not only unacceptable but absolutely illegal. The second thing we learn is that everybody, by mutual agreement,

## THE ROOT OF ALL EVIL?

In Jamaica there is a plant called both Lucky Lily and Dumb Cane. The latter name refers to the fact that if someone sucks its stem, it causes his salivary ducts to swell and makes it temporarily impossible for him to speak. Lucky lily is the name for the white-spotted variety of dumb cane, since there is a widespread belief that if a small amount of money is buried at its root, it will attract a great deal more.

In his novel *A Cool Day For Killing*, William Haggard tells a similar tale of the magnolia tree: 'It was widely believed the tree brought good fortune. It brought prosperity in general but in particular it bore that fine thing gold, and the sensible man who planted one buried gold amongst its seedling roots.'

``

## DON'T BLAME MONEY!

*'Money is the most convenient thing in the world: we could not possibly do without it. We are told that the love of money is the root of all evil; but money itself is one of the most useful contrivances ever invented: it is not its fault that some people are foolish enough or miserly enough to be fonder of it than of their own souls.'*

G. B. Shaw *The Intelligent Woman's Guide to Socialism, Capitalism, Sovietism and Fascism*

``

accepts money for buying and selling purposes, even though no one is going to use the metal coins as actual metal objects, or the paper for any of the purposes to which it is usually put as a material (writing, printing, wrapping, cleaning and the like).

Having reflected on this, we are likely to wonder further about money. Why, for example, do we specifically use metal and paper as the two materials for our currency? Who introduced coins and notes to serve as money? What did people do before there were coins and notes, when they wanted to buy or sell something?

## TRADING WITHOUT COINS

Coins were invented around 3000 years ago. Before that, payments were made in one of two ways.

The first way was to use currency other than coins. Archaeological and historical researches have shown that cowrie shells and bronze tools were used for payment in ancient China, for example. Gold rings were used in Egypt and grain served as money in Mesopotamia.

The second way, in which something closer to modern trading was involved, was to barter one object or commodity for another. A hunter, for example, would exchange his hides and meat for the corn that he wanted from the farmer, who in his turn needed the skins for clothing and the meat for food. Archaeologists have discovered a barter contract from ancient Egypt dating back to about

1100 BC. The contract is written on a stone, and details the bartering of a bull for a variety of goods, including grain, oil, honey, cloth and wood. One of the great disadvantages of a bartering system, however, is that the parties have to agree how much or how many of one commodity is worth an equivalent of the other. How many hides are worth how much corn? How many pigs are worth two cows? For that matter, in societies where women are commodities, how many goats are worth a bride?

One solution to this difficulty is to give the bartered goods a value by weight, and to relate that weight to a metal. This was what the Egyptian contract did, specifying that both bull and goods were worth 119 *deben* weight of copper.

From using metal weight as a value, it is clearly just one logical step to using the metal itself as the actual currency in the form of coins. This is why the names of many coins and currencies today still have a 'weight' meaning as well as a 'value' meaning. Britain thus has the pound sterling and the pound in weight, and until relatively recently France similarly had the *livre* as both a coin and a weight.

Both the use of non-coinage payment systems and the practice of bartering continued to exist long after the introduction of coins. Today, for example, cowrie shells are still traditionally used as money in parts of India, Thailand and East and West Africa, while salt is similarly used for payment in some areas of Ethiopia. In modern times of war, both cigarettes and alcoholic drink have been used for bartering purposes, while after

### MATE'S RATES

Bartering of a kind still goes on, even in modern western societies. New Zealanders, for example, who sell goods or offer some kind of professional service, recognize what they call 'mate's rates'—discounted rates offered to friends. A plumber will work cheaply for his friend who happens to be, say, a paper-hanger. Naturally, the paper-hanger will charge only mate's rates when he does some work for his friend the plumber.

World War II cigarettes were used as actual money in occupied Germany. The British soldier who was issued with 50 free cigarettes a week was thus being 'paid' as properly as the soldier elsewhere who was getting his weekly pay in coins and notes.

**Shells**, and cowrie shells in particular, make good money, for although they are nothing like coins to look at, they are relatively identical in shape and size, are easy to handle, easy to find nat-

urally, and easy to count. One could even say that, like the best coins, they are attractive in appearance. The popularity of cowrie shells for currency has led to one species being given the scientific name of *Cuprea moneta*, 'money cowries'.

**Cattle** have also been popular as currency from pre-classical times. They are a symbol of wealth, and the Mycenean coin called the 'talent' was made of bronze and actually shaped like a cow's

## BARTER IS BETTER

Thomas Ashe, author of *Travels in America in the Year 1806*, describes the bartering methods of farmers and store-keepers he encountered on the Allegheny River: 'Money is not always necessary as a circulating medium. The words *buy* and *sell* are nearly unknown here: in business, nothing is heard but the word *trade*. Will you trade your watch, your gun, pistols, horses, etc. means will you change your watch, gun, etc. for corn, pigs, meal. But you must anticipate all this from the absence of money.'

Ashe says that all the hard money goes to the great landholders who live in the cities. He describes what happens when the farmers visit the stores with their excess produce: 'They receive in return nothing but an order on a store for the value in goods; and as the wants of such persons are few, they seldom know what articles to take. The store-keepers turn this circumstance to advantage, and frequently force on the customer a thing for which he has no use, or which is worse, when the order is trifling, tell him to sit at the door and drink the amount, if he chooses. As this is often complied with, a market day is mostly a scene of drunkenness and contention, fraud, cunning and duplicity, the store-keeper denying the possession of a good article till he fails in imposing a bad one. I have known a person ask for a pair of shoes, and receive for answer that there were no shoes in the store, but some capital gin that could be recommended to him.' (See also RUMMY MONEY, p. 129.)

## THE TRUE MEANING OF MONEY?

'The true meaning of money yet remains to be popularly explained and comprehended,' says Theodore Dreiser in his novel *Sister Carrie*. He then goes on to give what is presumably his own 'popular explanation' of this important matter: 'When each individual realizes for himself that this thing primarily stands for and should only be accepted as a moral due—that it should be paid out as honestly stored energy, and not as a usurped privilege—many of our social, religious, and political troubles will have permanently passed.'

Having confused everybody thoroughly, Dreiser continues snobbishly: 'As for Carrie, her understanding of the moral significance of money was the popular understanding, nothing more. The old definition: 'Money: something everybody else has and I must get,' would have expressed her understanding of it thoroughly. Some of it she now held in her hand—two soft, green ten-dollar bills—and she felt that she was immensely better off for the having of them. It was something that was power in itself. One of her order of mind would have been content to be cast away upon a desert island with a bundle of money, and only the long strain of starvation would have taught her that in some cases it could have no value. Even then she would have had no conception of the relative value of the thing; her one thought would, undoubtedly, have concerned the pity of having so much power and the inability to use it.'

## WRITING ABOUT MONEY

J. K. Galbraith has an interesting essay on *The Language of Economics* in which he refuses to accept the common complaint that writers on economic subjects are especially obscure. The essay defines good economic writing as needing: to express the personality of the writer; to involve the reader in the matter being discussed; to display a certain amount of humour. The latter, says Professor Galbraith, shows that the writer is able to detach himself from his subject, a necessary ability in any scientific enquiry.

Professor Galbraith, whose own writing provides a model for all to imitate, particularly recommends Adam Smith's *The Wealth of Nations*, putting that author above John Stuart Mill. He also points to Thorstein Veblen, whose book, *The Theory of the Leisure Class* (1924), he believes to have influenced the behaviour of the American rich. It was Veblen who introduced the concepts of 'conspicuous consumption' and 'conspicuous leisure', subjecting the rich to sardonic disdain.

Veblen's prose, says Professor Galbraith, may be involuted and pretentious, constantly struggling for effect, but it resourcefully drives home his point. He quotes the following passage from Veblen's book to allow his readers to judge for themselves:

'Since the consumption of these more excellent goods is an evidence of wealth, it becomes honorific; and conversely, the failure to consume in due quantity and quality becomes a mark of inferiority and demerit.

'This growth of punctilious discrimination as to qualitative excellence in eating, drinking, etc. presently affects not only the manner of life, but also the training and intellectual activity of the gentleman of leisure. He is no longer simply the successful, aggressive male—the man of strength, resource, and intrepidity. In order to avoid stultification he must also cultivate his tastes, for it now becomes incumbent on him to discriminate with some nicety between the noble and the ignoble in consumable goods. He becomes a connoisseur in creditable viands of various degrees of merit, in manly beverages and trinkets, in seemly apparel and architecture, in weapons, games, dances, and the narcotics. This cultivation of the aesthetic faculty requires time and application, and the demands made upon the gentleman in this direction therefore tend to change his life of leisure into a more or less arduous application to the business of learning how to live a life of ostensible leisure in a becoming way.'

hide. In Latin, too, the words for 'cattle' (*pecus*) and 'money' (*pecunia*) were directly related. Other animals served similarly, as we are reminded in the old story of Jason, who in classical mythology led the Argonauts to capture the Golden Fleece—the fleece of pure gold that was the coat on a miraculous winged ram. The mythological hero was not searching for some exotic animal but for great wealth and riches. If he had been an American in the 19th century he would have been a gold rush pioneer!

**Stones** have also been used as money, and continued to be so until the last century in some of the Caroline Islands of the Pacific. There, 'small' coin-age existed in the form of circular aragonite stones measuring about 50 cm *20 in* across, while the 'large' coins, used for important payments, were bigger stones measuring up to as much as 4 m *12 ft* in diameter.

Although money, in its earliest forms, is certainly ancient in origin, its historical emergence is lost in the mists of time. The origin of **coins**, on the other hand, and certainly of **banknotes**, can be dated much more accurately. A key factor in the introduction of coinage—the use of metals as weights—has already been mentioned. For a more detailed look at the story of coins and modern currencies a separate chapter is needed.

## LOLLY, SPECIE, DIBS

The popularity of money at all levels of society is reflected in the number of slang terms it attracts. Many of the terms have only a temporary existence, or are restricted to a particular group of speakers. Some live on only because they were incorporated into literary works. In *The Lay of the Old Woman Clothed in Grey*, for instance, part of *The Ingoldsby Legends* by Richard Harris Barham, occurs the following piece of fractured verse:
'Money!
In one just at Death's door it was really
    absurd
To see how her eye lighted up at that word
Indeed there's not one in the language that I
    know,
(Save its synonyms 'Spanish', 'Blunt', 'Stumpy'
    and 'Rhino',)
Which acts so direct, and with so much effect
On the human sensorium, or makes one erect
One's ears so, as soon as the sound we
    detect.'

Charles Dickens has Sikes, in *Oliver Twist*, saying: 'It's all very well, but I must have some blunt from you tonight.' 'I haven't a piece of coin about me,' replies Fagin.

'The alpha and omega of it all was money,' writes Bob Shilling, in *All the Bees and Honey*. The pen-name has suitable monetary connections, and most British readers would recognize that the title of the novel is rhyming slang for 'money'. The author makes the point that other terms exist by continuing: 'Money, lucre, dough, ackers, readies, spondulicks, the folding variety. The secret of a happy life was to make enough of it not to have to go after it any more. Yes, money was what it was all about.'

In his *Times* column (February, 1990), Griff Rhys Jones writes: 'Think of the cost of going primitive! To lie in rags beneath a banyan tree eating fruits and nuts and doing bugger all needs serious dosh.'

The American writer Robert Gover, in his *One Hundred Dollar Misunderstanding*, has a passage where many slang expressions for money, or dollars, are used. He puts them into the mouth of a black working girl, and assumes that the middle-class white to whom they are addressed will not understand them. 'Ain you got no jack? He say, Huh? I say, Ain you got no skins, no kale? No bread? No bones, no berries, no boys?'

*Dog Day Afternoon*, by Patrick Mann, has a similar slang-laden conversation about money: 'I need bread,' Littlejoe said conversationally. 'Gonna ball Lana tonight, man, and that broad don't ball without I lay a few solid blasts on her.'
'How much bread you need, man?' Sam asked.
'Double saw?'
'Too heavy. I got two fives to my name.'

Tallulah Bankhead, in her autobiography *Tallulah*, writes: 'I succumbed to radio offers only when poverty-stricken. The need for moolah led me to make a frontal attack in the spring of '41, just as I was about to entrain for Reno . . .'

Below is a check-list of these informal terms for money, which are either used now or have been used in the past in different parts of the English-speaking world. A brief indication is given where possible of derivations, but many of the terms are very obscure.

Ace
Ackers
Actual
Addlings (nautical, for pay
    accumulated during
    voyage)

Allow (at Harrow School, for
    weekly pocket money)
Aste
Ballast (nautical)
Balsam (because of its
    healing qualities)

Bangers
Bank rags
Bawbees
Beans
Bees (for bees and honey)
Bees and honey (Julian

Franklyn, in his *Dictionary of Rhyming Slang*, thinks that 'this holds first place among rhyming slang terms on account of its appropriateness: bees symbolize work, work produces money, the possession of which is sweet.' He adds that the expression was first recorded at the end of the 19th century.)

Berries

Billies

Biockey

Bit

Blood

Blunt (hence blunted = in money)

Boodle (possibly from Dutch *boedel* 'property')

Boot (tailor's and shoemaker's slang for an advance on wages)

Brads (especially copper coins. Brads were shoemaker's rivets)

Brass

Bread (possibly from Bread and honey, a variant of Bees and honey. But gingerbread was in earlier use.)

Browns

Bullets

Bunce (also found as bunse, bunts. Possibly a form of 'bonus'.)

Buttons

Cabbage

Cake

Chinkers

Chinks ('Have chinks in thy purse' Ben Jonson)

Chips

Clams

Cod's roe

Cog

Coigne

Coin

Cole

Courage

Cush(el)

Darby

Dibs

Dimmock

Dinero (Spanish for 'money')

Dirt

Do-re-mi

Dosh (West Indian)

Dots

Dough

Duckies

Dues

Dust

Folding stuff

Funds

Gelt (Yiddish, from Old High German *gelt* = reward)

Gent (probably from French *argent* 'money')

Gingerbread

Gold

Gravy ('Is Luke in the gravy?' 'What a gross expression. He shows no signs of being rich at all.' J. I. M. Stewart *The Last Tresilians*)

Green

Greenbacks

Greenies

Hay

Hoot

Iron

Jack

Jimmy O'Goblins

Juice

Kale (seed)

Kotchel

Kylege

Lean green

Lettuce

Lolly (from lollipop, rhyming slang for drop, in its meaning of to tip or bribe someone.)

Long green

Loot

L.S.D. (see p. 21)

Lump

Mazuma, the old

Means

Metal

Mint sauce

Mon

Moolah

Mopus

Moulies (copper coins)

Muck

Mulla

Necessary

Needful, the

Nuggets

Ochre (from colour of gold)

Oday

Oof, ooftish (Yiddish, ultimately from German *auf dem Tisch* 'on the table'. This was where the money had to be before one played cards for money. An oofbird was a supplier of money, oofless meant poor, oofy was another word for rich)

Oscar (from Oscar Ashe (1871–1936), a well-known actor at one time, rhyming on cash.)

Packet

Paint

Palm soap (especially for money used as a bribe)

Pazaza

Pelf

Pile

Pitch

Pocers

Possible

Potatoes

Readies

Ready

Reek

Rhino (see p. 117)

Ripple

Rivets
Rocks
Roll
Rowdy
Rubbish
Sausage and mash (rhyming on cash)
Scads
Scramble
Scratch
Sea-coal
Shekels
Simoleons
Smash (loose change, rhyming on cash)
Snow

Spanish
Specie
Splosh
Spondulix (thought to derive from a Greek word for a species of shell once used as currency)
Stumpy
Suds
Sugar (originally rhyming slang, sugar and honey?)
Syrup
Tin (and hence the rhyming slang expression 'tin tank' for a bank. 'Monstrous nice girl . . . Lots of tin, I

suppose, eh?' William Thackeray, *Vanity Fair*)
Tom and funny
Toot (from 'whistle and toot' rhyming on loot.)
Tusheroon
Velvet
Wad
Wampum
Whackers
What it takes
Wherewithal
Whistle and toot
Wonga
Wood
Yennom (back slang)

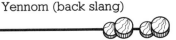

## ECONOMICAL ECONYMY

The word 'economy' is derived from Greek and literally means 'house-management'. In onomatology, or the study of names, the word 'econymist' is sometimes used. It is pronounced in exactly the same way as 'economist' and means either someone who names a house or a person who studies house-names.

What appear to be house-names with a money connection are sometimes seen in English suburbs. 'Farthing', however, is usually a reference to a measure of land,

while 'The Pound' normally refers to an enclosure. At least one house called 'Sixpence' is owned by a Tanner family. References to mortgages are found in 'Cobwebs' (currently owned by the Woolwich Equitable Building Society) and the rather poetic 'High Loaning'.

Perhaps 'Conclusion' would make a suitable house-name for an economist, alluding to the well-known saying, attributed to G. B. Shaw, that 'If all economists were laid end to end, they would not reach a conclusion'.

# 2
# MONEY IN THE ROUND

## COINS

It was the only way we could fit you on the coin your excellency

The story of money is essentially the story of coins. So where did the first **coins** originate?

It has now been conclusively established that coins were invented in the late 7th century BC by the Lydians. These were a Greek people who lived in what is now western Turkey. Before this time, as elsewhere, the Lydians had been using weighed pieces of metal for payment. But they realized that it would be sensible and helpful to stamp such pieces of metal with marks that guaranteed their value when they were presented for payment. The idea soon caught on, and within a hundred years of the Lydian innovation, coins were widely adopted throughout the Greek world.

However, by our standards, such early coins were crude and cumbersome, and simply looked like roundish, heavyish pieces of metal with a stamp on one side. The stamps themselves varied, and at first were not the familiar human heads that we now expect to see on coins. Coins issued in Athens, Corinth and Aegina in the 6th century BC

showed either a badge of state, a winged horse (Pegasus) or a turtle. These latter symbols were specifically linked with the last two cities mentioned, so that a trader from Corinth took his 'Pegasus badge' with him to other cities, and anyone from Aegina could be recognized by his 'turtle' money.

### COINS AND METALS

One important question when introducing actual coins, of course, is the choice of **metal** for making them. And the more basic question arises: why metal and not any other material?

Clearly, a medium for making coins was needed that was durable, malleable and easily handled. As value, too, was essentially involved, whatever was used should have intrinsic worth.

As mentioned in the previous chapter, metals were already in use for payment in the form of weighed, sized pieces. Since these pieces already possessed the desired qualities, especially for purposes of stamping, it was logical to continue to use them in the new adapted form.

The matter of value was obviously important. Ideally, a coin was to be regarded as actually worth the value of the object or service for which it was exchanged. For this reason, it was the so-called precious metals, **gold** and **silver**, that were at first exclusively used for making coins.

But there was, and is, a difference between these two! Gold is more valuable than silver, so how did it happen that silver was the metal that was chiefly used for making coins? Why not use the most valuable metal, rather than the next most valuable?

The reason is that, for standard, everyday coinage, gold was *too* valuable. Although both metals were found naturally in rock formations, gold was scarcer, as it was found only in a free state, that is, in uncombined form. Silver, on the other hand, although not common, could be found both in the free state and in combination with other metals. This scarcity of gold posed difficulties of size and quantity when used to make a coin that was worth the value of a purchased object. The amount of gold needed to buy a loaf of bread, for example, would have been tiny—so small that it would have been impractical to make a coin of such size. Gold would therefore have been of use only for extremely large transactions. (Even as recently as the 19th century, when gold guineas were in use, other metals were used to provide the coins needed for everyday transactions.)

Silver was therefore the prime metal used for coins in the early stages. It was just right: it was valuable, but not too valuable, and there was enough silver available in the ground naturally for it to continue to be mined and utilized for the foreseeable future. Moreover, it had not only all the ideal qualities mentioned for making a coin, but it also looked attractive, with a brightness and sparkle that hinted at its special value.

Not for nothing does the ordinary French word for 'money', *argent*, still have its main basic meaning of 'silver', from Latin *argentum*.

Of course, there are other metals besides gold and silver, some precious, some not. But the best known would have been, again, either too valuable, like platinum (discovered in South American gold mines in the 18th century) or too common, like iron.

What the Lydians often did, however, to get the best of both worlds, was to issue not only silver coins but coins made from an alloy of silver and gold. This could be obtained naturally from the sands of river beds, as one of the combinations in which silver was found, and was known as **electrum** (from the Greek word *elektron*, meaning 'amber', referring to its pale yellow colour). One such Lydian electrum coin, dating from about 600 BC, had a design showing a horse's head.

## THE PHILOSOPHER'S STONE

It was commonly believed in medieval times that there existed a substance which would turn any base metal into gold. The search for this 'philosopher's stone' was one of the chief pursuits of the alchemists, who were also trying to discover the 'elixir of life', which would enable them to live for ever. The experiments of the alchemists occasionally led to discoveries of genuine value, and gave rise to the modern science of chemistry.

One of Ben Jonson's best comedies is *The Alchemist* (1610). Face, Subtle and Dol Common delude various people, holding out to them the promise of the philosopher's stone. Charles Dickens deals with the subject in a minor way in *The Lamplighter*.

## DOLLAR COINS

In 1989 yet another attempt was being made by two American congressmen to introduce legislation which would lead to a dollar coin. Mr Morris Udall and Mr Jim Kolbe suggested that the coin should be made of American-mined copper. Three-fifths of that copper comes from Arizona, as do the congressmen.

Although there are strong arguments in favour of a dollar coin, the American public does not seem to favour the idea. When the Susan B. Anthony dollar was introduced in 1979, complaints from all sides forced it to be withdrawn almost immediately. There are said to be 465 million Anthony dollars stored in mints and Federal Reserve banks across the country.

Another, of about the same date, was rather more ornate, showing a feeding stag and a Greek inscription translating as 'I am the seal of Phanes'. No one knows who Phanes was, but clearly the stag was his personal seal. By having the coin stamped with his badge like this, Phanes was guaranteeing the coin's value as money.

## OTHER COIN INVENTORS

Although the Lydians are now generally accepted as the inventors of coinage, it is fair to mention that there are two rival claimants. These are the Indians and the Chinese. Recent scholarship disputes both these bids, since it seems likely that India derived her coinage from the Greeks in about the 4th century BC. Although the Chinese may well have invented coinage independently, it is almost certain that they did so later than the Lydians.

Gold and silver were not, of course, the only metals to be used for coins. It was in the late 5th century BC that Greek cities in what is now southern Italy and Sicily began to make coins from **copper**. They introduced these to replace the small silver coins that up till then had been used for relatively small payments. The new copper coins were given a value that was actually more than they were worth as metal objects, so that they

were much more like the coins that we know today. The current British £1 coin, for example, is really a virtually worthless brass alloy token.

About a century after the Greeks, the Romans introduced *their* copper coinage, with the one difference that the original coins were valued according to their actual metal content, as the earlier gold and silver coins had been. At the eastern end of the Greek world, in the city of Olbia (near modern Nikolaev, in the Ukraine), on the northern shore of the Black Sea, a third copper coinage arose, based on the earlier use of uncoined **bronze** as currency. Subsequently, both the Romans and Olbians used their bronze coinages instead of silver coins, as the Greeks had originally done.

From that time on, gold, silver and bronze coins soon came to be adopted in other countries of the western world.

## THE GOLD STANDARD

Although gold was used only sparingly for coinage, for the reasons mentioned, the metal itself came to be regarded as the accepted standard by which currencies were measured internationally. This is the origin of the **Gold Standard**, as it is now known. In a sense, gold has become a kind of world currency (rather than actual coinage), which countries use for settling international debts. Moreover, the Gold Standard long served as a benchmark for exchange rates, that is, for the prices at which one country's currency could be converted into another. But World War I disrupted world trade and international payments, and all participant countries then dropped the Gold Standard. Although Britain returned to the Standard in 1925, it proved almost impossible to equate a particular amount of gold with the value of a pound. The result was that the Gold Standard broke down, and the pound was 'floated', finding its own level against other currencies.

The United States, on the other hand, preserved a limited form of Gold Standard for the dollar until as recently as 1971, when President Nixon put an end to the convertibility of the dollar into gold.

**"**

## THE YELLOW SLAVE

Timon: *What is here?*

*Gold? Yellow, glittering, precious*
   *gold? . . .*
*Thus much of this will make black*
   *white, foul fair,*
*Wrong right, base noble, old young,*
   *coward valiant.*
*. . . This yellow slave*
*Will knit and break religions, bless*
   *th'accurs'd,*
*Make the hoar leprosy ador'd, place*
   *thieves,*
*And give them title, knee, and*
   *approbation,*
*With senators on the bench. This is it*
*That makes the wappen'd widow wed*
   *again.*
*. . . Come, damn'd earth,*
*Thou common whore of mankind, that*
   *puts odds*
*Among the rout of nations, I will make*
   *thee*
*Do thy right nature.*

William Shakespeare *Timon of Athens* 4.iii

**"**

The Gold Standard illustrated a curious paradox: whereas gold had been chosen as money because it was valuable, it actually became valuable because it was used as money, in particular for minting coins of the highest or rarest denominations.

## GOLD, SILVER AND COPPER COINS IN MODERN TIMES

Despite the demise of the Gold Standard, gold coins do still exist. They are normally not for ordinary circulation, but are for sale to collectors as an investment. One well-known example is the present krugerrand of South Africa, exactly one ounce of gold in weight.

Britain had gold sovereigns (value £1 each) as ordinary circulating coins till World War I. There

 **BRITANNIA**

The Britannia gold bullion coin was launched by the Royal Mint on 13 October 1987. The coin comes in four sizes, having face values of £100, £50, £25 and £10 according to weight. Their price varies from day to day depending on fluctuations in the gold market.

The issue of these coins represented the first major development in the gold coinage of the United Kingdom for more than a century and a half. The gold sovereign had been extremely popular with collectors, but had come under attack from such coins as the South African krugerrand, the Canadian Maple Leaf, the American Eagle and the Australian Nugget.

Britannia herself has been associated with coins since the reign of the Roman emperor Hadrian (AD 117–138). She reappeared on the new copper halfpennies and farthings, authorized by Charles II in 1672, as a seated figure with spear and shield. Her face, it is thought, was that of Frances Stuart, Duchess of Richmond, the King's favourite. Sir William Petty wrote in 1682: 'Upon the account of beauty our *Britannia* half-pence were almost all hoarded as medals till they grew common'.

were also gold coins with a value of £5, £2 and half a sovereign (10 shillings). After the War no gold coins circulated, and in 1966 a law was passed which made it illegal for any British residents to hold more than four gold coins unless they had been licensed as genuine coin collectors by the Bank of England. This order was revoked in 1971, so that today residents of the United Kingdom may freely buy, sell and hold gold coins.

Silver coins have really gone the same way as gold coins. Until as recently as the turn of the 20th century, the value of an ounce of silver was that of one-sixteenth of an ounce of gold. Up to 1920 all British silver coins were actually struck in standard silver, this being a 92.5 per cent alloy of pure silver. The coins included the crown (five shillings), half-crown (two shillings and sixpence), shilling, and sixpence. In 1920 the proportion of silver in the alloy was reduced to 50 per cent. From 1947 all so called 'silver' coins have been struck from cupro-nickel, with the exception of Maundy money, still struck in sterling silver, and the 20p piece, which is minted from an alloy of 84 per cent copper and 16 per cent nickel, so that it is even 'baser' than the other silver coins.

Even copper coins have been 'downgraded'. In 1860, bronze coins were introduced in Britain to replace the former copper coinage, mainly for the penny, halfpenny and farthing. Today, 'bronze' means an alloy of 97 per cent copper, 2½ per cent zinc and ½ per cent tin. (These proportions have varied a little over the years.)

Of all silver coins, one of the best known was not the crown or shilling but the **dollar**.

The original silver dollar was struck in the early 16th century from silver mined at Joachimsthal ('St Joachim's valley') in northern Bohemia, now

### SILVER DOLLAR JIM

The nickname of James M. West, a Texan millionaire, was 'Silver Dollar Jim'. He used to carry pocketfuls of silver dollars and throw handfuls of them onto the ground because he enjoyed watching people scramble for them. When he died, nearly 300 000 silver dollars were found hidden in his house.

### FACE VALUE

*The Enchanted Profile* is a short story by O. Henry. It concerns a very rich woman who wants to adopt a young woman as her daughter, because 'her face is exactly like a dear friend of mine, the best friend I ever had'. At the end of the story we learn that the profile of the young lady is a 'dead ringer for the lady's head on the silver dollar'.

Jáchymov in northwest Czechoslovakia. It was known as the *Joachimsthaler*, and later simply as a *Thaler*. The word, on transatlantic soil, then gave the word 'dollar'. A whole family of silver dollars arose in different countries throughout Europe, as the chief standard silver coin, until the first American dollar was struck in 1794. It was issued as a silver coin until 1935, so has a more or less parallel history to the British silver shilling as far as its metal content is concerned.

### NAMING THE COINS

As coins became more sophisticated, they mostly adopted a regular format, especially in Europe and subsequently in the New World. They were uniformly round, flat, sometimes had milled edges, and came to be recognized by their distinctive pictorial features and inscriptions, normally with a portrait on the obverse ('heads' side) and some other national or regional device on the reverse ('tails'). To serve as actual currency, their value also needed to be stated in single or multiple units. The head on the obverse (hence 'heads') was usually that of a reigning monarch or ruler, or of the mintmaster who had issued the coin. The reverse often bore a religious or patriotic device, such as a cross or the representation of a national personage such as Britannia.

But before any of the finer points could be regularized, the coins themselves needed to have names. As with older or historic names generally, these frequently developed naturally. So it was not surprising that many coins came to be named after the particular **weight** that they had come to represent. The *pound* is a classic example. In the UK it is still sometimes necessary to define 'pound' when buying something: does the purchaser (or seller) mean 'pound in money' or 'pound in weight'? Some foods, such as meat and vegetables, are even 'a pound a pound', i.e. 1 lb costs £1. The names of both the former French *livre* (as a coin) and present Italian *lira* go back to the Roman *libra*, which was the basis for all monetary dealing and which was divided into 12 ounces (*unciae*). (In actual weight, though, the Roman pound was lighter than the present avoirdupois pound, equalling 327.45 g as against the present metric correspondence of 453.56 g.)

Reminders of this particular origin exist in the modern standard abbreviation for each kind of pound, for 'lb' is simply short for 'librae' and the pound sign (£) is just a crossed letter 'L', standing for the same word.

A similar name is that of the tiny copper coin called the *grano* ('grain'), formerly circulating in Italy and Malta. Some still current coins have an even more basic name to mean simply 'weight' itself. Examples are the South American *peso* and the familiar Spanish *peseta*. The latter word is a diminutive, meaning 'little weight'. The Israeli (and biblical) *shekel* also has 'weight' as its meaning, as did the biblical *talent*. (English 'tolerance' in the sense 'permissible range in weight or other variation' derives directly from the same source.)

Even more basically, some coins came to be known by a word that merely means 'money' or just 'coin' itself. This is more common for eastern countries, such as the Chinese *cash* (*not* related to English 'cash'!), the Japanese *sen*, which was based on it, and the well-known Japanese *yen*. These last two mean exactly the same: 'round thing', 'coin'.

Many coins took their names from the **metal** in

## RAZOO

In Australian and New Zealand slang this is a non-existent coin of trivial value, a 'farthing'. The word often occurs in the phrase 'brass razoo' (and is also spelt rahzoo, razhoo). It is always used negatively, as in statements like: 'Richards never has a rahzoo.' 'I wouldn't give you a razoo for that.' 'He hasn't got two brass razoos to rub together.' Razoo has been in use since at least 1930, but its origin is unknown.

## L.S.D.

These letters were used to refer to British money in general before decimalization. They are usually explained as the first letters of the Latin words *librae* 'pounds', *solidi* 'shillings' and *denarii* 'pence', though since many early money-men in Britain were Italian, they may represent Italian *lire*, *soldi* and *denari*.

In *The Small House at Allington*, by Anthony Trollope, Amelia comments on John Eames's interest in L.D. She means Lilian Dale, the heroine of the story. 'L.S.D.', replies Eames. 'That's my love—pounds, shillings and pence, and a very coy mistress she is.'

Hood says of his Miss Kilmanegg that she learns her L.S.D. before her ABC (see p. 178—THE WOMAN WITH THE GOLDEN LEG). Dickens has a character in one of his *Christmas Stories* use the word 'L.S.D.-ically' to mean financially.

It is, of course, pure coincidence that L.S.D. is also the popular name of the hallucinatory drug Dextro-lysergic acid diethylamide 25.

which they were minted, and which earlier would in a number of cases have been used as weights. They include the *aureus*, the standard gold coin of Ancient Rome, the Dutch *guilder* and Polish *zloty*, whose names also mean 'gold', the Roman *argenteus* ('silver') and the homely American *nickel*. This last name is that of the 5-cent piece and refers to the cupro-nickel alloy (25 per cent nickel, 75 per cent copper) from which it has been regularly minted since the 19th century.

Some coins came to be named after their **colour, size** or **shape**. A run of former French silver coins were known as the *blanc* ('white'), while the formerly popular *anna* had a name that meant simply 'small'. Some size and shape names are really nicknames, such as the English *cartwheel* penny (both size and shape), the heavy 2-penny piece struck in the reign of George III, and the crudely minted 50-dollar gold coin called the *slug*, issued in California during the mid-19th-century gold rush.

Size, too, lies behind the names of such coins as the former Italian *grosso*, which derives from Latin *grossus*, so merely means 'big'. In fact, several coins got their 'big' names from this origin, such as the *gros*, the *groschen* (literally 'little gros'), and *grosz*. It may come as a surprise to find that the *groat* has the same meaning, despite having been a small coin. This is because the name was used in the Middle Ages for all thick silver coins, and the better-known little silver groat worth 4 pence was a much later development, struck only in the 19th century.

A similar name was that of the Roman *solidus*, the standard gold coin introduced by Constantine the Great in place of the aureus (see above). Its name means what it says, 'solid', otherwise 'thick and heavy'. It came to be divided into 12 denarii (silver 'pennies'), and with them and the larger Roman libra, of which it was one seventy-second part, set the pattern for the English pounds, shillings and pence, abbreviated as '£.s.d.', or *librae, solidi, denarii*. Not only that, for it gave the name of the French *sou* and Italian *soldo*. (Today, the normal Italian word for 'money' is the plural of this, *soldi*.) Nor does the influence of the *solidus* end there, for it gave the standard English word *soldier*, originally referring to the pay given to men who joined the army, then coming to be used of the men themselves, the 'paid ones'.

It is possible, too, that the *shilling* may have a

## MISS PENNY—MEET MR FARTHING

Many surnames that look like money names actually *are* money names.

If your name is **Farthing**, your ancestor could have been a person who paid a farthing's rent. Or he could have been nicknamed Farthing because he was small. The original farthings were pennies cut into four to make change, and one of these pieces would have been small in both size and relative value. Otherwise, the name could have been used for a person who lived on a 'farthing' of land, the fourth part of a larger area.

A person called **Halfpenny** could have been similarly named: either for the rent he paid or because he was small in size or significance. As with farthings, the original halfpennies were pennies cut in two.

By contrast, a person nicknamed **Penny** would have been regarded as someone of value. The penny was the only unit of coinage until the 14th century, when the gold noble was introduced. The name **Pennyman** means 'servant of Penny'.

More obviously, a person named **Money** would have been given the nickname because he was rich, or because he was a moneyer by trade.

Someone named **Moneypenny**, though, could have been rich or miserly. The name actually means 'many pennies', so the 'money' is misleading.

The surname **Shilling** probably came to England from German-speaking countries (as *Schilling*), and like Penny could refer to a rent or fee paid or have resulted from some anecdote involving a shilling.

The name **Besant** is still found. This comes from the name of a gold coin that circulated in medieval times. It took its name from Byzantium, where it was originally minted. A person named Besant would have been rich, or possibly a coiner.

The surname **Minter** means what it says, 'moneyer', 'person who works at a mint'. **Coyne** means the same—although it could also refer to a miserly person.

But if your name is **Pound**, this will not have come from the monetary value. The name arose to describe someone who lived near a pound where animals were kept. Even so, in the Royal Navy people named Pound are often nicknamed 'Quid'

The name **Cash** does not mean what it says, either. It originally denoted a maker of cases, otherwise chests or boxes.

The surnames **Stirling** and **Dollar** both derive from Scottish place names.

name somehow derived from *solidus*, although the link has not been definitely proved.

Easily one of the most common names for a coin is the one that describes its **value**, almost always in multiples. (The roman *as*, however, had a name that simply meant 'unit': first unit of weight, then monetary unit.)

Bearing in mind that the most common multiples are 2, 4, 10, 100 and 1000, and the most common divisions correspondingly ½, ¼, 1/10th, 1/100th and 1/1000th, here are some of the best known such coin names, after their English numerical equivalent:

2: *double* (and so *doubloon* as 2 pistoles);

4 or ¼: *farthing* (¼ of a penny), *quarter* (25 cents, or ¼ of a dollar);

10 or 1/10th: *denier*, *dime* (10 cents or 1/10th of a dollar), *dinar*. (The American dime gets its name from French *dixième*, 'tenth': the other coin names come from Roman *denarius*, whose own name means 'containing 10', as it was originally a silver coin containing 10 *asses*.)

100 or 1/100th: *cent* (100 to a dollar), *centime* (100 to a franc), *centimo* (100 to a peseta), all from Latin *centum*;

1000 or 1/1000th: *mill* (1000 to a dollar), *millime* (1000 to a dinar), both from Latin *mille*.

Almost as common as value names are names referring to a distinctive **feature** represented on the coin. The American 10-dollar coin known as

## PENNY PLACES

Some places in the British Isles have a name based on 'Penny' or other money words, but they are not always what they seem.

**Penny Bridge**  a village near Ulverston, Cumbria, is named after a local family called Penny.

**Pennycomequick**  a district (and pub) of Plymouth, Devon, is named after a former prosperous farm.

**Pennyfarthing Street**  Salisbury, Wiltshire, was formerly a small and insignificant lane.

**Sixpenny Handley**  a village near Cranborne, Dorset, has a name that really means 'Hill of the Saxons'. Even so, it was designated on signposts as '6D HANDLEY' before decimalization, and as '6P HANDLEY' after.

**Shillingford**  Shillingstone and Shillington, respectively villages in Devon, Oxfordshire and Bedfordshire, have names that derive from a personal name such as Sciella or Scytla.

**Stirling**  the town in central Scotland, has a name of uncertain origin.

**Dollar**  not far from it (and so 'in the Stirling area'), has a name that probably means 'ploughed field'.

However, field names usually do have a specific reference to money, and denote either their value or the rent paid. John Field's *English Field Names* (1972) includes the following under the different values:

Penny Bank, Penny Close, Penny Croft, Penny Field, Penny Furlong, Penny Hill, Penny Lands, Penny Mead, Penny Meadow, Penny Moor, Penny Patch, Penny Piece, Penny Pingle, Penny Prick, Penny Wood. (Some of these may have been round in shape, like a penny.)

Twopenny Close, Threepenny Copse, Fivepenny Slack, Sixpenny Mead, Tenpenny Bit, Twelve Pence, Four Shillings Croft, Five Shilling Meadow, Seven Shilling Worth, Twenty Shilling Field, Five Pound Piece.

Fields called Farthing were often so named as they were the fourth part of a larger area, although some may have been ironically nicknamed for the value of the land. Others may have belonged to a family named Farthing. Fields named Halfpenny were probably also named ironically, although some may have been named for their rent or value in the normal way. One such name has become famous as the birthplace of cricket: Broad Halfpenny Down, near Hambledon, Hampshire.

an *eagle*, for instance, had this bird on its reverse in a heraldic pose, the 'eagle displayed'. The former British *florin* preserved the name of the gold coins of Florence, which in the 13th century bore a lily, or fleur-de-lys, on the reverse, this flower being the badge of Florence itself. (The precise origin lies in the Italian word *fiorino*, 'little flower'.)

Perhaps best known are those coins whose names derived from the religious or royal symbol that they bore or still bear. Among them are the *crown*, the *cruzeiro* ('cross'), the *escudo* ('shield') and the *leu* ('lion'). Since such symbols are virtually international, at any rate in the western world, names of identical meaning can be found in different languages. Among other 'crowns', for example, are the *corona*, *krona* and *krone*, and other 'lions' include the former Dutch *leeuw*, Venetian *leone* and present Bulgarian *lev*.

The intimate relation between heraldry and currency is everywhere evident, therefore, in both figures represented and names given.

**Personal names** are equally prominent for coins, and as mentioned are often those of the ruler in power when the coin was first struck. They can range from the silver Roman *antoninianus*, named after the emperor Marcus Aurelius Antoninus, who introduced it in AD 215, to the *george*, the 5-dollar coin issued in Canada in 1912 which bore the head of George V, and from the Swedish *carolin* introduced in 1664 by Charles XI (whose name in Latin is Carolinus) to the projected but never realized British *Victoria*, planned as a possible decimal issue at the end of the 19th century, and named after the Queen.

This last name could equally have been regarded as a tribute to the Roman goddess of victory, Victoria, so it should not be assumed that all coins with personal names derive from that of a monarch or ruler. The *george noble*, for instance, issued under Henry VIII in 1526, bore a representation of St George and the Dragon, and the small 17th-century Irish coin called a *patrick* was similarly named after the country's patron saint.

Sometimes coins have been named after the ruler's **title** rather than his or her name. Familiar examples are the *sovereign* and the different coins that simply have the word 'royal' in the appropriate language, such as the *real*, *rial* and *riyal*.

In recent times, some currencies have been named after their **country of origin**, or after the race of that country. Among them are the *afghani*, introduced in 1926, the *somalo*, which was current from 1950 to 1960, and the *zaïre*, first circulated in 1967. Names of this type can also be much older. The obvious example is the *franc* as the French national currency.

This last well-known name probably originated from the actual inscription on the coin in the 14th century, which was FRANCORUM REX, 'king of the Franks', referring to Jean le Bon (John the Good) who was reigning at its time of issue.

One other equally familiar coin name, that of the *ducat*, also derives from its Latin inscription. The first gold ducat was issued in Venice in 1284 and bore the motto, in abbreviated form (because of the limited space): SIT. T. XTE. D. Q. T. V. REG. ISTE. DUCAT. This stood for the rhyming couplet:

Sit Tibi, Christe, Datus
Quem Tu Regis, Iste Ducatus.
('Unto Thee, O Christ, be dedicated this Duchy which Thou rulest.')

These two inscriptions have thus given the names of two of the best-known European coins, with the franc still familiar today.

## PECUNIARY PET-NAMES

In a *Times* article (November, 1989), Bernard Levin wondered how the British public had fallen into 'the horrible usage' of referring to a penny or pence as 'pee'. He thought this was a reflection of the fact that, with the introduction of decimal currency, the British people had ceased to love their currency. They had previously humanized their coins, and more importantly, had given them nicknames. Mr Levin cited the 'throopnee joey', the 'tanner' or 'sprasi', the 'bob', the 'two-bob bit' and the 'half-a-dollar'.

It would have been possible, said Mr Levin, to nickname the decimal coins. (He suggested 'nothing' for the 5p, 'garbage' for the 10p, 'useless' for the 20p, 'dross' for the 50p, 'ugly' for the £1. Nicknames were not given to the new coins and notes, however, since they no longer had a meaning apart from their function.

British coins and notes had indeed attracted a large number of nicknames over the centuries. Most have disappeared from normal speech, but references to them occur in literature. In *Down and Out in Paris and London* (1933), for example, George Orwell gives the following conversation in which two Londoners use nicknames for money which were current at the time:

'In front of the fire a fully dressed man and a stark-naked man were bargaining. They were newspaper sellers. The dressed man was selling his clothes to the naked man. He said:
'''Ere y'are, the best rig-out you ever 'ad. A tosheroon for the coat, two 'ogs for the trousers, one and a tanner for the boots, and a 'og for the cap and scarf. That's seven bob.''
"You got a 'ope. I'll give yer one and a tanner for the coat, a 'og for the trousers, and two 'ogs for the rest. That's four and a tanner.''
"Take the 'ole lot for five and a tanner, chum.''
"Right y'are, off with 'em.'' '

A check-list of British nicknames for coins and particular sums of money is given below:

**Farthing**   Covent Garden (rhyming with farden); fadge; fudge; Harrington (Lord Harrington obtained the patent of coining brass farthings in 1613); jack; rag

**Half-penny**   brown; meg (also used for a guinea); tanyok; tiddler (the decimal half-penny, half-heartedly known by this name. It was the smallest coin ever minted in Britain)

**Penny**   Abergavenny; coal heaver or heaver, rhyming slang for stiver; debblish (South Africa); Kilkenny; nose and chin (rhyming on 'win'); robin

**Twopence**   dace

**Threepence**   currant and plums (rhyming with thrums); Dora Gray (rhyming with tray = three); joey (used earlier for the fourpenny piece); thrumbuskins; thrummop; thrumms

**Fourpence**   Flag (for the groat, which was a coin worth fourpence); joey

**Sixpence**   bandy; bender; buck (as a final element in expressions like 'three-and-a-buck'); crinkle-pouch; cripple; crook; crook-back; downer; engineer's spanner (Merchant Navy); gen; goddess Diana; fiddler (fiddler's money meant small change, especially sixpences); kick (in later use as final element—'two-and-a-kick', etc); lord of the manor (sometimes lady of the manor); pig; sice; sow's baby (alluding to its size in relation to the hog, or shilling); sprarser; sprasi; sprat; syebuck; tanner; tartan banner (World War I army slang); tilbury; tizzy

**Tenpence**   (old style) dacha-saltee (from Italian *dieci soldi*)

**Shilling**   Abraham's willing; Barney Dillon (Scottish, to rhyme with shillun); beong; bianc; bionc; black dog (counterfeit); blow; bob; borde; breaky-leg; deener/deaner; dog's dinner (to rhyme with deaner); door knob; hog; kettle (on the hob); one for his (k)nob; riverina (to rhyme with deaner,

Australian); Robert; rogue and villain (rhyming with shillun); Thomas Tilling—a man well-known as a supplier of horse-drawn vehicles and horses; touch me, short for touch me on the knob. ('Touch someone for a touch me' meant to borrow a shilling)

**Two shillings** swi (Australian, suggested by German *zwei* 'two')

**Half a crown** Alderman; half-a-dollar; half an Oxford (rhyming slang, short for Oxford scholar); Poddy calf (Australian, rhyming on half. A poddy calf or lamb is motherless and brought up on a bottle); trooper; tusheroon (also tosheroon)

**Four shillings** ruof (back slang)

**Five shillings** caser; dollar; Oxford (scholar), rhyming on dollar; shirt and collar

**Ten shillings** cock and hen, (rhyming on ten); cow's calf (rhyming on half); half a bar; regent (i.e. half-a-sovereign)

**£1** bar; berry; bradbury; cow's lick = nick(er); couter (cooter); dragon; glistener (i.e. the sovereign); harlequin; heartsease; jane; jemmy (O'Goblin); lost and found; merry go round; nicker; oncer; quid; rainbow (suggested by rhino?); saucepan lid (rhyming on quid); stranger; sufferer; wuffler (also used for a guinea); yellowboy

**Guinea** bean/bien; Jimmy O'Goblin (sovereign); meg; ned; remedy; stranger (also used of a sovereign); wuffler

**£5** fiver; flimsy; handful; horse; Jack's alive; Lady Godiva; pangy; pennif

**£6** exes

**£10** Big Ben

**£20** score

**£25** pony; macaroni

**£50** half a ton

**£100** big one; C; C-note; century; hun; long one; one bill; oner; ton

**£200** twoer

**£500** monkey

**£1000** big one; cow; grand; g; k (in recent use).

The Americans have also bestowed pet names on coins and notes. Some of those recorded in various slang dictionaries are given below:

**1 cent** meg; red

**2 cents** dace

**5 cents** fish scale; jip; jit; jitney; medio; nickel; picayune (mentioned e.g. in *Uncle Tom's Cabin*); thrip

**10 cents** deemer; dime; dimmer; dimmo; hogg; short bit; skinny; smooth; thin one

**12.5 cents** bit; real; yorker

**25 cents** bird; cute or kute; quarter; quetor; two bits

**50 cents** turkey

**$1** ball; banger; bat; berry; boffo; bone; buck; buckeroo; can; cartwheel; case; Charlie Roller; checker; clam; copek; crum; dollo; fish; frog-skin; hoot and holler; iron man; lamb's tongue; one-spot; peso; piastre; plug; plunk; rag; seed; shekel; shiner; simoleon; single; sinker; slug; smacker; thumb nail; wagon wheel; whacker; wheel

**$2** deuce; two case note

**$5** Abe's cabe (from world of jazz. Cabe refers to cabbage, slang term for money. Abe to Lincoln, who is on a five dollar bill); fin; finiff; five-case note; fiver; five-spot; V; V spot

**$10** ned; sawbuck—a kind of wooden trestle with the legs projecting above the crossbar, so that they form an X at each end. The X taken as Roman ten; tenner

**$20** double sawbuck

**$25** hat

**$50** F; half C

**$100** bill; C note; century; yard

**$150** buck and a half

**$500** five C note; monkey

**$1000** grand; horse; thou

**$5000** five yards

**$10 000** X-ray

# 3
# HAMMERING IT OUT

## MINTS

All modern coins, of course, emanate from a mint. The word 'mint' has long implied not simply an establishment that literally 'makes money', by striking coins and in many cases printing bank-notes, but the official state body of a country that does this, to the strictest specifications.

Originally, a mint was simply a basic forge, as used by the Lydians in the 7th century BC to hammer out their electrum coins, or later by the Greeks and Romans to beat out their gold and silver pieces. The Chinese and Japanese would have produced coins in a similar way.

The method of manufacture was quite rudimentary, and usually involved two stages. First, the blank pieces were cast in moulds or cut out of sheets of metal. Then each piece was placed between two dies with designs cut into them, and the designs were stamped on to the pieces by hammering. The earliest coins had designs on one side only.

The whole process was of course carried out purely by hand. Even so, the designs were often sophisticated, and the coin itself could be a work of art.

Modern mints arose in early medieval times. When the different countries and states of the world were themselves gradually becoming established, a need arose for each country to issue its own distinctive coinage. In many countries there were several local mints before there was a state one. With the development of commerce several

### UP-TO-DATE

Mr John Crawford, of Cardiff, was surprised to find amongst the change he received while shopping a pound coin dated 1987. He was surprised because at the time it was still 1986. The Royal Mint promised to investigate this curious piece of evidence that they were determined to keep up-to-date. The results of their investigation were not made public.

feudal authorities, such as counts, bishops and individual cities, set up their own mints. In Britain, regulations for the government of the state mint were made in the first half of the 10th century by King Athelstan. Even so, there were local mints long after this date, as in other countries, with provincial mints operating under the control of the chief mint in London. Some countries had a large number of mints. In 13th-century France, for example, there were already more than 50 separate mints, each issuing its own coinage.

In such cases, commerce was hindered rather than helped by the proliferation of different currencies.

The actual process of minting coins was still mainly carried out by hand in medieval times, and did not become anything like mechanized until the 16th and 17th centuries. Attention was increasingly paid to such matters as achieving a consistent weight for the blanks to be stamped, to

## FIRST THINGS FIRST

Charles Chaplin, in *My Autobiography*, relates some early monetary experiences. When he was three his brother Sydney showed him a conjuring trick in which he appeared to swallow a coin and make it come out through the back of his head. Young Charlie decided that he could do anything his seven-year-old brother could do, and promptly swallowed the coin. His mother hastily sent for a doctor.

Two years later young Charles made his first appearance as a performer. He began to sing a song, and an appreciative audience threw coins onto the stage. 'Immediately I stopped and announced that I would pick up the money first and sing afterwards. This caused much laughter. The stage manager came on with a handkerchief and helped me to gather it up. I thought he was going to keep it. This thought was conveyed to the audience and increased their laughter.' It was only when Charlie had seen the money handed over to his mother for safe-keeping that he consented to finish his act.

## OVER THE MOON

It was formerly believed that if, on the first day of the first new moon in the year, you shut your eyes and turned over the smallest silver coin in your pocket, you would have money all through the year.

improvements in the manufacture of the dies, and to ways of stamping the designs successfully on larger coins. At the same time, precautionary steps were taken to protect coins from such abuses as clipping and filing. Moneyers had found that the clipping (trimming of metal) or filing of the edges of hammer-struck coins enabled dishonest money-changers to make substantial profits with only a minimal risk of detection. This practice was even inadvertently encouraged by some governments when they reduced the weight of a particular denomination, thus giving the older, heavier coins in circulation a value greater than the new ones. It was only on the introduction of machine-made coins that the clipping and filing of coins was brought to an end.

Coins struck at a particular mint came to be given a distinctive **mintmark**. This was a mark that identified the mint at which a coin was struck. It was usually a simple device, such as a letter or small symbol. If a letter, it was often the first letter of the name of the town where the mint was located. Coins minted in Prague, for example, had a 'P'. Not all letters were so meaningful, and a favourite modern system of mintmarks evolved from the one introduced in France by Francis I in 1540, by which the country's main mint was allotted the letter 'A', and other mints were given subsequent letters of the alphabet.

Numismatists now acknowledge that some apparent mintmarks on coins are not really mintmarks at all, but were stamped as the personal symbol of an individual mintmaster, engraver or designer. This can aid the correct identification of coins but it also makes things more complicated. It is clearly helpful in cases where a mint did not stamp any individual symbol on a coin, since the mark enables such a coin to be traced to the mint where the mintmaster made the issue or where the engraver or designer was employed.

Outside Europe, the Spanish established mints in the 16th century in South America and Mexico to strike coins from the gold and silver discovered and mined there.

## AMERICAN MINTS

The earliest mint in the United States was set up at Boston, Massachusetts, in 1652, where it was authorized to strike silver shillings, sixpences and threepences, these being the coins in which the English colonists did most of their reckoning. The first issues bore the letters 'NE' (for New England) on one side and their value on the other. Within a few months the design was altered to a tree on one side and the value and date of minting on the other, with the coins now given an inscribed border to prevent clipping. The tree depicted was at first a willow. Eight years later it was changed to an oak, and several years after that to a pine.

At the same time, much of the coinage that circulated in New England was minted in London, and in 1659 silver shillings, sixpences and groats were struck and sent to Maryland for issue in that colony. The coins depicted a fine profile head of the Lord Proprietor, Lord Baltimore.

In the 1730s Samuel Highley of Granby, Connecticut, began to issue his own money, striking the coins at a mint he set up by a copper mine at Simsbury, Connecticut. He issued threepences made of pure copper, each with his own design, a crown and the date 1737. When his coins were found to be underweight, he added an inscription, reading: 'Value me as you please—I am good copper.'

In 1785, Reuben Harmon, Jr, first issued copper coins from his mint at Rupert, Vermont, with his design incorporating the Green Mountains and a plough, the latter as a symbol of liberty and peaceful farming.

It was the Connecticut mint that excelled in sheer quantity, however, issuing around 29 000 copper coins in the three years from 1785. These originally bore a figure in armour on one side, and a personalization of Liberty, based on Britannia, on the other. An inscription read 'Independence and Liberty', if only to establish that the figure in armour was not that of a British monarch! It

## THE TICKET, NOT THE DESTINATION

In a _Times_ article (December, 1989) which discussed the differences between Britain and America, Barbara Amiel said that 'in the United States, the amount of money an individual has all but determines his place in the social hierarchy. In Britain it is not governed by it.' She went on to say that Americans were 'hell bent on accumulating money' in order to improve their standing in the social hierarchy. 'Money is the ticket, not the destination.'

was on these same copper coins that there first appeared the motto of the United States of America, 'E pluribus unum' ('One out of many', referring to the single union formed from several originally independent colonies).

In the two years from 1786, Massachusetts produced copper coins portraying an Indian with bow and arrow and an eagle holding arrows and laurels in its talons. It was the first state to designate its coins as cents and half-cents, the former coin being the equivalent of one-hundredth of a Spanish silver dollar. A decimal currency thus existed in America before it was introduced by the French Revolutionary government in 1795.

Once the United States of America proper came into being after the Declaration of Independence in 1776, it was clearly important to establish a unified national currency, issued from one or more government mints. This was not so straightforward, since any new currency would have to blend with existing coinages. Moreover, there was the problem of what the various denominations should be called, and to what extent existing coin names should be retained.

The national currency did not come about immediately, and there was much debate on the subject. In 1782 Robert Morris, a New York financier, proposed the setting up of a national mint that would issue decimal values. By way of names for the new denominations, he suggested a basic monetary unit called a _mark_, which would be divided into _quints_ (one-fifth of this) and _cents_ (one-hundredth). Thomas Jefferson, however, as author of the Declaration of Independence and future US President, rejected Morris's system as 'too laborious'. Instead, he proposed that the existing Spanish dollar should be the basic unit, on the grounds that it was 'a known coin, and the most familiar of all to the minds of the people', adding that it 'is already adopted from South to North, has identified our currency, and therefore happily offers itself as a unit already introduced'. He recommended that the dollar's value should be defined in terms of a ratio of 15:1 between its silver content and the equivalent in gold. The stage was thus set for an innovative bimetallic decimal currency.

There was still the matter of the dollar's subdivisions, and also of any coin representing a multiple value. Jefferson proposed that there should be a gold coin valued at 10 dollars, two silver coins—the dollar itself and a coin worth one-tenth of a dollar—and a copper coin with the value of one-hundredth of a dollar. The name *cent* was obvious for the latter. As for the one-tenth piece, Jefferson suggested the name *disme* or *dime*, derived from the French *dixième*, 'tenth'.

Even now, though, the proposals remained on paper for some years, and despite many discussions between representatives from the different states, no decision was taken. Congress authorized the establishment of a mint, but that too remained merely a project.

Finally, in 1792, Congress drew up a system of coin denominations, values and weights that would remain unaltered. The Coinage Act listed 10 different coin values, as follows: a 10-dollar gold piece, named the *eagle* after the device it bore, a 5-dollar gold piece, a 2½-dollar gold piece, a silver dollar piece, a silver half-dollar piece, a silver quarter-dollar piece, a silver dime piece, a silver half-dime piece, a copper cent piece and a copper half-cent piece.

For the site of the first United States Mint, Philadelphia, then the nation's capital, was chosen. David Rittenhouse, a noted astronomer and Treasurer of Pennsylvania, was appointed as its first Director. He took up the post that same year. In October that year George Washington, now in his first term of presidential office, supplied the Mint with some silver, from which 1500 half-dimes were struck for him to present to his friends and to foreign visitors. The Philadelphia Mint's first regular issue of coinage followed in 1793, in the form of copper cents and half-cents.

The history of American minting does not end there, however, and later mints arose in different parts of the country. With the 1820s gold rush in North Carolina and Georgia, for example, a boom in gold resulted, and new privately owned mints were set up in Gainesville, Georgia, Dahlonega, Georgia, and Charlotte, North Carolina, as well as at New Orleans, Louisiana. The first of these, owned by one Templeton Reid, issued gold 10-dollar, 5-dollar and 2½-dollar coins bearing the minter's name and the identification 'Georgia Gold'.

But the most famous gold rush in history, that of 1848 in California, did not have the same consequence. Although much actual gold changed hands, very few gold coins were minted locally, and payment was made by simply using gold dust. Nationwide, though, there was a marked increase in the minting of gold pieces. One of these was the famous 20-dollar gold piece, called the *double eagle*. At the same time a new, smaller gold dollar was issued.

In 1852 an important law was passed in the

## YOUNG AND OLD

*'Blessed are the young for they shall inherit the national debt.'*
Herbert Hoover

*'Young people, nowadays, imagine that money is everything, and when they grow older, they know it.'*
Oscar Wilde

*'You can be young without money, but you can't be old without it.'*
Tennessee Williams

*'Old people are accused of being forgetful; but they never forget where they have put their money.'*
Oliver Wendell Holmes

USA by which so-called **fiduciary coinage** was minted—that is, coins whose metal content was intrinsically lower than their nominal value. The silver content of the half-dollar, quarter-dollar, dime and half-dime was then reduced by 7 per cent. In 1857 a further law was passed which stated that foreign coins were no longer legal tender. This meant that the Spanish dollar and its divisions went out of circulation, after serving as the country's most famous and widely used currency since its introduction as the *peso* (the famous 'piece of eight') 200 years earlier.

There had been some initial debate as to the portrait that the new American coinage should bear and George Washington's head was considered as a possibility. In the end, though, it was a personification of Liberty that was chosen, as symbolizing the country's new-found independence and freedom, and it is her figure that has largely featured on American coins ever since.

The Philadelphia mint is still active, as is the mint at Denver, Colorado, which began operations in 1906. Before then, the main subsidiary United States mint was the one at San Francisco. This began operating in 1854, but the regular issue of coins ceased in 1955. In 1965 it resumed operations to strike specimen sets of coins for collectors. The New Orleans mint, meanwhile, had closed in 1909.

The United States Mint issued 90 per cent silver coins until 1965, when the Coinage Act that year phased out such coins and introduced cupro-nickel coinage. All silver was removed from the dime and quarter, and the silver content of the half-dollar was reduced to 40 per cent. A further act of 1970 removed the remaining silver from the half-dollar.

The first silver dollar piece showed the head of Liberty, facing right, with flowing hair, and the next type, which continued until 1798, showed a draped bust. That same year the 'heraldic eagle' dollar was introduced, with a stylized bird carrying the United States shield and in its beak a banner with the words E PLURIBUS UNUM. This continued until 1803, when the striking of silver dollars was interrupted until 1840. The new type, the 'Liberty seated' dollar, had a different eagle design on the reverse and the designation ONE DOL. This type continued until 1873, when striking once again ceased. It resumed in 1878 and continued to 1904. The following issue was 17 years later, in 1921, when the new 'Peace Dollar' was introduced. This was so called from the word PEACE inscribed on the rocky crag on which the eagle on the reverse was perched. This would be the last regular issue silver dollar struck in the USA, and the 'Eisenhower Dollar' of 1971 was cupronickel clad. In 1979 a smaller cupronickel dollar coin was issued bearing the portrait of the reformer and suffrage campaigner, Susan B. Anthony, and a representation of the Apollo 11 Moon landing.

The United States Mint, like most mints, also produces numismatic coins and coin sets. Recent issues have included a 90 per cent silver half-dollar of 1982, marking the 250th anniversary of George

### AWE-INSPIRING MONEY

Washington's birth, two 90 per cent silver dollars of 1983 and 1984, commemorating the 1984 Olympic Games, a further 90 per cent silver dollar coin and a cupro-nickel half-dollar of 1986 for the Statue of Liberty Centennial. There was also the 90 per cent gold $5 coin and 90 per cent silver dollar coin of 1987 in honour of the 200th Anniversary of the US Constitution.

## THE ROYAL MINT

There had been a mint in London since the 9th century, when it came to be established in the Treasury and Exchequer buildings. In 1300 it was transferred to a site between the inner and outer walls of the Tower of London. By the end of the century it had become the pre-eminent mint in England. Coins were struck according to an official indenture drawn up between the King and the Master of the Mint, with the latter post held by a number of noted persons, including Sir Isaac Newton in the first quarter of the 18th century. The separate post of Master of the Mint was finally abolished in 1870, and is now held as an *ex officio* office of the Chancellor of the Exchequer. At first, the London Mint issued only pennies, with smaller values obtained by cutting the penny into two (for halfpennies) or four (for farthings). From the 14th century on, however, the Mint produced other coins.

With the introduction of machinery, and pressure for space from the garrison at the Tower, it became necessary to move the Mint at the beginning of the 19th century to a new building on Little Tower Hill, where coins were first struck in 1810.

The London Mint had been striking coins for other countries besides those of Britain since the

### A MINT OF MONEY

The British Royal Mint is responsible not only for the 13 billion coins which are currently circulating in Britain, but for coins used in 65 other countries. It is a government department, run by Civil Servants, but operates like a company. In 1987/88 it declared a trading profit of over £6 million.

### THE GODLESS FLORIN

The first florins, or two shilling pieces, were minted in 1849. Their introduction appeared to be a victory for those in favour of a decimal coinage, since they were valued at a tenth of a pound, but the familiar shillings, sixpences, threepences and other awkward coins stayed in circulation.

Queen Victoria was not amused by the first florins. They omitted the Latin words *Dei Gratia*, 'by the grace of God', and became known as godless florins. The queen gave orders that this design was to be discontinued.

16th century. A great increase in demand for coins of all kinds, as well as impending decimalization, with all its new issues, finally necessitated the removal of the Royal Mint from London to large new buildings at Llantrisant, South Wales, in 1968. (Decimalization was introduced three years later.) The production of coins in the Tower Hill premises was then run down, and no new coins were struck after 1975. Five years later even the shop and exhibition centre there were closed as a result of impending new development on the site.

### OTHER MINTS

Mints in other countries were established at different dates.

In Russia, the first state mint was set up in Moscow in 1534. There were also mints in Ekaterinburg (modern Sverdlovsk), Nizhny Novgorod (modern Gorky), Yaroslavl, Kherson and Arkhangelsk. Many of these operated only for a short time. A mint was then founded by Peter the Great in St Petersburg in 1724, and from 1876 it became the only one in the country. It is now (in modern Leningrad) the sole mint to issue coins for circulation in the USSR. The Moscow Mint, reorganized in 1942, issues medals only.

In Australia, mints were established at Sydney in 1855 and at Melbourne in 1872.

In South Africa, the present Mint was opened at Pretoria in 1923, originally as a branch of the Royal Mint in London.

## THE TRIAL OF THE PYX

In the process of minting, great care is taken beforehand to ensure that the coins meet the precise agreed specifications regarding size, shape, weight and metal content. To ensure that the required specifications are being observed, most countries have established an official procedure for testing the coins *after* they have been minted, and before they are issued.

In Britain, this testing procedure is known as the Trial of the Pyx, a 'pyx' being a special box. (The word comes from Greek *pyxis*, 'box', originally referring to a box made of boxwood, with the modern English word 'box' also deriving from this Greek source.)

The ceremony, at first held four times a year but

## DESIGNING A SET OF COINS

In 1926, as a result of the Free State Coinage Act, the Irish Free State was faced with the task of designing a complete set of coins. A committee was appointed, with the poet W. B. Yeats as chairman, to advise the Minister of Finance about which designs to adopt. It was decided that the obverse impression of all eight coins would be the harp. The Minister ruled that the heads of modern persons should not be shown on the coins, and the committee soon decided that it would be unwise to depict national heroes such as Brian Boru. Thomas Bodkin, one of the committee members, later explained why he personally had been opposed to the use of religious symbols or saintly effigies on the coins. He said that it would be encouraging irreverence, and cited the common habit of spitting on a coin for luck. He also thought that such effigies would encourage large numbers of people to break the law. They would bore holes in the coins in order to convert them into medals or amulets.

In a lecture at the Metropolitan School of Art in November, 1928, Dr Bodkin continued: 'It occurred to us that the opportunity presented by the issue of an entirely new series of eight coins was one unparalleled in the modern history of numismatics. Every other European State which has enjoyed the privilege of a national coinage for centuries is bound by tradition to one or more symbols or emblems, which prevent their coinage, as a whole, from being a series of related designs. We, therefore, determined to seize the opportunity of making our coinage an artistic unit—of securing that each coin should, as it were, tell a part of the one story.

'Coins are the tangible tokens of a people's wealth. Wealth in the earliest times was always calculated in terms of cattle. Thence comes the word *pecunia*, "money", derived from *pecus*, "the beast". The wealth of Ireland is still derived in overwhelming proportion from the products of her soil. What, therefore, could be more appropriate than the depiction upon our coinage of these products? We remembered, too, that some of the loveliest coins of antiquity, which artists have admired for a thousand years, are adorned with the Bull of Thurium, the Horses of Carthage and of Larissa, and the Hare of Messana.'

As a result of these deliberations, the Irish Free State issued in 1928 coins with the following designs: half-crown—Irish hunter; florin—a salmon; shilling—a bull; sixpence—a wolfhound; threepence—a hare; penny—a hen and chicks; halfpenny—a pig; farthing—a woodcock. The hen and chicks were allocated to the penny because 'this, we considered, would be the coin most frequently used by the women of the house and by the children; and it seemed part of our duty to cater for their pleasure'.

The Irish farthing and halfpenny were demonetized in 1969, and other coins were withdrawn in 1971 when decimal currency was introduced. Some of Percy Metcalfe's original animal designs can still be seen, however, on the modern Irish fivepence, tenpence, twentypence and fiftypence pieces.

now annually, was initiated in the Chapel of the Pyx in Westminster Abbey, and dates back to at least the 13th century. Almost from the beginning it has been carried out by the Goldsmiths' Company of London, who now hold it in the Hall of the Company, in Foster Lane, near St Paul's Cathedral.

In March every year, samples of coins are sent from the Royal Mint to be tested by an independent jury of goldsmiths in the presence of the Queen's Remembrancer, an officer originally appointed to collect the debts due to the sovereign. The verdict of the jury is then delivered in the presence of the Chancellor of the Exchequer.

Original regulations required a penny to be taken from each ten-pound batch of coin produced and to be placed in a locked box ('pyx') to await weighing and assaying, this being the actual testing ('trial'). The coins are checked against special 'Trial Plates', made up to the prescribed standards and provided by the Goldsmiths' Company.

The earliest surviving Trial Plate, used for checking gold coins, dates from 1477 and is now in the possession of the Royal Mint. The plates were stamped with the dies of a coin of the same metal standard as those to be tested, and made up in metal that conformed exactly to that legally required of the coins. In the case of the 1477 Plate,

## A DEAR DINAR

A small gold dinar established a record as the most expensive coin in the world when it was sold by Sotheby's in September, 1988 for £165 000. The coin was minted in AD 696 by Caliph Abd al Malik, 64 years after Mohammed died. At the time Byzantine coins dominated world trade. The dinar introduced a new Islamic coinage which was meant to break that domination.

Unlike most western coins, the dinar bears no head. The Koran forbids the use of human imagery on coins and such-like objects. It does, however, carry a religious message: 'God is one, eternal, does not beget and is not begotten.'

## THE LOSABILITY FACTOR

Mr Terence Volk, one of Britain's leading numismatists, put forward the theory in 1988 that pennies were disappearing from circulation because people could not be bothered to pick them up if they dropped them. The new penny, he thought, was of too little value, and was physically insignificant. The old, heavier penny would have attracted more attention in dropping to the floor and was worth retrieving because it had more purchasing power.

the coin used as the norm was an angel of the time of Edward IV, which had a metal standard of 23 carats 3½ grains of pure gold and half a grain of alloy. At the Trial, a piece of metal was cut from the Plate and placed in the furnace with the coins being tested to act as a 'control'.

Although every effort was made to regularize and standardize the Plates themselves, there have been occasions when errors have occurred. In 1710, for example, Sir Isaac Newton, then Master of the Mint, was surprised to find the Trial jury giving a verdict that declared the gold coins as below standard. It was later discovered, however, that it was not the coins that were at fault but the Plate itself. Prepared three years earlier, it was made of gold that was *too* good, 917.1 parts in 1000 fine instead of the prescribed 916.67.

### COLLECTING COINS

Coin-collecting is an absorbing, if often expensive, interest for many people, and when undertaken seriously or professionally is known by the formal name of **numismatics** (from Greek *nomisma*, 'current coin'). Traditionally, numismatics also covers the collecting of tokens (see below) and medals, despite the fact that the latter are not pieces of currency.

It is not easy to define exactly what numismatics is, since it can be different things to different people. On the one hand, it is the collection of coins as objects in their own right. On the other, it is the study of coins related to their historic, economic, geographical, archaeological and artistic background. Whatever the case, coins cannot be studied in isolation and numismatics is bound to be a 'comparative' science, even where the collector confines his interests to the coins of a single country, reign, or mint.

Even the amateur coin collector will need to be a patient and skilful observer and classifier, noting carefully the smallest of differences in the coins, from their years of issue to the distinctions in their mintmarks. All numismatists, too, will benefit by studying an authoritative book on the subject, such as Ewald Junge's *World Coin Encyclopedia* (see Bibliography, p. 186), or by a visit to a professional coin collection, such as the one at the British Museum, London or those held by the universities of Oxford, Cambridge and Glasgow.

## TOKENS

**Tokens** interest some collectors just as much as standard coins. Although today all coins are in a sense 'token money', the word is properly used for those coins that were struck privately in historic times to fulfil a need when the government failed to issue enough money. They were thus 'emergency money' and provided the change needed for everyday commerce.

Tokens were similar to coins in most respects, and usually bore their place and date of issue and value. However, there were far more tokens struck in copper or some other base metal than there were in silver or gold, if only because they were needed for small change rather than large payments.

The majority of tokens were issued by tradesmen, including the traditional butcher, baker and candlestick-maker, and in the 17th century farthing tokens were particularly common. Most of these were struck before the Great Fire of London in 1666, so are valuable to collectors for the information they preserve about the commercial activities of their day, and for their ability to serve as a 'guidebook' to the streets and buildings of London that would soon be destroyed.

Because of their unprofessional origin, tokens were inevitably not so technically or artistically sophisticated as coins, but this 'amateur' aspect makes them attractive to many collectors, who admire their rather crude designs and wording. The trade of the issuer was often represented

## THE OTHER HALF

'Half a Sixpence' is the title of the musical based on *Kipps* by H. G. Wells. It was suggested by the idea of lovers' tokens. Kipps reads in *Tit-Bits* about lovers dividing a coin and keeping the halves, but it is harder than he thinks to split a sixpence in two. "When they met again the sixpence was still undivided.

He had not intended to mention the matter to her at that stage, but it came up spontaneously. He endeavoured to explain the theory of broken sixpences and his unexpected failure to break one.

'But what you break it for?' said Ann. 'It's no good if it's broke.'

'It's a Token,' said Kipps.

'Like—?'

'Oh, you keep half and I keep half, and when we're sep'rated, you look at your half and I look at mine—see? Then we think of each other'."

In the end it is Ann who files the sixpence in half and gives him back a piece. When they meet years later they still have the two halves and eventually marry.

by a picture rather than in words, with a flagon denoting a wine merchant, for example, or a pen, representing a scrivener.

In the 18th century, most of the tokens issued were halfpennies, and although there were fewer of them, their execution was generally rather more polished. Several tokens of this period had their edges inscribed with the places where they could be cashed, and the differences in such inscriptions make a special interest for token collectors today.

The 19th century saw the issue of a small number of silver tokens, as well as the appearance of individual 'coins' that are now genuine collector's pieces. They include a 40-shilling bank token in gold introduced in Reading, and a copper 'half-guinea' struck in Liverpool. The former is now very rare, since the token's manufacturer, Sir Edward Thomason, was infringing the royal prerogative, and its circulation was thus declared illegal and was halted.

## SOME SEVENTEENTH-CENTURY ADVICE ON MAKING MONEY

Francis Bacon first published his famous essays in 1597, though the revised and much expanded edition appeared in 1625. *Of Riches* contained his thoughts about wealth. He first commented on its evils, saying that wealth made it more difficult for a man to be virtuous and that it was of 'no solid use' to the person who possessed it. He could after all merely store it, give it away or display it to others in order to excite their admiration.

He went on to advise those who desire wealth not to be too greedy nor too impatient. Riches obtained honestly would come slowly; wealth which came quickly would be from the Devil.

To those already possessing great wealth he gave the following advice—that they should not believe anyone who pretended to despise wealth, that they should not be 'pennywise' in managing their money, that they should decide with great care who was to inherit it. He added: 'Defer not charities till death; for certainly, if a man weigh it rightly, he that doth so is rather liberal of another man's than his own.'

Knowing that most of his readers would be rather more interested in hearing how to acquire wealth, Lord Bacon provided a list of suggestions:

1. By parsimony, i.e. being extremely careful about spending whatever money one already has, though this 'is not innocent, for it withholdeth men from works of liberality and charity'.
2. By agriculture, or 'the improvement of the ground, but it is slow'.
3. By means of 'ordinary trades and vocations' pursued honestly and with diligence.
4. By snapping up bargains, though this is usually at the expense of others who are in financial difficulties. 'The gains of bargains are of a more doubtful nature, when men shall wait upon others' necessity.'
5. By means of partnerships, 'if the hands be well chosen that are trusted'.
6. By means of usury, lending money to others at a high rate of interest—'the certaintest means of gain, though one of the worst'.
7. By inventing something new, or being the first to fulfil a need. 'If a man can play the true logician, to have as well judgement as invention, he may do great matters, especially if the times be fit.'
8. By means of monopolies—these were commonly granted to royal favourites in Bacon's time, but were made illegal by James I. 'A great means to enrich,' according to Bacon.
9. By holding a lucrative office at court or in a nobleman's household, though Bacon goes on to say that if such posts are obtained by flattery 'and other servile conditions, they may be placed amongst the worst'.
10. By 'fishing for testaments and executorships'. Bacon quotes Tacitus on the subject of the philosopher Seneca: *Testamenta et orbos tanquam indagine capi*—'Wills and childless persons were caught (by Seneca) as though with a hunting-net.' This practice, says Bacon, is degrading.

A more general comment made by Lord Bacon in his essay was: 'The ways to enrich are many, and most of them foul.'

# 4
# FOLDING STUFF

## PAPER MONEY

After coins, the next most important development in the history of money was **paper money**.

How did this come about, and why?

Metal money in the form of coins had its advantages, but it also had one big disadvantage—it could easily be stolen. A merchant or trader carrying a quantity of coins could quite easily be set upon and robbed. Fairly early on such merchants must have developed the habit of taking not coins with them when travelling but a written document stating that they actually possessed the necessary money in order to trade. Such a document—a forerunner of the modern letter of credit and traveller's cheque—served as a substitute for

actual money. More importantly, it did not matter too much if the document was lost or stolen, for the money itself would still be intact in the merchant's home town or country and could not be released without his signature.

The document would not of course be drawn up by the merchant but by some other person or group of persons in his home town. They would vouch that he, the merchant, had deposited a particular sum of money (as actual coins) with them for safe keeping and that he had undertaken to pay any claim made by a debtor out of his deposit. The guarantors of such a document were therefore the forerunners of modern bankers.

**"**

### DOUBLE YOUR MONEY!

*I'll tell you a plan for gaining wealth,*
*Better than banking, trade, or leases;*
*Take a bank note and fold it across,*
*And then you'll find your money*
   *IN-CREASES.*
*This wonderful plan, without danger or*
   *loss,*
*Keeps your cash in your hand, and with*
   *nothing to trouble it;*
*And every time that you fold it across*
*'Tis plain as the light of the day that you*
   *double it!*

An anonymous poem quoted in C. C.
Bombaugh's *Oddities and Curiosities of
Words and Literature.*

**"**

This sort of document was still only a substitute for money, and not regarded as money itself. In due time, documents of this type *did* actually come to be used as money. In that respect they were rather like present-day traveller's cheques. Officially, the latter are still cheques, which need to be cashed at a bank like any other cheque in order to release actual money. But a traveller abroad will find in practice that the hotel where he stays will accept traveller's cheques as payment without any need for them to be encashed. It is almost as if each traveller's cheque is a bank note worth the amount printed on it.

The merchant's promissory document similarly altered its function. Originally, it would have been a certificate to the effect that he, Joe Bloggs, had deposited the sum of 123 pounds 4 shillings and 5 pence (or any other currency) and that he promised (hence 'promissory') to pay any sum up to that amount to honour any deal or bargain made. In course of time the document was not made out in favour of a particular person, but simply its bearer, that is, the person who happened to possess it at the time. The amount of money stated, too, was a convenient round sum, say £1, £5 or £10, instead of a totalled personal deposit. The issuer of the document promised to pay that stated sum (£1, £5 or £10) to whoever presented it. In

this way, the person who held the document was regarded as the owner of the sum given.

The result was now a fully fledged banknote. Even today, many such notes or bills bear a written guarantee of payment as witness to this origin. Every Bank of England note, for example, bears the wording: 'I promise to pay the bearer on demand the sum of £10' (or whatever), with this promise being made 'For the Governor and Company of the Bank of England' by the Chief Cashier, with his signature as proof.

Even so, although the banknote had arrived, it was still only a receipt for cash deposited. It was used as money, but was not thought of as actual money. It was like the traveller's cheque that the hotelier accepts in payment of his guest's bill. He may accept it at its face value, but he still hurries along to the bank to deposit or cash it, so that he has its value in *real* money.

After these first two stages in the evolution of paper money, it was a logical step for the third and final stage to arrive. This was when the primitive banknote was not just used for one transaction and then cashed, but was passed around from one person to another and used to settle a number of transactions. In other words, it circulated, as ordinary coins did. Like them, it became real money. It was as if the hotelier had come to use his traveller's cheques to pay his staff, and they in turn used the cheques to make purchases and payments of their own.

This development had an interesting consequence for the banker who had issued the note in the first place. If his notes circulated as real money, they did not come back to him to be cashed, or at most only a small proportion came back to be

 **A BED OF ROSES**

Before banks were established, people hoarded wealth or carried it around with them, in the form of gold chains. When Richard III led his army to the Battle of Bosworth, in 1485, he took his own bed with him. It was later found to have a secret compartment containing treasure worth £300, a huge sum at the time.

## " KNOWING ONE'S STUFF

Sterling: 'What signifies your birth and education, and titles? Money, money, that's the stuff that makes the great man in this country.'

George Colman and David Garrick
*The Clandestine Marriage* (1766)

"

## " THE INTELLIGENCE TEST?

Money made is the accepted measure of brains. A man who makes a lot of money is a clever fellow; a man who does not, is not.

Bertrand Russell *The Conquest of Happiness*

"

changed into smaller values in actual coins. He consequently needed to issue more notes than he was going to get back.

## FORESTALLING FORGERY

In the early days of paper money, there was much abuse of the system, especially by the issuers of the notes. There was distrust, too, on the part of the public. The man in the street naïvely supposed that if a banker apparently 'made money', by printing and issuing banknotes out of thin air, then he was likely to be a dishonest person, even a dangerous criminal. Also, lacking experience in paper money, many bankers issued too many notes. This resulted in a sharp increase in prices, so that eventually the money issued either became worthless, 'not worth the paper it was printed on', as we say, or it was redeemed in metal coins (or in promises to pay in metal coins), at a small fraction of its original value.

There was also the matter of **forgery**. Minting a coin is a precise science (or art), with special tools and equipment. But it is relatively easy to print a piece of paper that looks like a banknote. At least it was in the early days.

Not surprisingly, the banks devoted much attention to this aspect, and thus had three main objectives when making their issues. First, the notes had to be instantly recognizable to the public for what they were. One had to ensure that they could not be confused with any other kind of legal or financial document or certificate. Second, it had to be possible to issue them in sufficiently large numbers. Third, they had to be as difficult as possible to forge.

It goes without saying that a banknote should also not simply be functional but, like a coin, be a

work of art. Early notes were usually fairly simple in design and were printed in black ink on white paper from an engraved copper plate. Precise information such as the date, value, signature and serial number was frequently filled in by hand. But a simple copperplate engraving was easily forged, despite the fact that the hand-writing acted as a security check, and it also made the issue of large numbers of notes impracticable.

Printers and engravers of banknotes therefore had to devise new techniques. They progressed, for a start, to colour printing. Then, to foil forgers, they added coloured fibres in the paper and incorporated a watermark. By the end of the 19th century banknotes were entirely printed, with no handwriting involved in the process of manufacture.

The **watermark** was certainly a deterrent to forgers. In its earliest form it was made by attaching a wire mesh of the required design or pattern to the mould where the paper was made. The pulp for the paper was 'thinned' where it pressed against the wire of the mesh, with the result that the pattern was visible in contrast to a bright or dark background. Today, a much more sophisticated type of watermark is that of a portrait of a national figure 'built in' to the note, with a conventional

 **PART PAYMENTS**

The actor George Raft is said to have earned some ten million dollars in the course of his career. He once said that 'part of the loot went for gambling, part for horses and part for women. The rest I spent foolishly'.

## " A CHANGE FOR THE BETTER?

*'Women give to men the very gold of their lives, but they invariably want it back in small change.'*

Oscar Wilde

"

portrait of the same person actually printed on the note. Hold the reverse of a British £10 note up to the light, for example, and to the right of the portrait of Florence Nightingale you will see, in the white area of the note, an identical watermark portrait of her in surprising detail. This same portrait is also visible on the front of the note.

An important progression in the printing process, too, was a move from copper plates to steel plates. Steel is better for printing banknotes than copper because the hardness of the metal allows the intricate designs and wording to be reproduced accurately on thousands of identical notes. Such minute detail is in itself an added foil against forgery.

At first, the printing machinery used to produce banknotes operated only slowly, and could issue as few as four notes a minute. This figure should be compared with modern presses, which can print as many as 7500 notes a minute, or 9000 sheets an hour, each containing 50 notes.

The words 'I promise to pay' on early banknotes meant that the issuing bank would give the bearer of a note its value in gold. Once this fact became publicly known, banknotes themselves began to be more favourably accepted by the public. They felt that the notes were even worth their stated value in gold. Because it was both troublesome and unnecessary to change paper money for gold in this way, people soon came to accept the notes as money in their own right. In Britain, the Bank of England had since its foundation in 1694 come to occupy a special position, and now, 300 years later,

## FOOL'S GOLD

A cynic has been heard to mutter that a fool and his money are soon married.

it still has a virtual monopoly of note issue. Although other banks still issue notes in Scotland, Ireland and the Isle of Man, the Bank of England has the sole right of issuing notes in England and Wales. Moreover, since 1833 its notes have been officially recognized as 'legal tender', meaning that they are recognized by the law as fully discharging a debt.

Notes issued by the Bank of England are thus not only ordinarily used as money in Britain, but they are declared by the law actually to *be* money.

Today, however, it is no longer possible to convert banknotes into gold, as it was before World War I, when a £1 note could be exchanged for a gold sovereign (which is what the pound coin was actually called). During the War, the export and melting of gold was prohibited. There was therefore no point in converting paper money into gold. Eventually, in 1925, an Act was passed which freed the Bank of England from the obligation of converting every £1 note presented to it into a gold sovereign. People could still get gold for their notes, but only if they were prepared to accept a bar of gold instead, not a coin or coins. Such a bar would have been the equivalent then of about £1700 in notes.

Finally, in 1931, when the Gold Standard was suspended, it was no longer possible to convert notes into gold. So the words 'I promise to pay'

## " SHORT CHANGE

*You pays your money and you takes your choice.*
*Punch* caption

*One can never be too thin or too rich.*
Duchess of Windsor Attributed

*One man's wage rise is another man's price increase.*
Harold Wilson quoted in *The Observer* Jan 1970

*The insolence of wealth will creep out.*
Dr. Samuel Johnson

"

### INFRA DIG

A gold-digger, in the days when guinea coins were still in circulation, might justifiably have been called a kind of guinea-pig. These days such a person might be better described as a gimme-pig.

that remain on Bank of England notes today are absolutely meaningless. One could take £1700 *million* in notes to the Bank, and still not get any gold. In theory, the Bank could honour its promise by giving an equivalent in silver coins, but who would want that?

All this means that the banknote today, unlike the former gold coins of historic times, is simply a piece of printed paper, itself virtually worthless, except perhaps as a work of art or an example of the engraver's and printer's craft! Yet, increasingly, it is notes rather than coins that serve as money. In fact, there are now several countries in the world where the currency exists *only* in banknotes, so that there are no coins at all. They include Laos, the Maldives, Paraguay and Peru. Ironically, one of the countries that no longer issues coins is Guinea in West Africa, the very country that gave its name to the famous English coin, which was struck from gold shipped from that region of the African coast in the 17th century.

## BANKNOTES AS MONEY
So, when and where did **banknotes** begin to circulate as money, and how did they come to be issued in their present form?

The earliest known banknotes were issued in China in the 11th century. But the main period of emergence of banknotes as we know them today was during the 17th and 18th centuries.

The first bank to issue notes in Europe was the Swedish Stockholms Banco, founded in 1656. It began to issue notes in 1661 as a temporary alternative to devalued copper 'plate money' which had ceased to circulate. A royal decree declared that the notes were legal tender for use in circulation, so that they were the earliest examples of European banknotes as we know them today.

The Stockholms Banco was then followed by the Bank of England, which first issued banknotes

in its year of foundation, 1694. People depositing money with the Bank were able to have receipts in the form of a note, which could subsequently be redeemed for either the whole of the sum deposited or a portion of it.

A year later, the Bank of Scotland was founded, and began to issue its own notes. Although paper money was accepted more readily in Scotland than in England, Scottish banks sometimes had difficulties in redeeming notes for coins.

The first French paper money was issued by the Banque Générale, established in 1716 by the Scottish financier, John Law. Law believed that if banks issued paper money to increase the money supply, this would improve trade and boost employment. Two years after its foundation, his bank became the Banque Royale, and its notes were guaranteed by the Crown. Despite Law's undertaking that his notes would always retain their value because 'there will always be as much Money as there is Occasion or Imployment for, and no more', the government withdrew its support in 1720 and the bank failed, simply because it issued too many notes.

## BANKNOTES ROUND THE WORLD
In North America, paper notes for small sums began to circulate at about the same time as they did in Europe. In 1690, for example, Massachusetts Bay issued local notes to pay for a military expedition to Canada. Later, other colonies issued their own bills of credit to finance local projects. A fourpenny note issued in Pennsylvania in 1755 had the explicit wording: 'THIS BILL by Law shall pass current for FOUR PENCE, within the Pro-

### PRINTER'S ERROR

Europe's first printed banknotes were issued in 1661 by Johan Palmstruch of Stockholm. He printed too many notes (each with a face value of 10 thalers) and thus caused Sweden to suffer from inflation. For this, modern Chancellors of the Exchequer may care to note, he was sentenced to death, though he was subsequently saved by the personal intervention of the king of Sweden.

## " ────────────────────────

### SEEING THE LIGHT

*Engaged for fifty-four years (he had been admitted a solicitor on the earliest day sanctioned by the law) in arranging mortgages, preserving investments at a dead level of high and safe interest, conducting negotiations on the principle of securing the utmost possible out of other people compatible with safety to his clients and himself, in calculations as to the exact pecuniary possibilities of all the relations of life, he had come at last to think purely in terms of money. Money was now his light, his medium for seeing, that without which he was really unable to see, really not cognisant of phenomena.*

John Galsworthy *The Man of Property*

────────────────────────────── "

vince of *Pensylvania*. Dated Oct. 1, 1755.' At the top of the bill was printed '*Four* Pence', and at the bottom 'A Groat'. The value was also printed in different forms around the border of the note, in order to discourage any alteration.

Among the best known of the original notes were the so-called **assignats** issued by the French Republic in 1790. The revolutionary government aimed to raise money by issuing such notes, which were backed by the sale of land and property that had been confiscated from the Church and the aristocracy. The name *assignat* refers to the fact that the notes had been assigned, i.e. secured, in this manner.

During the American Revolution, paper money was issued by individual states and the Continental Congress. The notes were supposed to be backed by money raised from state taxes but by 1780 they were worth only one-fortieth of their face value. The phrase 'not worth a Continental', still in use in American English, refers to the public's general lack of confidence in the notes. Later, notes from private American banks replaced the depreciated Continental currency. (Many such notes became collectors' pieces because of their lavish engraving and artistic portraits.)

In the early 19th century a number of provincial banks in England obtained licences to issue their own notes. Control over their issue was sometimes lax, so that when there was a time of financial or commercial crisis, banks that had issued too many notes were unable to repay those customers who hastened to demand an equivalent in coin. When there was such a 'run on the bank', the bank in question would simply have to suspend payment and might well go out of business.

In Australia, meanwhile, gold had been discovered in the 1850s, resulting in the establishment of a number of new banks. Gold diggers were all too ready to deposit their precious findings with the banks and receive notes in exchange, if only because paper was much lighter and easier to carry around from site to site than gold nuggets!

Revolutionary governments, like that of France just mentioned, often chose to issue money in paper rather than coin. In Poland, the first paper money was issued in 1794 by the Supreme National Council, a military insurgent government, in order to support the struggle for independence. The leader of the revolution, Tadeusz Kościuszko, was also treasurer of the Council, and in his handling of the issue drew on his experience in the French Revolution the previous year. Similarly, in Peru the first notes were issued in 1822 by the revolutionary José de San Martín, in order to boost the economy after the declaration of independence the previous year.

The Confederate States of America issued a vast quantity of paper money in 1861 to finance

### LEGENDARY LANGUAGES

Indian banknotes reflect the polyglot nature of the country. On the same note there is likely to be a phrase such as 'Government of India' in eight languages—English, Bengali, Gujarati, Kannada, Oriya, Tamil, Telegu and Urdu. All these are living languages, actually spoken in different Indian states. British coinage still has a 'legend', as it is called, in Latin, a dead language which fewer and fewer British people understand.

*PAY-DAY*

'There is something exhilarating about pay-day, even when the pay is poor and already mortgaged for necessities. With that morsel of gold in their pockets, the men stepped out more briskly and their voices were cheerier than ordinary. When they reached home they handed the half-sovereign straight over to their wives, who gave them back a shilling for the next week's pocket money. That was the custom of the countryside. The men worked for the money and the women had the spending of it. The men had the best of the bargain. They earned their half-sovereign by hard toil, it is true, but in the open air, at work they liked and took an interest in, and in congenial company. The women, kept close at home, with cooking, cleaning, washing, and mending to do, plus their constant pregnancies and a tribe of children to look after, had also the worry of ways and means on an insufficient income.'

Flora Thompson *Lark Rise To Candleford*

the Civil War, some such notes not being redeemable until two years after the official notification of peace, i.e. not till 1867.

World War I saw the issue of notes instead of coins in several countries, simply because of the shortage of the necessary metals for minting coins. Soon after the outbreak of the War, the British Treasury started issuing £1 and 10-shilling notes to compensate for the shortage of gold coins, and the new notes were declared to be legal tender to pay any amount. The first such issue was of the famous so-called '**Bradburys**', named after the neat signature of the Secretary to the Treasury, 'John Bradbury', that appeared on them. In 1928 the issue of such low-value notes was taken over by the Bank of England, and it was in that same year that the Bank first issued its own 10-shilling note, as well as its first new £1 note for more than a century.

The 1920s, after World War I, were a period of financial and economic crisis in many European countries, with consequent hyperinflation. The high-value notes issued in Germany at this time have become legendary, and circulated with values of 500 million marks or more. The same thing happened as a result of World War II, when Greek notes for 25 million drachmas were issued, and Hungarian notes with a value of 100 000 *billion* pengö.

Recent developments in the issue of paper money have included the introduction of further foils against forgery, such as the insertion of a metallic strip into British notes, and the issue of plastic notes. The latter measure was intended to solve the problem caused by the heavy use of British £1 notes in the early 1980s, when they became thin and soiled and had to be replaced every few months. Plastic £1 notes were introduced in the Isle of Man in 1983. In the rest of the British Isles the straightforward replacement of notes by coins was found to be the logical and simpler solution, and the Bank of England ceased to issue £1 notes at the end of 1984.

### BRITAIN'S BANKNOTES

In the 20th century, there have been more issues of new bank notes and withdrawals from circulation of old ones than there have for coins (see p. 53).

Until 1943, there were white bank notes in circulation for values of £10, £20, £50, £100, £500 and £1000, but these ceased to be legal tender in 1945.

The old white £5 note issued between 1945 and 1956 ceased to be legal tender in 1961.

The £5 note issued between 1957 and 1963, bearing a portrait of Britannia, ceased to be legal tender in 1967.

The £5 note issued between 1963 and 1971, the first of the series to bear a portrait of the Queen, ceased to be legal tender in 1973.

The series of £1 notes issued from 1928 to 1960 and the 10 shilling notes of the same type issued from 1928 to 1961 (those without the royal portrait) both ceased to be legal tender in 1962.

The £1 note first issued in 1960 (with a representation of Britannia on the back) and the £10 note first issued in 1964 (with a lion on the back), each with a portrait of the queen on the front, both ceased to be legal tender in 1979.

The 10 shilling note was replaced by the 50p coin in 1969 and ceased to be legal tender in 1970.

('Ceased to be legal tender' meant that the notes could no longer be used for regular financial or commercial transactions. They could, however, be 'redeemed' in new currency when presented at the Head Office of the Bank of England.)

The first of the present series of British bank notes was the £20 note issued in 1970. This was followed by the £5 note in 1971, the £10 note in 1975, the former £1 note in 1978, and the £50 note in 1981. The £1 note was superseded by the £1 coin introduced in 1983 and ceased to be legal tender in 1988.

The current notes portray a famous figure from British history on the back by way of a distinctive identifying feature. The figures are: £5, The Duke of Wellington; £10, Florence Nightingale; £20, William Shakespeare; £50, Sir Christopher Wren.

All these Bank of England notes are legal tender throughout the United Kingdom. Additionally three Scottish banks issue their own notes. These are the Royal Bank of Scotland and the Bank of Scotland (values of £1, £5, £10, £20 and £100) and the Clydesdale Bank (£1, £5, £10, £20, £50 and £100). Strictly speaking, Scottish notes are not legal tender, although in Scotland they are

## MONEY TO BURN

Money is regularly burned when old bank notes, too worn out to remain in circulation, are destroyed. The *Observer* columnist, Sue Arnold, described in June 1988 how she watched two and a half million pounds-worth of ten-pound notes being incinerated. It made her think of a man she knew who, had he been there, 'would probably have thrown himself into the boiler on top of the blazing notes and become the first Scot to commit suttee'.

## " A ROSE BY ANY OTHER NAME

*... all bearers of the Forsyte name would feel the bloom was off the rose. He had no illusions like Shakespeare that roses by any other name would smell as sweet. The name was a possession, a concrete, unstained piece of property, the value of which could be reduced some twenty per cent at least.*

John Galsworthy *In Chancery*

"

accorded a status equal to that of Bank of England notes.

In Northern Ireland four banks issue their own notes. These are the Northern Bank and the Ulster Bank (values of £5, £10, £20, £50 and £100) and the Allied Irish Bank and the Bank of Ireland (£5, £10, £20 and £100). As with Scottish notes, Northern Irish notes are not legal tender but they circulate widely and hold a status comparable to that of Bank of England notes.

In the Channel Islands, the State of Jersey issues its own notes and coinage. The notes are for £1, £5, £10, £20 and £50, and the coins are for £1, 50p, 20p, 10p, 5p, 2p and 1p, as in mainland Britain. The States of Guernsey issues notes and coins similarly, but has no £50 note.

The Isle of Man government issues notes for 50p, £1, £10, £20 and £100. These are legal tender only in the Isle of Man, although they are also accepted at face value by banks in mainland Britain. The Isle of Man also has its own coins in the same values as in mainland Britain with, however, an additional £5 coin.

Although these Scottish, Northern Irish, Channel Islands and Isle of Man notes are not legal tender in the United Kingdom, they will normally be accepted by British banks regardless of their place of issue.

### AMERICAN BILLS

In the United States, the largest **bill** (banknote) currently being issued is that for $100, and issuance of currency in denominations higher than this was discontinued in 1969. As large denomina-

## THE ALMIGHTY DOLLAR

It was Washington Irving, in *The Creole Village* (1836), who wrote: 'The almighty dollar, that great object of universal devotion throughout our land, seems to have no genuine devotees in these peculiar villages.' The phrase was picked up by Charles Dickens in his *American Notes* (1842). Ben Jonson, however, had already referred to 'almighty gold' in 1616.

Dickens has a lengthy piece on the almighty dollar theme in *Martin Chuzzlewit*, where he describes a conversation young Martin has with a group of Americans: 'Dollars! All their cares, hopes, joys, affections, virtues and associations seemed to be melted down into dollars. Whatever the chance contributions that fell into the slow cauldron of their talk, they made the gruel thick and slab with dollars.

'Men were weighed by their dollars, measures were gauged by their dollars; life was auctioneered, appraised, put up and knocked down for its dollars. The next respectable thing to dollars was any venture having their attainment for its end. The more of that worthless ballast, honour and fair-dealing, which any man cast overboard from the ship of his Good Name and Good Intent, the more ample stowage room he had for dollars.'

A more recent 'dollar' word is *Dollardom*: a place where people's main aim is to amass dollars; also those who live in such a place; rich Americans collectively. 'Dollar' phrases in general use include: 'You look like a million dollars', 'dollar crazy' for a person who is money-mad, and 'bet one's bottom dollar' on something that is felt to be a certainty. 'Scream and holler' has been used as rhyming slang for a dollar.

The dollar sign ($) is said to have begun as a combination of the letters US.

O. Henry, in *The Octopus Marooned*, is responsible for: 'Whenever he saw a dollar in another man's hands he took it as a personal grudge, if he couldn't take it any other way.'

tion bills reach the Federal Reserve Bank (see p. 98), they are withdrawn from circulation. Even so, there are certainly many people who hold the discontinued currency. A description of such bills is included in the details below.

All American bills have a portrait of a past President on the front, and up to and including the $100 bill a representation of a historic or important event or place on the back.

| Amount | Front | Back |
|---|---|---|
| $1 | Washington | Great Seal of US |
| $2 | Jefferson | Signers of Declaration |
| $5 | Lincoln | Lincoln Memorial |
| $10 | Hamilton | US Treasury |
| $20 | Jackson | White House |
| $50 | Grant | US Capitol |
| $100 | Franklin | Independence Hall |
| $500 | McKinley | (ornate design) |
| $1000 | Cleveland | (ornate design) |
| $5000 | Madison | (ornate design) |
| $10 000 | Chase | (ornate design) |
| $100 000 | Wilson | (ornate design) |

The highest value bill, that for $100 000, is used only in transactions between the Federal Reserve System and the Treasury Department.

## THE WORTH OF A PENNY

Henry Peacham's *The Worth of a Penny* was first printed in 1641. (The title-page of this little book announced it as 'The Worth of a Penny: or a caution to keep money. With the causes of the scarcity and misery of the want hereof, in these hard and merciless times. As also how to save it in our diet, apparel, recreations, etc. and also what honest courses men in want may take to live.')

It was reissued by William Lee in 1664 with some additions and was sold out within a few days. Lee promised readers that if they had a penny, the book would teach them how to keep it; if they had no penny, the book would teach them how to get one.

The Great Plague and the Great Fire of London caused the next edition of the book to be delayed until 1667. Lee now promised that it would advise readers on how to have 'a penny to spend, a penny to lend and a penny for thy friend'. Our own present readers would no doubt wish to be in that happy position. The extracts from the book which we give below may or may not help in that respect, but as a varied collection of comments on money they are at least entertaining in themselves. We have used the 1883 edition of Peacham's work, included by Andrew Lang in his *Social England Illustrated*.

'Most true it is, that money so heaped up in chests and odd corners, is like, as one saith, to dung; which while it lieth upon a heap doth no good, but dispersed and cast abroad, maketh fields fruitful. Hence Aristotle concludeth that the prodigal man is more beneficial to, and deserveth better of, his country, than the covetous miser. Every trade and vocation fareth the better for him.'

'One very well compared worldly wealth or money unto a football: some few nimble-heeled and nimble-headed run quite away with it; when most are only lookers-on, and cannot get a kick at it, in all their lives.'

'A pleasant fellow came, not long since, to a usurer in Moor Fields, and desired him that

he would lend him £50. Quoth the usurer, "My friend, I know you not." "For that reason only, I would borrow the money of you," said the other, "for if you knew me, I am sure you would not lend me a penny." '

'If words and promises would pass for coin; there would be no man poor.'

'Have you a daughter, by birth well-descended, virtuous, chaste, fair, comely, endued with the most commendable qualities that may be required in a young, beautiful and modest maid: if you have not been, in your life-time, thrifty to provide her a portion, she may live till she be as old as Creusa, the wife of Aeneas, ere you shall get her a good match. *Nam genus et formam Regina Pecuniam donat*: "Money's a Queen, that doth bestow beauty and birth to high and low." Hence the Dutch have a proverb, that "Gentility and fair looks buy nothing in the market." '

'If you happen to be sick and ill; if your purse hath been lately purged, the doctor is not at leisure to visit you. But unto monied and rich men, they fly as bees to the willow palms. The sick is in more danger of them than his disease.'

'Misery is ever the companion of borrowed money.'

'Infinite are the casualties that are incident to the life of man, whereby he may fall into poverty: as misfortune by fire, loss at sea, robbery and theft on land, wounds, lameness, sickness and the like. Men run out of great estates and have undone themselves by over-sumptuous building, above and beyond their means and estates. Others have been undone by carelessness and thriftless servants, such as waste and consume their masters' goods. Some, yea, a great many, have brought themselves to beggary by play and gaming. Others affect unprofitable, yea, impossible inventions and practices, as the philosopher's stone, or the discovery of the new world in the moon by these new devised perspective glasses (i.e. telescopes).'

'If any would be taught the true use of money, let him travel to Italy! For the Italian, the Florentine especially, is able to teach all the world thrift.'

'Thrift, next to the serving of God, is the first thing we ought, even from children, to learn in the world.'

'From the Saxons' time until Edward III, the penny of this land had a cross struck so deep in the midst thereof, that you might break out any part of the four, to buy what you thought good; which was, in those days, their farthing' (fourth part).

'Northern nations are, of all others, the greatest eaters and drinkers; and of those, the French say we of England have the best stomachs and are the greatest trenchermen of the world. But they are deceived; those of Denmark and Norway exceed us, and the Russians, them. I confess we have had, and yet have, some remarkable eaters amongst us. Not long since Wood of Kent ate up, at one dinner, fourteen green geese, equal to the old ones in bigness, with sauce of gooseberries. But the truth is, that those men live the longest, and are commonly in perfect health, who content themselves with the least and simplest meat; which not only saves the purse, but preserves the body.'

'Execrable is the miserable and base humour of many who, to save their money, will live upon vile and loathsome things, as mushrooms, snails, frogs, mice, and the like.'

'You must, if you would keep your money in your purse to uphold your credit, at all times be frugal and thrifty also in your apparel; not dogging the fashion, or setting your tailor to work at the sight of every Monsieur's new suit. There is a middle, plain and decent garb, which is best and most to be commended. What money might be saved, if we were so wise as the Dutch or Spaniards who, for these two or three hundred years, have kept themselves to one fashion.'

'I see no reason why a Frenchman should not imitate our English fashion, as we do his. What! have the French more wit than we in fitting clothes to the body, or a better invention or way in saving money, or making of apparel? Surely, I think not.'

'The most ordinary recreations in the country are football, skales or nine-pins, shooting at butts; quoits, bowling, running at the base, stoolball, leaping, and the like: whereof some are too violent and dangerous. The safest recreations are within doors, but not in regard of cost and expense; for thousands sometimes are lost at dicing-houses.'

Peacham's advice about how to make money was mainly to 'be diligent and industrious' in whatever trade or profession one had been trained. 'If brought up to no trade,' he added, 'you may find entertainment among our new plantations in America; as New England, Virginia, the Barbadoes, St Christopher's and the rest; where with a great deal of delight, you may have variety of honest employment, as fishing with the net or hook, planting, gardening, and the like, which, besides your maintenance, you shall find it a great content to your conscience to be in action, which God commands us all to be.'

'In a word, for a conclusion, let everyone be careful to get and keep money. Know the worth of a penny!'

# 5
# FOUNDING THE POUND

## BRITISH MONEY

Just think how much we could be worth when we've retired!

BANK OF ENGLAND
ONE POUND
£1
Collector's item £5

We have already mentioned British bank notes, but let us now look more closely at the British monetary system. How about the humble **penny** for example? How did it come to be so called? The familiar British coin traces its history back to the 8th century, when it was introduced as a small silver piece under Charlemagne.

Because its origin is so ancient, its name unfortunately remains obscure. It *may* be related to the modern word 'pan', with reference to the original shape of the coin. Or it may even be an onomatopeic name, describing the 'ping' it makes, or made, when dropped. Moreover, in Old English its name was spelled *pennig*, suggesting a further link with other coins ending in *-ing*, such as the *farthing* or *shilling*. But this may purely be coincidental.

Coin names such as 'dollar' and 'penny' became so familiar in the English-speaking world that other coins have been named after them. They include the Hawaiian *dala*, Samoan *tala*, German *pfennig* and Finnish *penni*.

### POETICAL PROMPTING

Geoffrey Chaucer wrote a *Complaint to his Purse* and sent it to Henry IV. It was a hint that he could do with an increase in the pension that had been granted to him by Richard II in 1394. Chaucer called his purse his 'lady dear', and said how sorry he was that she was now so light. He wanted his purse to be heavy again, and to be able to hear the blessed sound of yellow coins chinking in it. The King was evidently amused by this approach, and Chaucer's pension was increased.

## STERLING

In Britain, the *pound* is the key unit of currency, both for national and international purposes and rates of exchange. So how did British currency come to be known as **sterling**?

Originally, *sterling* was the name of a number of different coins in medieval times, especially the silver penny. Some Norman coins of this type bore the representation of a star (in Middle English, *sterre*), and this probably gave the coin its name, with perhaps the final *-ing* based on existing names such as the *shilling* and *farthing*.

Chaucer mentions the coin in his *Canterbury Tales*:

> Myn hooly pardon may yow alle warice
> So that ye offre nobles, or sterlynges,
> Or elles siluer broches.

(That is: 'My holy pardon will save you from all this if you offer nobles, sterlings, or silver brooches' *The Pardoner's Tale*, 1385.)

A similar coin circulated on the Continent, and was known in Old French as the *esterlin*, with this name of the same origin.

The name of the silver coin came to be adopted to denote a standard of purity, almost as if it was 'star quality', and was applied to money regarded as meeting this standard. This sense of *sterling* is first recorded in 1565 in Thomas Cooper's *Thesaurus Linguae Romanae et Britannicae*, a Latin-English dictionary, where he defines the word *centussis* (a Roman coin) as 'A rate of Romaine money conteyning 10 Denarios, that is, x grotes of old sterlynge, when viii grotes went to an ownce'.

Soon after, *sterling* acquired the further sense of 'English money', as distinct from foreign money. This usage is first recorded in 1601, where a history of Ireland refers to Irish money 'being brought back againe to the Exchange to be converted into sterling'.

But the term *sterling silver* was in use earlier than this, and a text dated 1551 refers to groats made of 'sterlinge siluer'. This meant pure silver, and gave the general sense of the word as we now use it to mean 'excellent', as in 'sterling work'. If silver was of sterling quality, it was stamped with a lion passant (walking with its far forepaw raised).

*Sterling* was therefore the general term that defined all lawful coins of the realm in Britain, and

## FIGHTING INFLATION

The plague that occurred in the 14th century in England wiped out large numbers of farm workers and craftsmen. Those who survived knew that they were in a strong position. Many tried to take advantage of that fact. In his *Chronicon*, Henry Knighton reported on the situation in 1349:

'In the meantime the king made proclamation throughout every shire that reapers and other labourers should not take more money than was the custom of old time, upon penalty under the Statute, which to that end he renewed. The labourers, however, were so high-stomached and arrogant that they would not obey the king's behest. If any master wished to employ them needs must he give them what they asked; either lose his fruits and crops or satisfy to the full the greedy wishes of the workers.

'When it came to the ears of the king that his commands were not obeyed—that higher wages were being given to the labourers, he levied heavy fines on the abbots, priors, and knights of all conditions and on the gentry both great and small; on some 100 shillings, on others 40 shillings, on others 20 shillings, and on others according to their means.

'Furthermore the king caused many labourers to be arrested and cast them into prison. Many such betook themselves to the woods and forests for a time. They who were taken were heavily fined. The leaders swore they would not take a daily wage higher than of aforetime, and they were then set free. In the same manner did the king act with regard to craftsmen in the boroughs and villages.'

These measures had some success, but Knighton reports that in the winter following the Black Death 'all necessaries became so dear that what in times past had been worth a penny, at that time was worth fourpence or fivepence.'

(From *Illustrations to British History*, edited by J. Turral)

## SPILLING THE BEANS

A 'bean' in British slang of the early 19th century meant a guinea coin. Eric Partridge tentatively suggested that the word in this sense was connected with the French word *bien*, in the sense of 'something good'. With the withdrawal of the guinea coin from circulation (it was no longer struck after 1813), 'beans' came to mean money in general. The expression 'not worth a bean', however, meaning valueless, had been in use for centuries. In this case the reference was to the vegetable. That also seems to be the case with 'I haven't a bean', as a phrase meaning 'I'm penniless'. This began to be used at the end of the 19th century.

'Old bean' as a friendly term of address derives from bean, i.e. head, a comparison of the shape of the head with the shape of a bean. This usage began some time after the use of bean for the guinea coin, but the head stamped on the coin may have influenced its slang name.

implied a particular standard of weight and purity. Eventually, some years after coins had ceased to be minted out of absolutely pure metal, the Coinage Act of 1870 defined the respective standards as follows:

> For gold coin: fine gold, alloy, or millesimal fineness 916.66;
> For silver: fine silver, alloy, or millesimal fineness 925;
> For bronze: mixed metal, copper, tin, and zinc.

('Millesimal' here means simply 'thousandth parts', so that silver must have a purity of 925 parts in 1000, or 92.5 per cent.)

Until 1931, as mentioned, the Gold Standard marked the official exchange rate for converting currencies (i.e. money) into gold, with gold itself then usable as a currency. But when the Gold Standard was abandoned in 1931, and the British government stopped selling gold at a fixed price in exchange for sterling, a **Sterling Area** was established. The term was applied to those countries that tied their currencies to sterling (i.e. British money) rather than to gold, and who held their assets (gold and other currency reserves) in London. In practice this meant Commonwealth countries and certain other countries as varied as Denmark, Estonia, Iceland and Siam. The whole system was based on the fact that sterling was the world's main currency.

After World War II, however, many members of the Sterling Area started to diversify their reserves by holding other currencies besides sterling, dollars in particular. As a result of this, Britain had to negotiate an agreement with members by which they undertook to maintain a proportion of their reserves in sterling in exchange for a guarantee in terms of dollars.

Eventually, with each country building up its own reserves, even within the Commonwealth, the Sterling Area was reduced by 1978 to just the United Kingdom, Ireland, the Channel Islands, the Isle of Man, and Gibraltar.

Today, therefore, the Sterling Area as originally organized no longer exists.

### THE INTRODUCTION OF NEW COINS

The issuing into circulation of a new coin is both a formal and a popular event, frequently accompanied by public praise or criticism, especially if the coin markedly differs from the traditional in its size, weight or shape. In Britain, opinions were divided on the 'acceptability' of the seven-sided 20p and 50p coins when they were first introduced, and on the new £1 coin similarly. Coins, after all, are an important familiar feature of every-

**❝**

### WAITING IN THE WINGS

Riches, like insects, when conceal'd
  they lie,
Wait but for wings, and in their season,
  fly.
This year a reservoir, to keep and
  spare,
The next a fountain, spouting thro' his
  heir.

Alexander Pope *Epistle to Bathurst*

**❞**

## A NIMBLE NINEPENCE

An old proverb says that 'a nimble ninepence is better than a slow shilling'. The meaning is that in business a quick profit is better than a slow one, even if it is smaller. Brewer's *Dictionary of Phrase and Fable* prefers to explain the nimble ninepence as a silver coin that was 'pliable', but nimble has at no time had such a sense. *Chambers English Dictionary* contains the even more extraordinary statement that ninepence can refer to 'a high standard of nimbleness'.

'Ninepence' seems to have featured in many different expressions. The *Oxford English Dictionary* quotes 'as neat as ninepence', 'as grand as ninepence', 'as easy as ninepence', 'as right as ninepence'. The latter expression might still be heard, used by a speaker to mean that he was in good health.

It seems to have been possible in former times to describe someone as 'ninepence to a shilling', meaning that he was not quite right in the head, 'not the full quid' as they would say in New Zealand. The English saying may have referred to the Elizabethan shilling that was intended for circulation in Ireland. It depreciated in value and was treated as a coin worth only ninepence.

day life, and as in anything traditional, there can be an initial resistance at a popular level.

Today, in the final years of the 20th century, the issuing of new coinage is not as momentous an event as it was in the early years of the same century. Then, almost a hundred years ago, the Edwardian era was characterized by opulence and ostentation, and this was duly reflected in the inscriptions and pictorial images of the coins, as well as in the manner of their formal issue.

King Edward VII acceded to the throne in January 1901, so that new coinage was obviously required for a new monarch. The following royal proclamation, now historically interesting for its descriptive detail, accordingly appeared in the *London Gazette* on 10 December that year:

## By the KING
## A PROCLAMATION

*EDWARD*, R.I.

WHEREAS under section eleven of 'The Coinage Act, 1870' We have power, with the advice of Our Privy Council, from time to time by Proclamation to determine the design for any coin:

And whereas it appears to Us desirable to determine new designs for the gold and bronze coins mentioned in the First Schedule to 'The Coinage Act, 1870':

We, therefore, in pursuance of the said enactment and of all other powers enabling Us in that behalf, do hereby, by and with the advice of Our Privy Council, proclaim, direct, and ordain as follows:

1. The designs for the said gold and bronze coins shall be as follows:–

### GOLD COINS

(1) Five-Pound Piece.—Every five-pound piece shall have for the obverse impression Our effigy with the inscription 'Edwardus VII. Dei Gra: Britt: Omn: Rex Fid: Def: Ind: Imp:' and for the reverse the image of Saint George armed, sitting on horseback, attacking the dragon with a sword and a broken spear upon the ground, and the date of the year, with a graining upon the edge.

(2) Two-Pound Piece.—Every two-pound piece shall have the same obverse and reverse impression and inscription in all respects as the five-pound piece, with a graining upon the edge.

(3) Sovereign.—Every sovereign shall have for the obverse the aforesaid effigy with the inscription: 'Edwardus VII D.G. Britt: Omn: Rex F.D. Ind: Imp:' and for the reverse the same impression in all respects as the five-pound piece, with a graining upon the edge.

(4) Half-Sovereign.—Every half-sovereign shall have the same obverse and reverse impression and inscription in all respects as the sovereign, with a graining upon the edge.

### BRONZE COINS

(1) Penny.—Every penny shall have for the obverse impression Our effigy with the inscription: 'Edwardus VII Dei Gra: Britt: Omn: Rex Fid: Ind: Imp:' and for the reverse impression the figure of Britannia seated on a rock surrounded by the

## FARTHING

The farthing was a familiar coin in Britain for 1000 years, until it ceased to be legal tender on 31 December, 1960. Its name indicated that it was a 'fourth-ing', a quarter of a penny, though in the Bible farthing was used as a translation for the Roman *as*, the tenth part of a *denarius*, as well as the *quadrans*, the fourth part of a *denarius*.

The farthing was usually a silver coin until the 17th century. It was made of copper alloys, and later of bronze. There was also a gold farthing, a quarter-noble, but normal references to farthings in literature are to the less valuable coin.

Although the coin has disappeared from circulation, people might still say that they don't care a brass farthing about something, or that an article isn't worth a brass farthing. In London slang of the 19th century an insignificant person could be referred to as a 'farthing-faced chit'. People at that time were also likely to eat a farthing-dip, which was a piece of bread dipped in hot pork fat, sold by butchers.

In Cockney rhyming slang a farthing was a Covent Garden, since the colloquial pronunciation of farthing was 'farden'. This seems to have been normal at all levels of society, since in Thackeray's *Vanity Fair* it is used by Sir Pitt Crawley in the following scene:
'Where's the farden? I gave you three-half-pence. Where's the change, old Tinker?'
'There!' replied Mrs Tinker, flinging down the coin; 'it's only baronets as cares about farthings.'
'A farthing a day is seven shillings a year; seven shillings a year is the interest of seven guineas. Take care of your farthings, old Tinker, and your guineas will come quite nat'ral.'

sea, her right hand holding a shield which rests against the rock, while in her left hand she grasps a trident, and the inscription 'One Penny,' with the date of the year and a plain edge.

(2) Half-penny.—Every half-penny shall have the same obverse impression and inscription as the penny, and for the reverse the figure of Britannia seated as described for the penny, and the inscription 'Half-Penny,' with the date of the year and a plain edge.

(3) Farthing.—Every farthing shall have the same obverse impression and inscription as the penny, and for the reverse the figure of Britannia seated as described for the penny, and the inscription 'Farthing,' with the date of the year and a plain edge.

2. This Proclamation shall come into force on the first day of January nineteen hundred and two.

Given at Our Court at Saint James's, this tenth day of December, in the year of our Lord one thousand nine hundred and one, and in the first year of Our Reign.

GOD save the KING.

The abbreviated Latin inscription, which is even further abbreviated on the smaller coins, reads in full *Edwardus VII Dei Gratia Brittaniarum Omnium Rex Fidei Defensor Indiae Imperator*, otherwise 'Edward VII by the Grace of God of All the Britains King, Defender of the Faith, Emperor of India'. The title 'Ind: Imp:' was subsequently omitted on coins from 1949 onwards, as India had become a republic in 1947, and the title 'Britt: Omn:' was further omitted from 1954 by royal proclamation. (In the proclamation quoted above, the abbreviation 'R.I.' after the King's name stands for *Rex Imperator*, 'King Emperor', the latter word relating to his sovereignty over the British Empire.)

### THE MODERN £1 COIN

The £1 coin and 1p piece of the late 1980s, by contrast, have the simple inscription 'Elizabeth II D.G. Reg.F.D.', with 'Reg.' for *Regina*, 'queen', as the female equivalent to *Rex*.

The £1 coin, introduced in 1983, raised some eyebrows on account of its edge inscription, as this was not only novel but baffling in meaning. The

## WEALTHY ALLUSIONS

Modern authors would probably not expect their readers to recognize immediately an allusion to Dives. *Dives* is actually the Latin word for 'rich', but is traditionally the name given to 'the rich man' in the parable of The Rich Man and Lazarus (*Luke* xvi.19). As for Croesus, this king of Lydia (560–546 BC) was so wealthy that the saying 'as rich as Croesus' became proverbial.

William Thackeray took it for granted that his readers would be familiar with both names. In *Vanity Fair* occurs: 'Your friendship for Dives is about as sincere as the return which it usually gets. It is money you love, and not the man; and were Croesus and his footman to change places, you know who would have the benefit of your allegiance.'

wording was DECUS ET TUTAMEN, a Latin phrase from Virgil meaning 'An ornament and a safeguard'. The words had appeared on the edge of a number of earlier coins from the time of Charles II, and were designed to be a protection against clipping and other damage to the metal. (The phrase was said to have been devised by the diarist John Evelyn, and since it appeared on the 17th-century crown, led to the actual nicknaming of that coin as a 'decus'.)

The £1 issue of 1983 was a specifically 'English' one, so that when the coin was struck in a Scottish issue in 1984, the edge inscription changed to NEMO ME IMPUNE LACESSIT, 'No one provokes me with impunity', the motto of the Order of the Thistle and of three Scots regiments: the Scots Guards, the Royal Scots and the Black Watch. The origin of the motto itself is lost in antiquity.

In 1985 the Welsh £1 coin had the inscription: PLEIDIOL WYF I'M GWLAD, 'True am I to my country', words from the Welsh national anthem, 'Land of My Fathers', and in 1986 the Northern Ireland issue (which could hardly have had Irish wording) returned with the DECUS phrase, as did the 1987 English one.

Each issue circulated freely throughout the UK.

## IN WITH THE NEW, OUT WITH THE OLD

As in earlier centuries, the 20th century has seen the introduction of a number of new coins in Britain, as well as the withdrawal from circulation of others. Decimalization in 1971 resulted in a greater number of new coins than would otherwise have been likely.

Coins were *introduced* from 1901 as follows:

| | |
|---|---|
| 1968 | 5p (to replace 1 shilling) |
| | 10p (to replace 2 shillings, or florin) |
| 1969 | 50p (to replace 10 shilling note) |
| 1971 | ½p |
| | 1p |
| | 2p |
| 1982 | 20p |
| 1983 | £1 (to replace £1 note) |
| 1986 | £2 |

(Decimal coins issued before 1982 had their value in 'New' pence.)

Coins *ceased to be legal tender* from 1901 as follows:

| | |
|---|---|
| 1960 | Farthing (¼d) |
| 1969 | Pre-decimal halfpenny (½d) |
| 1970 | Half-crown (2s 6d) |
| 1971 | Threepence (3d) |
| | Pre-decimal penny (1d) |
| 1980 | Sixpence (6d = 2½p) |
| 1984 | Decimal halfpenny (½p) |

## THREE FARTHINGS

'Remuneration' is from a Latin word which means 'reward'. It is still a very formal word for 'pay', and was a learned word in Shakespeare's time. He has fun with it in *Love's Labour's Lost* (3.i), where Armado gives Costard three-farthings, saying 'there is remuneration'. Costard then says to himself: 'Now I will look to his remuneration. Remuneration! O, that's the Latin word for three farthings. Three farthings—remuneration. . . . Why, it is a fairer name than French crown. I will never buy and sell out of this word'.

In 1990 the original shilling (1s = 5p) and florin (2s = 10p) were still in circulation, although in decreasing numbers. They will presumably cease to be legal tender in due course, as the sixpence did.

Not everyone is satisfied with the present British coins, however. One of the objectors is the Treasury, who say that the range of coins is not right and who point out that some of the lower values will cost more to mint than their face value. Also, it is illogical to have a large 10p piece that is worth half the small 20p coin.

In 1986 a team at Nottingham University, after carrying out research on British coins among the public and industry on behalf of the Royal Mint, made a number of recommendations. They included the following:

1. The heavy seven-sided 50p piece should be replaced by a comfortable, light, round coin, just a little larger than the existing 5p coin.
2. The weighty 10p coin should be replaced by one the size of the old sixpence.
3. The 2p bronze coin should be abolished altogether.
4. The 5p coin should be cut to the size of the silver threepenny piece of the 1930s.
5. As well as a £2 coin for general use, a new £5 coin should be introduced.
6. The lightweight 20p piece should *not* be replaced or abolished.

Such changes have not yet been implemented, although it is planned to mint the 1p and 2p coins in copper-plated steel from 1991, instead of in the present alloy of copper and tin. This is because the alloy is actually worth more than the face value of the coins themselves. The new coins will be slightly thicker than the present ones, but will weigh the same.

Looking further ahead, however, it seems quite possible that all coins will be gradually phased out with the arrival of the cashless society (see Chapter 14, p. 181). New mintings and issues will then be matters of purely academic or historic interest.

**" ——————————————**

### MACHO MONEY?

*'A 15 000-a-year man makes love better than a pauper. There is virility in a large salary and women can sniff this out. Often they are accused of being mercenary but this is not necessarily true; it is not the money they want but the strength and potency that go with it.'*

Michael Fisher *The Executive*

**—————————————— "**

 COINS OF ENGLAND AND SCOTLAND

**angel**  gold coin of England struck 1465 and originally known as an 'angel noble', for its value of 6s 8d (see **noble** below). Not minted after 1634.

**angelet**  gold coin of England struck 1465 at a value of 3s 4d, i.e. half an angel (see above). Discontinued 1619.

**bawbee**  silver coin of Scotland struck 1542 at a value of three Scottish pennies (later six, or the equivalent of the English halfpenny).

**bodle**  copper coin of Scotland struck 1677–87 at a value of two Scottish pennies or one-sixth of an English penny.

**bonnet piece**  gold coin of Scotland struck 1539 at a value of 40 Scottish shillings. Named for its portrait of James V wearing a flat cap or 'bonnet'.

**bun penny**  (see p. 58).

**cartwheel**  nickname of heavy copper twopenny English coin struck 1797. Its size, weight and raised edge suggested a cartwheel.

**crown**  gold coin of England ('crown of the rose') struck 1526 at a value of 4s 6d and modelled on the French *écu au soleil*. Superseded same year by 'crown on the double rose' at a value of 5s, and supplemented 1551 by a silver coin, still valued at 5s. In modern times struck only as a commemorative piece, with the sole exception of the Churchill crown of 1965, now a collectors' item.

**demy**  gold coin of Scotland of late 14th century at a value of half a crown. Hence its name, meaning 'half'.

**farthing**  silver coin of England, originally struck 1279 as a fourth of a penny. Struck as a copper coin 1672, and as a bronze piece in 1860.

**florin**  gold coin of England struck 1344 at a value of 6s. Abandoned soon after, and not struck again until 1849, as a silver piece, at a value of one-tenth of a sovereign, i.e. 2s. Word 'florin' dropped from 2s piece 1937. Still in circulation with a value of 10p long after decimalization (1971).

**george noble**  gold coin of England struck 1526–33 as a noble, i.e. at a value of 6s 8d. Name relates more to representation on reverse of St George slaying the Dragon than to George III, under whom first issued.

**groat**  silver coin of England struck 1279 at a value of 4d as a copy of the French *gros tournois*. In use until 1662, after which issued as Maundy money. Reissued as 'Britannia groat' 1836–55, still as 4d coin.

**guinea**  gold coin of England struck 1663 and in circulation to end of 18th century, initially as an ordinary sovereign or 20s piece, but from 1717 having a value fixed at 21s. In modern times purely a money of account, especially for professional fees, but rarely so after decimalization (1971), when its value became £1.05.

**half-crown**  gold coin of England struck 1526 at a value of 2s 6d, and current to 1625. From 1551 also issued as a silver piece (to 1946), then as a cupro-nickel coin to 1971, when it was withdrawn on introduction of decimalization.

**halfpenny**  at first a piece obtained by cutting a silver English penny in two, but struck as an individual silver coin in 13th century. From 1672 issued as a copper piece, then from 1860 as a bronze coin. Last struck as a pre-decimal coin in 1967, and first as a decimal one in 1971. The latter withdrawn from circulation in 1985.

**hatpiece**  gold coin of Scotland struck in 1591 at a value of 80s. Named for its portrait of James VI wearing a tall hat.

**leopard**  gold coin of England struck in 1344 at a value of 3s, or half a florin.

**lion**  gold coin of Scotland struck at end of 14th century at a value of 5s.

**merk**  silver coin of Scotland struck 1580 at a value of 13s 4d, with name based on the mark. After Union of Scotland and England in 1604, declared to have a value of 13½d when circulating in England.

**noble**  gold coin of England struck 1344 at a value of 6s 8d, and superseding the original florin.

**penny**   originally a silver coin of England current in the 8th century, copied from the Roman *novus denarius* ('new denier'), hence its former abbreviation as 'd'. A gold penny was struck in 1257. The copper penny dates from 1797, and the bronze coin from 1860. The decimal penny ('p') was introduced 1971.

**pound**   the first £1 piece was struck as a silver coin of England in 1642 and 1643 in Shrewsbury and Oxford, during the Civil War. Later issued with this value as the sovereign (see below). The present £1 coin was first struck 1983.

**rider**   gold coin of Scotland struck 1475, acquiring a value of 23s from 1491. Named for its portrait of James III on horseback.

**sceat**   silver coin of England current in the 7th and 8th centuries, as the precursor of the silver penny. Name, pronounced 'shat', is Old English for 'treasure', 'money' (cp modern German *Schatz*, 'treasure', 'wealth').

**shilling**   silver coin of England struck 1504, originally as a testoon (see below). The name 'shilling' had been in earlier use, however, as a money of account. Superseded in value (originally 12 pence) by the decimal 5p piece in 1971, but still circulating even now.

**sixpence**   silver coin of England struck 1551 and circulating until 1980, when ceased to be legal tender. Name had been in earlier use as a money of account.

**sovereign**   gold coin of England struck 1489 at a value of 20s, and so serving as a piece worth £1. Under Edward VI (second half of 16th century) had a value of 30s, but under Elizabeth I reverted to 20s. First of modern sovereigns struck 1817. Ceased to be legal tender during World War I.

**testoon**   name used for shilling (see above) introduced 1504, and also for silver coin of Scotland struck 1553–62 at a value of four Scottish shillings.

**threepence**   silver coin of England struck 1551, and in later issues. Modern nickel-brass 12-sided piece struck 1937 and issued to 1967. Ceased to be legal tender 1971, on introduction of decimalization.

**thrymsa**   gold coin of England issued 6th and 7th centuries, deriving its name from Roman *tremissis*, a version of the triens, on which the English piece was based.

**unicorn**   gold coin of Scotland struck 1486 at a value of 18 Scottish shillings.

**unite**   gold coin of England and Scotland struck 1604, at a value of 20s, to mark union of the two kingdoms.

## QUIDS IN

'Quid' has been a British slang term for a sum of money since the 17th century. It was at first applied to a guinea, later to a sovereign, or pound. The word's origin has been the subject of much speculation, but it remains a mystery. It has naturally been linked with Latin *quid*, 'what', with scholars pointing to the use of 'wherewithal' (with what) in its sense of 'money'. The link is a tenuous one, however.

If a story someone tells is not the full quid, the suggestion is that he is keeping something back.

In the Royal Navy HMS *Royal Sovereign* was quickly dubbed Tiddley Quid, 'tiddley' meaning 'smart'. In a similar way the nickname of Admiral Sir Dudley Pound, though not one used to his face, was Phoney Quid, with a pun on the Dud of his first name.

Australian slang has 'fiddley did' as 20th-century rhyming slang for a quid. In London slang a quid could be a 'saucepan lid' or 'Yid'.

 *A GOOD PENNYWORTH*

The penny (the word itself is of obscure origin) has been part of the English currency system since the 8th century. It has appeared in many forms, as a silver, copper or bronze coin, with differing values. Until 1971 there were 240 pennies to the pound; there are now 100. In Canada and some parts of America, penny has long been used to refer to a cent.

Before decimalization in 1971 the abbreviation d. was used for the penny, (for Latin *denarius* or *denarii*). Some people therefore used the form 'dee' when talking about it. Writing to the *Times* newspaper in November, 1989, Mr John Tapp recalled that in his school tuckshop in the late 1930s one asked for a 'dee drink' or a 'two-dee drink'. Amongst the boys transactions took place in 'dees' and 'haydees' (halfpence). In the same newspaper Mrs Josephine Parkin mentioned a music-hall song which ran:
O Kitty is pretty and Kitty is fair,
She works in the City in Finsbury Square,
She sells cups of coffee; her price is two d.
She's sending me off my C.H.U.M.P.

This 'dee' usage, however, was by no means as general as the post-decimalization use of 'pee' (based on the new abbreviation of p.), ugly though most English speakers consider the latter term to be.

A penny is now of such insignificant value that it would be difficult to compile a list of things that could be done, or purchased, for a penny. Henry Peacham had less difficulty in compiling such a list in the 17th century. In his *Worth of a Penny* he says that it could be: 'bestowed in charity upon a poor body' in order to earn a heavenly reward; it could buy a small quantity of aniseed, which when distilled in water might 'save one's life in a fainting fit'; it could add considerably to your education, since 'for a penny you may hear a most eloquent oration upon our English kings and queens, if you will listen seriously to David Owen, who keeps the monuments at Westminster Abbey'; it would pay for a

crossing of the Thames by ferry, thus avoiding a long detour; it would provide 'all the news in England and other countries, of murders, floods, witches, fires, tempests and what not' in one of the weekly news books; it would enable you to have 'your horse rubbed and walked after a long journey'; it would buy you 'a fair cucumber, but not a breast of mutton'.

'For a penny,' Peacham continued, 'you may have your dog wormed, and so be kept from running mad; for a penny, you shall tell what will happen a year hence in some almanack; for a penny, you may be advanced to that height that you shall be above the best in the city.'

To achieve this dramatic effect the penny had to be spent, together with a good deal of energy, in St Paul's Cathedral. The penny gave one the right to climb to the top and thus be 'above the best in the city'.

The long history of the penny in England has led to the inclusion of the word in many idiomatic phrases, some of which remain in daily use. 'This mourning (i.e. the clothes for it) will cost a pretty penny,' says a character in *Mary Barton*, by Elizabeth Gaskell, and a modern speaker might use exactly the same phrase to mean that something is expensive. This may originally have been a reference to the so-called gold penny minted by Henry III in 1257. This was a gold coin but not actually a penny—the word was occasionally used in the more general sense of 'coin'.

'We told you he'd turn up like an old bad penny' occurs in *The Black Prince*, by Iris Murdoch. A bad penny was a counterfeit coin, which no one was pleased to find amongst his change. 'In for a penny, in for a pound' is likely to be the philosophical utterance of someone who has begun something and feels that it should be completed, whatever the cost. 'Pennies from heaven' refers to money obtained unexpectedly, and without effort.

Something which is cheap may be said to be 'two (or ten) a penny'. 'To spend a penny' remains a rather coy euphemism for going to the lavatory, recalling a time when public conveniences had cubicles to which entrance could only be obtained by inserting a penny in a slot. Slot-machine usage also underlies the statement, made to someone who finally seems to have grasped one's point, that 'the penny has dropped'.

We still offer someone 'a penny for your thoughts', though we are likely to be told that the thoughts are not worth even that small amount, or that they are worth much more. To earn money legally is 'to turn an honest penny'. 'To turn an honest hundred pounds' might be more meaningful, but the penny expression lives on.

Listed below are some other penny expressions which have been used in English at one time or another:

**Arles penny**   see Earnest penny. This term was used especially in Scotland.

**Bargain penny**   see Earnest penny.

**Bun penny**   the penny (struck 1860–94) which shows Queen Victoria with her hair gathered in a bun at the back of her neck. The coin portrays her as a young woman, but she was 40 years old when the coin first appeared. A bun penny could no doubt have been used at the time to buy a penny bun in any baker's shop.

**Catchpenny**   used in the 18th century to describe something that was worthless, such as a publication, but which was designed to trap the unwary into purchasing it.

**Cock penny**   this was a customary payment at Shrovetide, made to a schoolmaster in certain schools in the North of England by the pupils or their parents. Cock-pence were theoretically meant to defray the expense of cock-fighting or cock-throwing, but the money came to be a necessary supplement to a teacher's income. One such teacher is quoted in the *Oxford English Dictionary* as saying that his annual salary in the early part of the eighteenth century was £10 a year, 'and entrances and cock-pennies amounted to as much more.'

**Earnest penny**   a small sum of money, originally a penny, put down as a deposit to secure an object that one intends to buy or to seal a bargain. Also called an arles penny, bargain penny, fastening penny, God's penny. Earnest penny was frequently used metaphorically in religious senses in the 17th century.

**Eight-penny**   used by Shakespeare, in *1 Henry the Fourth* 3.iii, to mean 'of little value'—'a trifle, some eight-penny matter'.

**First penny**   in the 16th and 17th centuries a phrase which meant 'cost price', as in 'seven butts of sack, which cost the first penny seventeen ducats the butt'.

**God's penny**   a penny paid to indicate that a bargain had been struck, e.g. an agreement between a master and a servant. The actual penny would originally have been devoted to some religious or charitable purpose, hence the name.

**Hanse penny**   a penny levied by a medieval trading guild.

**Hearth penny**   see Peter's penny.

**Homage penny**   money or a gift given under Feudal Law to a lord in acknowledgement of allegiance.

**Lickpenny**   an obsolete term for something which absorbs one's money. 'Law is a lick-penny' occurs in *St Ronan's Well*, by Sir Walter Scott. John Lydgate (1375–1440) has a long poem called *London Lyckpenny*. Its theme is the difficulty of living in London if one has no money.

**Penny ale**   poor quality beer sold for a penny a gallon.

**Penny-a-liner**   a freelance writer for the newspapers who was paid a penny a line. Since this put the emphasis on quantity rather than quality, it led to writing that was unnecessarily wordy. The penny-a-liner was not always concerned with facts, which took time and effort to gather. The fictional efforts of such hacks led to the alternative popular name penny-a-liar.

**Penny-a-mile**   a hat, rhyming on 'tile'.

**Penny-ante** used mainly by American speakers to mean 'trivial'. The original reference was to a poker game in which the minimum wager was one penny. 'I'm not talking about the penny-ante handy man for hire. I'm talking about the man who thinks he is serving a higher cause than his country and wouldn't accept a penny for the risks he undergoes.' Isaac Asimov, *Yankee Doodle Went to Town*.

**Penny a pound** rhyming slang for 'ground'.

**Penny arcade** an amusement arcade with slot machines that were originally operated by a penny.

**Penny bank** a savings-bank at which a deposit as low as a penny could be deposited.

**Penny bird** an Irish dialect name for the Little Grebe, also called the drink-a-penny.

**Penny black** the first adhesive postage stamp issued in Britain, 1840.

**Penny-boy** a boy found at cattle markets who did occasional droving at the rate of a penny per animal.

**Penny-buster** late 19th-century slang for a small new loaf, or a large bun, costing a penny.

**Penny-catcher** a derisive term in Jamaica for anyone who is willing to work for too little money.

**Penny death-trap** the popular name for the penny paraffin lamp imported from Germany at the end of the 19th century. It was dangerous and caused many accidents.

**Penny dog** an expression which has been variously used to describe a kind of dog-fish, a shark, a dog of inferior breed or a dog that constantly follows its master.

**Penny dreadful** a penny publication containing crime stories written in a sensational and lurid manner.

**Penny-farthing** the nickname of the 'ordinary' bicycle which was fashionable in the 1870s, the name deriving from the large front wheel and the small rear one.

**Penny-father** an old, miserly man. The expression was used mainly in the 16th and 17th centuries.

**Penny fish** the John Dory, from the round spots on its sides.

**Penny flower** the plant 'Honesty', from its round pods.

**Penny gaff** a low class theatre or music-hall with a penny entrance-fee. A gaff was originally a slang word for a fair.

**Penny grass** an alternative name for pennywort.

**Penny loaf** a slang term of derision in the 19th century for a man afraid to steal. The implication was that he was content to live on a penny loaf.

**Penny locket** rhyming slang for 'pocket'.

**Penny lottery** in his *Everyday Book*, William Hone describes the Penny Lottery which was drawn at the Theatre Royal in London on 19 October, 1698. Tickets cost a penny each, and the prize was £1000.

**Penny packets** wartime Royal Air Force slang for small parties of soldiers, less than a platoon, seen from the air.

**Penny pies** moneywort.

**Penny pig** an earthenware pot shaped like a pig used as a money-box.

**Penny pincher** a miser, also known at one time as a penny-peeler.

**Penny plain (and tuppence coloured)** a catch-phrase contrasting the plain with the fancy. The exact origin of the phrase is disputed, but it clearly referred to printed matter that was more expensive if coloured.

**Penny pool** another form of 'penny ante'.

**Penny post** normally a reference to the postal system introduced by Rowland Hill in 1840, enabling a letter to be sent anywhere in Britain for a penny. There had been an earlier scheme in the London area.

**Penny pots** low 19th-century slang for the pimples on the face of a heavy drinker.

**Penny readings** parochial entertainments where a penny was charged for entrance. *Lark Rise to Candleford*, by Flora Thompson, has a full description: 'The Penny Reading was a form of entertainment already out of date in most places; but at Candleford Green it was still going strong in the 1890s. The pennies taken at the door paid for heating and light. It was a popular as well as an inexpensive entertainment. Everybody went; whole families together, and all agreed that the excitement of going out after dark, carrying lanterns, and sitting in a warm room with rows and rows of other people, was well worth the sum of one penny, apart from the entertainment provided. The star turn was given by an old gentleman from a neighbouring village, who, in his youth, had heard Dickens read his own works in public and aimed at reproducing in his own rendering the expression and mannerisms of the master.'

**Pennyroyal**   a kind of mint, formerly believed to have medicinal properties. The name corrupts an earlier *puliol real*, ultimately Latin *pulegium*, 'thyme'.

**Penny-stinker**   a bad cigar in London slang of the 1880s.

**Penny-stone**   a flat, round stone used as a quoit.

**Penny weddings**   weddings at which the guests contributed small sums of money to help pay for the wedding-day entertainment. Any surplus money went towards furnishing the marital home. Penny weddings were especially common in Scotland, Wales and Ireland.

**Pennyweight**   24 grains of Troy weight, the original weight of a silver penny.

**Pennyweighter**   in US criminal slang, one who steals jewellery or precious stones, typically by entering a shop, palming something and hiding it under the counter for an accomplice to pick up later. A pennyweighter is also one who substitutes paste for real stones. In a mining camp he is one who steals very small quantities of gold at a time.

**Penny white**   17th- and 18th-century slang for an ugly but rich woman.

**Penny wise**   used of a person who is niggardly.

**Pennywort**   the name of several plants with rounded leaves.

**Peter's penny, or Peter penny**   an annual tax of a penny paid by each householder having land of a certain value to the papal see at Rome. This was before the Reformation, and was discontinued in 1534. Also known as hearth penny, Rome penny.

**Potation penny**   an obsolete term for money given as a contribution towards a drinking party.

**Rome penny**   see Peter's penny.

**Scot penny**   a penny paid as one's share of the bill for an entertainment.

**Sixpenny**   used by Shakespeare in *1 Henry the Fourth* 2.i to mean paltry. 'Sixpenny strikers' is used to refer to highwaymen who would knock a man down for sixpence, a paltry sum.

**Slut's pennies**   a dialectal term in the 18th century for hard pieces in a loaf that were due to imperfect kneading of the dough.

**Soul penny**   a penny subscribed for a mass said for the soul of a dead person.

**Teind penny**   a penny paid as a tithe. Teind is a Northern and Scottish word for 'tenth'. Tithing penny is another form of this expression.

**True penny**   an epithet for an honest, trustworthy man. In *Hamlet* the term is used in direct address.

**Tuppeny, or twopenny**   in 19th-century slang this could mean the head. Head in rhyming slang was 'loaf of bread' and a loaf cost twopence. A child playing leap-frog would be told: 'Tuck in your tuppeny!'

**Victor penny**   this is connected with cock-penny (see above). It was a penny paid to a schoolmaster by the pupil owning the victorious cock.

**Ward penny**   in Feudal Law this penny was paid to a superior in lieu of military service.

## SHILLING

The shilling was a familiar coin in Britain for nearly 500 years. It continued for a while after the decimalization of British currency in 1971, pretending to be a five-pence piece. Older speakers may still refer to the latter coin as a shilling, but the term is no longer officially recognized. It is frequently mentioned in literature, and acceptance of the King's or Queen's shilling once signified that a man had enlisted as a soldier. Victorian fathers were also likely to issue threats to their offspring, to the effect that they would be cut off with a shilling, i.e. disinherited.

At some levels of society, a shilling was a substantial sum of money. G. B. Shaw has Professor Higgins make the point in *Pygmalion*, Act 2. Eliza Doolittle has offered him a shilling to give her an elocution lesson, and he remarks: 'You know, Pickering, if you consider a shilling, not as a simple shilling, but as a percentage of this girl's income, it works out as fully equivalent to 60 or 70 guineas from a millionaire.

'Figure it out. A millionaire has about £150 a day. She earns about half-a-crown . . . She offers me two-fifths of her day's income for a lesson. Two fifths of a millionaire's income for a day would be somewhere about £60. It's handsome. By George, it's enormous! It's the biggest offer I ever had.'

Liza is alarmed at the turn the conversation is taking: 'Sixty pounds! What are you talking about? I never offered you sixty pounds. Where would I get . . .?' 'Hold your tongue,' says Higgins.

John Philips (1676–1709) has a long poem called *The Splendid Shilling*, written in the style of John Milton. A typical verse runs: 'Happy the man who, void of cares and strife, In silken or in leathern purse retains A Splendid Shilling: he nor hears with pain New oysters cried, nor sighs for cheerful ale; But with his friends, when nightly mists arise, To Juniper's, Magpie, or Town Hall repairs.' The references in the last line are probably to public houses. The poem continues by saying that the poet is being chased by a dun or catchpole because he has no money.

Other references are found to a 'bob', as the shilling was universally known. No one has been able to explain the origin of this nickname, though it appears to be the diminutive form of Robert. Hence the remark by Dickens in *A Christmas Carol*, to the effect that 'Bob had but fifteen "Bob" a week

himself; he pocketed on Saturdays but fifteen copies of his Christian name.'

Jerome K. Jerome, in *The Idle Thoughts of an Idle Fellow*, comments: 'Years ago, when my whole capital would occasionally come down to what in town the people call a bob, I would recklessly spend a penny of it, merely for the sake of having the change, all in coppers, to jingle. You can't feel nearly so hard up with elevenpence in your pocket as you do with a shilling.'

An altogether more powerful literary allusion of this kind occurs in the *Ballads and Songs* of John Davidson (1857–1909). There is a long poem called 'Thirty Bob A Week', its theme being the difficulty of trying to survive in London in the 1890s on a wage of 30 shillings a week. Davidson was not just using his imagination. The son of a Scottish minister who came to London in 1889, he suffered great poverty and ill health. He eventually committed suicide.

His 'Thirty Bob A Week' poem ends:
I was the love that chose my mother out;
I joined two lives and from the union burst;
My weakness and my strength without a
    doubt
Are mine alone for ever from the first:
It's just the very same with a difference in the
    name
As 'Thy will be done'. You say it if you durst!

They say it daily up and down the land
As easy as you take a drink, it's true;
But the difficultest go to understand,
And the difficultest job a man can do
Is to come it brave and meek with thirty bob a
    week,
And feel that that's the proper thing for you.

It's a naked child against a hungry wolf;
It's playing bowls upon a splitting wreck;
It's walking on a string across a gulf
With mill-stones fore-and-aft about your neck;
But the thing is daily done by many and many
    a one;
And we fall, face forward, fighting, on the
    deck.

# 6
# FOREIGN FUNDS

## EUROPEAN MONEY

### MAKING A MARK

We begin with German currency, since it is the Deutschmark which is to be the central currency unit of the European Bank from 1992.

The **mark** traces its origin back to a weight and money of account (that is, existing in name only) to at least the 9th century AD, when it was originally valued at two-thirds of the Roman pound.

The first actual coin of the name was one struck in Lübeck in 1506, but the more familiar silver denomination was issued only in 1873 (until 1927). From 1933 to the outbreak of World War II, the mark was struck in nickel, and after the war, from 1950, circulated in cupronickel.

The **Deutschmark**, as the standard monetary unit of West Germany, was instituted in 1948, and was so called to be distinguished from the East German mark. This was also at first called a Deutschmark (which simply means 'German mark'), but later became officially a *Mark der Deutschen Notenbank* ('mark of the German issuing bank') then from 1968 the *Mark der Deutschen Demokratischen Republik* ('mark of the German Democratic Republic'), now often referred to as an Ostmark. If the two Germanies, East and West, reunite as a single state, there seems little doubt that monetary union will occur, with a reversion to the mark pure and simple as the basic currency. In April 1990 Helmut Kohl, the West German Chancellor, took the decision to convert East Germany's Ostmarks into Deutschmarks on a 'one to one' basis, thus opening the way to an eventual reunification between the two governments.

## WELL-HEELED

To be well-heeled is, in a way, the opposite of being down-at-heel, but the former expression derives from cock-fighting, where metal spurs were put on the cocks. The original meaning was thus 'armed' or 'equipped' with any kind of arm. In American slang a man was well-heeled if he was carrying a revolver. The modern meaning of well-heeled in the sense of comfortably provided with money arose at the beginning of the 20th century.

Being down-at-heel, not having enough money to have one's shoes repaired, is taken to be a general sign of destitution.

The Deutschmark is divided into 100 pfennigs. The **pfennig** (whose name is related to that of the penny) originated as a medieval silver coin, but from the 16th century was issued as a copper piece.

## FRANKLY SPEAKING

France is familiar for its **franc**, divided into 100 centimes.

The franc was first issued as a gold coin in 1360, and probably took its name from its original Latin inscription, FRANCORUM REX, 'king of the Franks', this being the title of Jean le Bon (John the Good) who was king of France when it was introduced. A silver franc was then introduced in 1577 under Henri III. Unusually, therefore, France is a country whose name, from a root word meaning 'free', is of identical origin to that of its native population and its basic currency.

The **centime** first made its appearance in 1795, when it was introduced by the revolutionary government as part of the new decimal system. It was struck at the same time as the third issue of the franc, which was again a silver piece.

## PIECES OF EIGHT

Spain has the **peseta**, divided into 100 centimos, as its currency.

The peseta, whose name is a diminutive of *peso*, 'weight', dates from the 18th century. It was struck for internal circulation as a 'companion' coin to the full **peso**, the famous silver coin known as the 'piece of eight', with reference to its value of eight reales. The peso was itself introduced in 1497, as a result of the monetary reforms of King Ferdinand and Queen Isabella of Spain. In the latter half of the 19th century, the peso was adopted as a gold coin by most South American countries.

## COATS OF ARMS

In Portugal, the main currency is the **escudo** (meaning 'shield'), divided into 100 **centavos**. The first escudo was the gold coin struck in 1537, and the shield that gave it its name was that of the Spanish coat of arms that it bore.

## FROM LIBRA TO LIRA

The basic currency of Italy is the **lira**, divided into 100 **centesimi**.

As its name shows, the lira evolved from the Roman libra, or pound, and it was a money of account from early medieval times. It did not become an actual coin until 1472, when it was issued by the Doge Nicolas Tron of Venice as a

**"**

### THE NIGHT WORD

*Fillmore is full of ideas about gold. The 'mythos' of gold, he calls it. He tells me that the French are hoarding their gold away in watertight compartments deep below the surface of the earth; he tells me that there is a little locomotive which runs around in these subterranean vaults and corridors. I like the idea enormously. A profound, uninterrupted silence in which the gold softly snoozes at a temperature of 17¼ degrees Centigrade. . . . Gold is a night word belonging to the chthonian mind: it has dream in it and mythos.*

Henry Miller *Tropic of Cancer*

(*Mythos* is the Greek word for 'myth, story, talk'. *Chthonian* means 'of the earth or the underworld and the deities that inhabit it; ghostly'. The word is pronounced *thonian*.)

**"**

silver piece. (It was also known as a testone, 'head', referring to the portrait of the Doge that it bore.) The lira was adopted as the equivalent of the French silver franc when Italy joined the Latin Monetary Union in 1865.

## GOING FOR GOLD

While Belgium and Switzerland, like France, have francs and centimes for their currency, Holland has the florin or **guilder**, divided into 100 **cents**.

The guilder (or gulden), as its name indicates, was originally a gold coin. It was current in different issues in various countries and states of Europe, including Germany, Austria, Hungary and Sweden. In the Netherlands, however, the

**""**

### THE DILEMMA

*'Sell all thou hast, and give to the poor,' she heard on Sunday morning. That was plain enough, plain enough for Monday morning too. As she went down the hill to the station, going to school, she took the saying with her. 'Sell all thou hast, and give to the poor.' Did she want to do that? Did she want to sell her pearl-backed brush and mirror, her silver candlestick, her pendant, her lovely little necklace, and go dressed in drab like the Wherrys: the unlovely uncombed Wherrys, who were the 'poor' to her? She did not. She walked this Monday morning on the verge of misery. For she 'did want to do what was right. And she didn't want to do what the gospels said. She didn't want to be poor—really poor. The thought was a horror to her: to live like the Wherrys, so ugly, to be at the mercy of everybody.*
*'Sell all thou hast, and give to the poor.' One could not do it in real life. How dreary and hopeless it made her!*

D. H. Lawrence *The Rainbow*

**"**

guilder was a silver coin, first struck in 1601.

The Dutch guilder is still known by its alternative name of 'florin'. It took this name from the coin that circulated all over Europe from the 13th century, when it was first issued as a gold piece in Florence. (The florin took its name not so much from Florence, but from the badge of that city that it bore, a lily or fleur-de-lys, in Italian *fiorino*.)

## CROWNED HEADS

The Scandinavian countries of Norway, Sweden and Denmark have almost identically named currencies, called the **krone** in Norway and Denmark, and the **krona** in Sweden. The name obviously means 'crown'. In Sweden, this is divided into 100 **öre**, and in the other two countries into 100 **øre**. This name also has an obvious meaning, that of 'gold', ultimately from Latin *aureus*, 'gold coin'. The krone has been the main monetary unit of Norway and Denmark since 1895, when it was issued as a silver coin. The öre was originally a small unit of weight, but was issued as a silver coin in Sweden in 1522. Together with its equivalent in the other two countries, it became standardized as the one-hundredth part of a krona or krone in 1872.

Iceland has a similar currency, with the **króna** divided into 100 **aurar**. Here the larger value was adopted as a coin only in 1925.

### NOSE

'To pay through the nose' means to pay too much. One story accounting for the origin of the expression is that the Danes imposed a nose tax on the Irish in the 9th century. Those who could not pay had their noses slit.

The story has been linked since the 17th century to other oppressors and other victims, e.g. the Jews. Professor Weekley thinks it might be a playful variation of to bleed someone in the sense of extracting money from him. 'To bleed someone' certainly can mean to extort money, the most extreme form of such blackmail being 'to bleed someone white,' perhaps by 'putting the bite' on him.

## FINNISH FINANCE

Finland's national currency is the **markka**, divided into 100 **penniä**. These names are basically the same as the mark and pfennig of Germany. The markka was first struck as a silver coin in 1860, when it had a value of a quarter of a rouble, Finland then being part of the Russian empire (until 1917).

## RUSSIAN ROUBLES

In the Soviet Union itself, as formerly in Russia, the main unit of currency is the **rouble**, divided into 100 **kopecks**. The rouble has a name that means literally 'cut-off', referring to the portions of silver bars that served as both weights and money of account in the 14th century. The first coin of the name was introduced by Peter the Great as a silver piece in 1704. The kopeck, whose name means 'lance', from the depiction of the tsar on horseback holding a lance that it bore, was first struck as a silver piece in 1534. Under the monetary reforms of Peter the Great it became a copper coin in 1704.

## HUNGARIAN HELLERS

Hungary has the **forint** ('florin') as its main currency, divided into 100 **filler**. In its modern form, the forint was introduced in 1946 to replace the pengö (a name related to 'penny'), which had been current as a silver coin from 1925. The filler has a name directly corresponding to that of the heller of Austria and elsewhere. (See p. 66)

## SCHILLINGS AND GROSCHEN

Today, Austria's main currency is the **schilling**, divided into 100 **groschen**. The schilling was adopted as the country's basic monetary unit in 1925, but earlier was found as the name of various coins elsewhere in Europe, especially in certain northern German states. It clearly relates by name directly to the English shilling. The groschen was originally the chief silver coin of the Holy Roman Empire, taking its name from the French gros, in turn named after the Italian grosso, which meant simply 'large'.

## LOST LIONS

Bulgaria has the **lev** as its main unit of currency, divided into 100 **stotinki**. The lev has a name that

means 'lion', and originally bore a representation of this animal, since it was modelled on the French franc. The stotinka, like many 'one-hundredth' coins, has a name that simply denotes this fraction, from Bulgarian sto, 'hundred'. Both coins were introduced in 1880, when Bulgaria joined the Latin Monetary Union.

## GOLD AND SILVER

Poland's main unit of currency is the **zloty**, meaning simply 'golden'. The name was originally used of the gold coin introduced in the 16th century as a copy of the Hungarian goldguldiner. But silver zlotys have equally been issued in later times. The zloty is divided into 100 **groszy**, with a name related to that of the groschen, which circulated in the Holy Roman Empire. Its name in turn derived from the French gros, which literally means 'large', although the groschen and grosz are small coins. ('Groschen' is a diminutive, meaning literally 'little big'.)

## CZECH PAYMENTS

In Czechoslovakia, the main unit is the **koruna**, whose name means 'crown'. The present coin of the name was introduced in 1922. The koruna is divided into 100 **haléřů**, with 'haléř' the Slavonic equivalent of 'heller'. The **heller** was a small silver coin first struck in Germany in the 13th century, taking its name from the Swabian town of Hall (today Schwäbisch Hall) where it was originally minted.

## BRING ON THE PARAS

In Jugoslavia, the chief unit is the **dinar**, divided into 100 **paras**. The dinar has a name identical to that of the Arabic gold coin first struck in Syria in the 7th century. It in turn derived its name from the Roman denarius. The para has a name of Turkish (originally Persian) origin, and means simply 'piece'.

 LUCKY LUCRE

The word 'lucre' derives from Latin *lucrum* 'gain'. It often occurs in the phrase 'filthy lucre', which was Tyndale's translation of a phrase in the *New Testament* (*Titus* 1.11). The *Revised Standard Version* prefers 'base gain', and a more colloquial explanation would be 'money obtained dishonestly'.

Lucre is pronounced with a long vowel sound, like the name Luke, but in his well-known short story *The Rocking-Horse Winner*, D. H. Lawrence has the following: 'I thought when Uncle Oscar said *filthy lucker*, it meant money.'
'*Filthy lucre* does mean money,' said the mother. 'But it's lucre, not luck.'
'Oh!' said the boy. 'Then what is luck, mother?'
'It's what causes you to have money. If you're lucky you have money. That's why it's better to be born lucky than rich. If you're rich, you may lose your money. But if you're lucky, you will always get more money.'

 **“**

### WAS THIS THE FACE . . .?

*It is open to us, of course, to believe that Troy was besieged for ten years for the sake of a woman, as it is pleasant to read in Homer of Helen watching the battlefield from the tower above the Skaian gates, while the old men of the city marvel at her beauty, saying to one another 'Small blame it is that for such a woman the Trojans and Achaeans should long suffer hardships.' But if you ask me, do I believe that the Trojan war happened so, I am constrained to answer that I do not: I suspect there was money in it somewhere.*

Sir Arthur Quiller-Couch *The Commerce of Thought*

**”**

### WHEN IN ROMANIA . . .

Romania's chief unit of the currency is the **leu**, divided into 100 **bani**. The leu has a name of the same origin as the Bulgarian lev, so also means 'lion'. The present coin was introduced in 1867 as a gold piece equivalent to the French franc. The ban is a copper coin first issued the same year. Its name ultimately derives from the Persian title *ban*, meaning 'lord', but more directly relates to the title of a military ruler in time of war in certain Eastern European countries.

### TURKISH DELIGHT

Turkey, although only partly in Europe, has the Turkish lira as its 'pound', with this name the same as that of Italy's main unit of currency. The Turkish lira is divided into 100 **kurus**, a name of historic origin that is ultimately based on that of the groschen or grosso, so literally means 'large'.

### GREEK DRAMS

Greece, as might be expected, has currency units with ancient names. The main unit is the **drachma**, divided into 100 **lepta**. In Ancient Greece, the drachma was the basic silver coin, as

## THE TALENTED GREEKS:

Edward Gibbon remarks in his *Decline and Fall of the Roman Empire* that in her most flourishing time the 21 000 citizens of Athens possessed only 6000 talents, or £1200 sterling,

well as the term for a standard weight. The name corresponds to modern English 'dram' or 'drachm', and originally meant 'handful'. The historic concept was of a coin or weight equal to a 'handful' of obols (later standardized as equal to six obols). The lepton was similarly the name of both a small coin and weight. Its name means simply 'small'.

### ALEXANDER OF ALBANIA

In Albania, the main currency is the **lek**, divided into 100 **qindarka**. Both coins were introduced in 1925, before which time Albania had no currency of her own. The lek takes its name from the abbreviated name of Alexander the Great, who was associated with this region of Europe, and who himself established several mints as well as being responsible for the great influence of Greek coinage in various parts of the world. The qindar has a name that denotes its basic value, since it derives from Albanian *qint*, 'hundred'. The qindar is thus a coin with a name related directly to that of the cent.

### SMALLER CHANGE

The smaller European countries or principalities have currencies identical to those of their larger neighbours. Andorra, in fact, has no currency of its own, but uses French and Spanish currencies equally. Liechtenstein similarly uses Swiss currency. Both Luxembourg and Monaco have the franc as their main currency, while in San Marino and the Vatican, Italian currency circulates. Malta has the Maltese lira as its main unit, with this divided into 100 cents or 1000 mils, both self-explanatory names.

### THE COLONIAL HERITAGE

Many European countries, including Britain, settled colonies elsewhere in the world in historical times, and witness to this are the

currency names still found today outside their nation of origin.

The **shilling**, for example, still exists in Kenya, Somalia, Tanzania and Uganda (even though it is no longer issued in its native land!), and the **centavo**, of Portuguese origin, is found as the lesser unit of currency in many Central and South American countries (such as Argentina, Bolivia, Chile, Colombia, Cuba, Dominican Republic, Ecuador, Guatemala, Honduras, Mexico, Nicaragua and El Salvador) as well as in Africa (Guinea-Bissau and Mozambique). Among the few places outside Britain that still have pounds and pence, however, and that were either former colonies or part of the British Empire, only the Falkland Islands, Gibraltar and St Helena are notable. This is very modest when compared to the many countries round the world that have currency in dollars and cents, as a legacy of American history and settlement, or by way of adoption after the American pattern, as in Australia.

Just as the centavo is still found outside Portugal, so is the **céntimo** still used as the lesser currency of countries outside Spain, although only in Costa Rica, Paraguay, Peru and Venezuela.

The former French **franc** still exists as the main currency in many countries, with the 'Franc CFA' (Franc de la Communauté financière africaine) found in many African countries, and the 'Franc CFP' (Franc des Comptoirs français du Pacifique) in such Pacific countries as French Polynesia and New Caledonia. In all four French overseas departments (former colonies), French Guiana, Guadeloupe, Martinique and Réunion, as well as in the *collectivités territoriales* of Mayotte and St

## GOING TO THE DOGS

A young man with a wealthy, elderly aunt was anxious to please her. Knowing that she was especially fond of her two poodles, he visited her daily and took them for a walk. When she died he learned to his satisfaction that he was a beneficiary in her will. He was less satisfied when the lawyer read out: 'To my dear nephew, knowing that he loves them, I leave Fifi and Pierre.'

## ARGUE OR ELSE!

The poet and essayist Joseph Addison (1672–1719) had a friend with whom he used to have long discussions about many subjects. The two of them often disagreed, but after the friend had borrowed some money from him, Addison noticed that his friend now always agreed with him. This became very tiresome, until finally Addison felt obliged to tell his friend: 'Either contradict me, sir, or pay me my money.'

Pierre and Miquelon, whose status is midway between an overseas department and an overseas territory, the currency is exactly the same as that of France, in francs and centimes. But the German mark is found nowhere outside its native Europe, chiefly because the Germans did not colonize to anything like the same extent as the English, Portuguese, Spanish or French.

### COMMON CURRENCIES

When the European Economic Community (Common Market) was set up in 1957, it was intended that ultimately a common unit of currency should be established for it, if only as a money of account.

The result was the **ECU** (pronounced either 'aykew' or by its initials), the abbreviation for 'European Currency Unit', introduced in 1979 on the setting up of the European Monetary System (see p. 103). Its name, not entirely fortuitously, coincides with that of the *écu* ('shield'), a historic French coin of differing types and values that was first struck as a gold piece in the 13th century. (This kind of *écu* existed as recently as the 19th century as a 5-franc coin.)

The ECU was specifically created to settle debts among member countries of the EEC and to act as a standard in floating currencies. Its value is related at any given time to a group ('basket') of European currencies. But despite its obvious advantages—it could serve, like the dollar, as a real reserve currency, for example—the ECU has been slow to catch on, even in the sophisticated world of currency and finance. It is used, however, for the official business of the **European Invest-**

ment **Bank** (EIB), the bank set up in 1958 to finance capital investment projects in the EEC. In June 1989, the ECU equalled approximately 68p, or $1.06.

On the other hand, a wide range of 'Euro-' terms are now current to relate to the European money market, especially that of the EEC, suggesting that the concept of a unified monetary system for Europe is very real.

Here are some of the best-known:

**Eurobank** any European bank that holds deposits from European and other countries.

## " 

### MORTGAGE

The word *mortgage* came into English from French and literally means a 'dead pledge'. In the 17th century, lawyers explained that if the mortgagor did not repay the money he had borrowed within the stipulated time, his property was taken from him and was thereafter 'dead' to him. If the money was repaid, then the debt itself was 'dead'.

A mortgage is now generally used to buy a house or land, but occasional references are found in literature to other kinds of mortgage agreements: *Some times when the weekly income would not run to a sufficient quantity of fattening food, an arrangement would be made with the baker or miller that he should give credit now, and when the pig was killed receive a portion of the meat in payment. More often than not, one half of the pig-meat would be mortgaged in this way, and it was no uncommon thing to hear a woman say, 'Us be going to kill half a pig, please God, come Friday.'*

Flora Thompson *Lark Rise to Candleford*

"

## PORTRAIT OF A LADY

In *Amos Barton* George Eliot describes Mrs Patten, 'a childless old lady, who had got rich chiefly by the negative process of spending nothing. She is a pretty little old woman of eighty, once a lady's maid, and married for her beauty. She used to adore her husband, and now she adores her money, cherishing a quiet blood-relation's hatred for her niece, Janet Gibbs, who, she knows, expects a large legacy, and whom she is determined to disappoint. Her money shall all go in a lump to a distant relation of her husband's, and Janet shall be saved the trouble of pretending to cry, by finding that she is left with a miserable pittance.'

**Eurobond** a bond of the European Investment Bank issued in various currencies by a non-European company for sale in Europe. Like most bonds it is a long-term, fixed interest loan, and is provided by such long-term investors as insurance companies and pension funds. Eurobonds are dealt in chiefly by 'top borrowers' such as multinational companies, banks, and individual governments, and the term has come to be used in particular for the bonds of an American corporation that are sold outside the US and that are denominated and paid for in dollars, and that therefore yield interest in dollars. A Eurobond denominated in yen, and designed to benefit from the movement of shares in the Japanese stock market, is called a 'Euroyen Bond'.

**Eurocheque** a cheque issued by a British bank that is negotiable in a European bank (see also p. 97).

## THE POOR LAW

The British journalist Katharine Whitehorn rightly remarks in *How To Survive Children* that the easiest way for children to learn about money is for the parents not to have any.

**Eurocurrency** a currency that is deposited and lent in Europe outside its country of origin. The main Eurocurrency is the dollar, which has almost always accounted for over 70 per cent of the market. But there are also 'Euromarks' (or 'EuroDeutschmarks'), 'Euroyen', 'Eurosterling', and so on. Eurocurrency is used as a source of short-term or medium-term finance, in particular in international trade, and has the advantage of being easily convertible.

**Eurodeposit** a deposit of the currency of any country in the Eurocurrency market (see above).

**Eurodollar** an American dollar deposited in a bank outside the USA, especially (although not always) one in Europe. The Eurodollar is at present the leading Eurocurrency (see above).

**Euromarket** a financial market in a currency held outside its country of origin, in particular dollars held in Europe (the first formal such market). Most Euromarket transactions are between banks.

**Euromoney** an alternative, perhaps friendlier term for Eurocurrency (see above).

**Eurosterling** British pounds held in Europe as Eurocurrency (see above).

Support for the ECU, as mentioned, has been patchy, with its promoters mainly those professionally involved in finance and industry. Moreover, it is still essentially money of account. So why could not an actual pan-European coin be minted to circulate in EEC countries?

A proposal for such a coin was made by a reader of *The Times* (Stuart Campbell, Letter to the Editor, 10 November 1988). He suggested that the coin should be based on the florin, with each country minting and printing its florins with its own heraldry on the obverse and a common symbol, such as the original fleur-de-lys, on the reverse. Such florins, he argued, could be standardized for weight and size, and could be introduced to replace the ECU at its contemporary value. If subdivisions were needed, there could be ten 'denars' to the florin.

Attractive though such a proposal was, if only for its historic links (the florin was first minted in 1252 and circulated widely throughout Europe), it was not adopted.

## RATES OF EXCHANGE

Rates of exchange between the different currencies of the world vary slightly on a daily basis. The rate also varies according to whether one is buying or selling the foreign currency. This list serves as a very rough guide to the relative values of some of the world's major currencies. It averages out rates which applied against the pound sterling and the American dollar on 28 February, 1990. On that day one pound was worth approximately $1.70: one dollar was worth roughly 59 pence.

|  | Pound sterling | American dollar |
|---|---|---|
| Fr franc | 9.75 | 5.77 |
| D Mark | 2.88 | 1.71 |
| Gr drachma | 273.00 | 161.20 |
| Du guilder | 3.33 | 1.92 |
| It lira | 2135.00 | 1261.00 |
| Sp peseta | 183.50 | 109.50 |
| Sw franc | 2.55 | 1.50 |
| Can dollar | 2.05 | 1.19 |
| Aus dollar | 2.23 | 1.32 |
| Aust schilling | 20.10 | 12.04 |
| Bel franc | 59.50 | 35.53 |
| Dan krone | 11.10 | 6.56 |
| Fin markka | 6.98 | 4.00 |
| Nor krone | 11.10 | 6.56 |
| Port escudo | 252.50 | 149.90 |
| Sw krona | 10.45 | 6.15 |
| Japanese yen | 258.00 | 149.55 |
| Sd Arab riyal | 6.44 | 3.75 |

## WORLD CURRENCIES IN MODERN TIMES

| | |
|---|---|
| Afghanistan: | Afghani (Af) = 100 puls |
| Albania: | Lek (Lk) = 100 qindarka |
| Algeria: | Algerian dinar (A D) = 100 centimes |
| American Samoa: | US dollar ($) = 100 cents |
| Andorra: | Spanish peseta and French franc |
| Angola: | Kwanza (Kw) = 100 lwei (Angolan escudo until 10.1.1977) |
| Anguilla: | East Caribbean dollar (EC $) = 100 cents |
| Antigua and Barbuda: | East Caribbean dollar (EC $) = 100 cents |
| Argentina: | Austral (A) = 1000 pesos (from 14.6.1985) |
| Aruba: | Aruban florin (Afl) = 100 cents (from 11.1.1986) |
| Australia: | Australian dollar (A $) = 100 cents (Australian pound until 14.2.1966) |
| Austria: | Schilling (Sch) = 100 groschen |
| Bahamas: | Bahamian dollar (Ba $) = 100 cents |
| Bahrain: | Bahrain dinar (B D) = 1000 fils |
| Bangladesh: | Taka (Tk) = 100 poisha |
| Barbados: | Barbados dollar (Bds $) = 100 cents (East Caribbean dollar until 3.12.1973) |
| Belgium: | Belgian franc (B Fr) = 100 centimes |
| Belize: | Belizean dollar (Bz $) = 100 cents |
| Benin: | CFA franc (CFA Fr) = 100 centimes |
| Bermuda: | Bermuda dollar (Bda $) = 100 cents |
| Bhutan: | Ngultrum (Nu) = 100 chetrum (Indian rupee also used) |
| Bolivia: | Boliviano (Bs) = 100 centavos (from 1.1.1987) |

| | |
|---|---|
| Botswana: | Pula (Pu) = 100 thebe (SA rand until 23.8.1976) |
| Brazil: | New cruzado (NCz $) = 100 centavos (from 15.1.89) |
| Brunei: | Brunei dollar (Br $) = 100 cents |
| Bulgaria: | Lev (Lv) = 100 stotinki |
| Burkina: | CFA Franc (CFA Fr) = 100 centimes |
| Burma: | Kyat (Kt) = 100 pyas |
| Burundi: | Burundi franc (Bu Fr) = 100 centimes |
| Cameroon: | CFA franc (CFA Fr) = 100 centimes |
| Canada: | Canadian dollar (C $) = 100 cents |
| Cape Verde: | Cape Verde escudo (CV Esc) = 100 centavos (Portuguese escudo until 1.7.1977) |
| Cayman Islands: | Cayman Islands dollar (CI $) = 100 cents (Jamaican dollar until 1.5.1972) |
| Central African Republic: | CFA Franc (CFA Fr) = 100 centimes |
| Chad: | CFA Franc (CFA Fr) = 100 centimes |
| Chile: | Chilean peso (Ch $) = 100 centavos (Escudo until 29.9.1975) |
| China: | Yuan (Y) = 10 chiao (jiao) = 100 fen |
| Christmas Island: | Australian dollar = 100 cents |
| Cocos Island: | Australian dollar = 100 cents |
| Colombia: | Colombian peso (Col $) = 100 centavos |
| Comoros: | Comorian franc (CF) = 100 centimes (CFA franc also used) |
| Congo: | CFA Franc (CFA Fr) = 100 centimes |
| Cook Islands: | Australian dollar = 100 cents |
| Costa Rica: | Costa Rican colón (CR C) = 100 céntimos |
| Côte d'Ivoire | CFA Franc (CFA Fr) = 100 centimes |
| Cuba: | Cuban peso (Cub $) = 100 centavos |
| Cyprus: | Cyprus pound (C £) = 1000 mils |
| Czechoslovakia: | Koruna (crown) (Kčs) = 100 haléřů |
| Denmark: | Danish krone (D Kr) = 100 øre |
| Djibouti: | Djibouti franc = 100 centimes |
| Dominica: | East Caribbean dollar (EC $) = 100 cents |
| Dominican Republic: | Dominican Republic peso (DR $) = 100 centavos |
| East Germany: | Mark (M) = 100 pfennig |
| East Timor: | Indonesian rupiah (Rp) = 100 sen |
| Ecuador: | Sucre (Su) = 100 centavos |
| Egypt: | Egyptian pound (E £) = 100 piastres = 1000 millièmes |
| El Salvador: | El Salvador colón (ES C) = 100 centavos |
| Equatorial Guinea: | CFA Franc (CFA Fr) = 100 centimes (Equatorial Guinea peseta until 29.9.1973, when renamed ekwele, plural form bipkwele) (CFA Franc from 1.1.1985) |
| Ethiopia: | Birr (Br) = 100 cents (Ethiopian dollar until 14.10.1976) |
| Falkland Islands: | Falkland Islands pound (FI £) = 100 pence |
| Faroes: | Faroese krone (F Kr) = 100 øre |
| Fiji: | Fiji dollar (F $) = 100 cents (Fiji pound until 13.1.1969) |
| Finland: | Markka (F Mk) = 100 pennia |
| France: | Franc (Fr) = 100 centimes |
| French Guiana: | French franc (Fr) = 100 centimes (French Guiana franc until 1.1.1975) |
| French Polynesia: | CFP franc = 100 centimes |

| | |
|---|---|
| Gabon: | CFA Franc (CFA Fr) = 100 centimes |
| Gambia: | Dalasi (Di) = 100 butut (Gambia pound until 1.7.1971) |
| Ghana: | Cedi (C) = 100 pesewas (Ghanaian pound until 19.7.1965) |
| Gibraltar: | Gibraltar pound (Gib £) = 100 pence |
| Greece: | Drachma (Dr) = 100 lepta |
| Greenland: | Danish krone (D Kr) = 100 øre |
| Grenada: | East Caribbean dollar (EC $) = 100 cents |
| Guadeloupe: | French franc (Fr) = 100 centimes (Guadeloupe franc until 1.1.1975) |
| Guam: | US dollar ($) = 100 cents |
| Guatemala: | Quetzal (Q) = 100 centavos |
| Guernsey: | UK pound and Guernsey pound (G £) = 100 pence |
| Guinea: | Guinean franc (G Fr) = 100 centimes (Guinean franc until 2.10.1972 and syli until 6.1.1986) |
| Guinea-Bissau: | Guinea-Bissau peso (GB P) = 100 centavos (Escudo until 2.3.1976) |
| Guyana: | Guyanese dollar (G $) = 100 cents |
| Haiti: | Gourde (Gde) = 100 centimes |
| Honduras: | Lempira (La) = 100 centavos |
| Hong Kong: | Hongkong dollar (HK $) = 100 cents |
| Hungary: | Forint (Ft) = 100 fillér |
| Iceland: | Icelandic króna (I Kr) = 100 aurar |
| India: | Indian rupee (I R) = 100 paisa |
| Indonesia: | Rupiah (Rp) = 100 sen |
| Iran: | Rial (Rl) = 100 dinars |
| Iraq: | Iraqi dinar (I D) = 20 dirhams = 1000 fils |
| Ireland: | Punt (or Irish pound) (I £) = 100 pighne (or pence) |
| Isle of Man: | UK pound and IoM pound (IoM £) = 100 pence |
| Israel: | Shekel (Sk) = 100 (new) agorot (Israeli pound until 24.2.1980) |
| Italy: | Lira (L) = 100 centesimi |
| Jamaica: | Jamaican dollar (J $) = 100 cents (Jamaican pound until 8.9.1969) |
| Japan: | Yen (Y) = 100 sen |
| Jersey: | UK pound and Jersey pound (J £) = 100 pence |
| Johnston Island: | US dollar ($) = 100 cents |
| Jordan: | Jordan dinar (J D) = 1000 fils |
| Jugoslavia: | Jugoslav dinar (Ju D) = 100 paras |
| Kampuchea: | Riel (C Rl) = 100 sen |
| Kenya: | Kenyan shilling (K Sh) = 100 cents |
| Kiribati: | Australian dollar (A $) = 100 cents |
| Kuwait: | Kuwaiti dinar (K D) = 10 dirhams = 1000 fils |
| Laos: | Kip (Kp) = 100 at |
| Lebanon: | Lebanese pound (L £) = 100 piastres |
| Lesotho: | Loti (Lo) = 100 lisente (The plural form of loti is maloti (Mo). SA rand until 19.1.80) |
| Liberia: | Liberian dollar (L $) = 100 cents |
| Libya: | Libyan dinar (L D) = 1000 dirhams (Libyan pound until 1.9.1971) |
| Liechtenstein: | Swiss franc or Franken (S Fr) = 100 centimes or Rappen |
| Luxembourg: | Luxembourg franc (L Fr) = 100 centimes. The Belgian franc is also legal tender |
| Macao: | Pataca (Pat) = 100 avos |

| | |
|---|---|
| Madagascar: | Madagascar franc (Mg Fr) = 100 centimes |
| Malawi: | Malawi kwacha (M K) = 100 tambala (Malawi pound until 15.2.1971) |
| Malaysia: | Ringgit (Ma $) = 100 sen |
| Maldives: | Rufiyaa (Rf) = 100 laari (Maldivian rupee until 1.7.1981) |
| Mali: | CFA franc (CFA Fr) = 100 centimes (CFA franc until 1.7.1962 and from 1.9.1984) |
| Malta: | Maltese lira (M L) = 100 cents = 1000 mils |
| Martinique: | French franc (Fr) = 100 centimes (Martinique franc until 1.1.1975) |
| Mauritania: | Ouguiya (U) = 5 khoums (CFA franc until 29.6.1973) |
| Mauritius: | Mauritius rupee (M R) = 100 cents |
| Mayotte: | French franc (Fr) = 100 centimes (CFA franc until February, 1976) |
| Mexico: | Mexican peso (Mex $) = 100 centavos |
| Midway Islands: | US dollar ($) = 100 cents |
| Monaco: | French franc and Monegasque franc (Mn Fr) = 100 centimes |
| Mongolia: | Tugrik (or Togrog) (Tug) = 100 möngö |
| Montserrat: | East Caribbean dollar (EC $) = 100 cents |
| Morocco: | Dirham (Dh) = 100 centimes |
| Mozambique: | Metical (Mt) = 100 centavos (Mozambique escudo until 16.6.1980) |
| Namibia: | SA rand (R) = 100 cents |
| Nauru: | Australian dollar (A $) = 100 cents |
| Nepal: | Nepalese rupee (N R) = 2 mohur = 100 paisa (pice) |
| Netherlands: | Netherlands guilder or florin (Fl) = 100 cents |
| Netherlands Antilles: | Netherlands Antillian guilder (NA Gld) or florin (NA Fl) = 100 cents |
| New Caledonia: | CFP franc (CFP Fr) = 100 centimes |
| New Zealand: | New Zealand dollar (NZ $) = 100 cents (New Zealand pound until 10.7.1967) |
| Nicaragua: | Nicaraguan córdoba (C $) = 100 centavos |
| Niger: | CFA Franc (CFA Fr) = 100 centimes |
| Nigeria: | Naira (N) = 100 kobo (Nigerian pound until 1.1.1973) |
| Niue: | New Zealand dollar (NZ $) = 100 cents |
| Norfolk Island: | Australian dollar (A $) = 100 cents |
| North Korea: | North Korean won (NK W) = 100 chon (or jun) |
| North Yemen: | Yemen rial (Y R) = 100 fils |
| Norway: | Norwegian krone (N Kr) = 100 øre |
| Oman: | Rial Omani (O R) = 1000 baizas |
| Pacific Islands, US: | US dollar ($) = 100 cents |
| Pakistan: | Pakistan rupee (P R) = 100 paisa |
| Panama: | Balboa (Ba) = 100 centésimos |
| Papua New Guinea: | Kina (Ka) = 100 toea. (Australian dollar until 19.4.1975) |
| Paraguay: | Guaraní = 100 céntimos |
| Peru: | Inti (I) = 100 céntimos = 1000 soles (from 1.2.1985) |
| Philippines: | Philippine peso (P P) = 100 centavos |
| Pitcairn: | New Zealand dollar (NZ $) = 100 cents |
| Poland: | Złoty (Zl) = 100 groszy |
| Portugal: | Escudo (Esc) = 100 centavos |
| Puerto Rico: | US dollar ($) = 100 cents |
| Qatar: | Qatar riyal (Q R) = 100 dirhams |

| | |
|---|---|
| Réunion: | French franc (Fr) = 100 centimes (CFA franc until 1.1.1975) |
| Romania: | Leu = 100 bani (The plural form of leu is lei) |
| Rwanda: | Rwanda franc (Rw Fr) = 100 centimes |
| Sahara, Western: | Moroccan dirham (formerly Spanish peseta) |
| St Christopher and Nevis: | East Caribbean dollar (EC $) = 100 cents |
| Saint Helena: | St Helena pound (St H £) and UK pound = 100 pence |
| St Lucia: | East Caribbean dollar (EC $) = 100 cents |
| St Pierre and Miquelon: | French franc (Fr) = 100 centimes (CFA franc until 1.1.1973) |
| St Vincent: | East Caribbean dollar (EC $) = 100 cents |
| San Marino: | San Marino lira (SM L) = 100 centesimi. Italian and Vatican lira also in use. |
| São Tomé and Príncipe: | Dobra (Db) = 100 centavos (São Tomé and Príncipe escudo until 2.7.1977) |
| Saudi Arabia: | Saudi riyal (SA R) = 20 qursh = 100 halala(s) |
| Senegal: | CFA Franc (CFA Fr) = 100 centimes |
| Seychelles: | Seychelles rupee (S R) = 100 cents |
| Sierra Leone: | Leone (Le) = 100 cents |
| Singapore: | Singapore dollar (S $) = 100 cents |
| Solomon Islands: | Solomon Islands dollar (SI $) = 100 cents (Australian dollar until 24.10.1977) |
| Somalia: | Somali shilling (So Sh) = 100 cents |
| South Africa: | Rand (R) = 100 cents (South African pound until 14.2.1961) |
| South Korea: | South Korean won (SK W) = 100 chon (jun) |
| South Yemen: | Yemeni dinar (Y D) = 1000 fils |
| Soviet Union: | Rouble (Rub) = 100 kopecks |
| Spain: | Peseta (Pa) = 100 céntimos |
| Sri Lanka: | Sri Lanka rupee (SL R) = 100 cents |
| Sudan: | Sudanese pound (S £) = 100 piastres = 1000 millièmes |
| Surinam: | Surinam guilder (S Gld) or florin (S Fl) = 100 cents |
| Swaziland: | Lilangeni (Li) = 100 cents (The plural form of lilangeni is emalangeni (Ei). SA rand until 6.9.1974 but also still current) |
| Sweden: | Swedish krona (S Kr) = 100 öre |
| Switzerland: | Swiss franc or franken (S Fr) = 100 centimes or rappen |
| Syria: | Syrian pound (Sy £) = 100 piastres |
| Taiwan: | New Taiwan dollar (NT $) = 100 cents |
| Tanzania: | Tanzanian shilling (T Sh) = 100 cents (East African pound until 14.6.1966) |
| Thailand: | Baht (Bt) = 100 satang |
| Togo: | CFA Franc (CFA Fr) = 100 centimes |
| Tokelau: | New Zealand dollar (NZ $) = 100 cents |
| Tonga: | Tongan pa'anga (T $) = 100 seniti (Australian dollar until 3.4.1967) |
| Trinidad and Tobago: | Trinidad and Tobago dollar (TT $) = 100 cents |
| Tunisia: | Tunisian dinar (T D) = 1000 millimes |
| Turkey: | Turkish lira (T L) = 100 kurus or piastres |
| Turks and Caicos Islands: | US dollar ($) = 100 cents (Jamaican currency until 1973) |
| Tuvalu: | Tuvaluan dollar (T $) = 100 cents. Australian dollar also in use |
| Uganda: | Uganda new shilling (U Sh) = 100 cents (East African pound until 15.8.1966) |
| United Arab Emirates: | UAE dirham (UAE Dh) = 100 fils |

United Kingdom:      Pound (£) = 100 pence (Until 15.2.1971 one pound = 20 shillings, one shilling = 12 pence)

United States:      Dollar ($) = 100 cents

Uruguay:      Uruguayan new peso (Urug N$) = 100 centésimos

Vanuatu:      Vatu (VT) = 100 centimes (New Hebridean franc until 1.1.1981)

Vatican:      Vatican City lira (V L) = 100 centesimi. Italian lira also in use.

Venezuela:      Bolívar (B) = 100 céntimos

Vietnam:      Dông (D) = 10 chao (hào) = 100 sau (xu)

Virgin Islands, British:      US dollar ($) = 100 cents

Virgin Islands, US:      US dollar ($) = 100 cents

Wake Island:      US dollar ($) = 100 cents

Wallis and Futuna Islands:      CFP Franc (CFP Fr) = 100 centimes

Western Samoa:      Western Samoan tala (WS $) = 100 sene (Western Samoan pound until 10.7.1967)

West Germany:      Deutsche mark (DM) = 100 pfennig

Zaire:      Zaire (Z) = 100 makuta = 10 000 sengi (Congolese franc until 23.6.1967)

Zambia:      Kwacha (K) = 100 ngwee (Zambian pound until 16.1.1968)

Zimbabwe:      Zimbabwe dollar (Z $) = 100 cents

---

## WORLD CURRENCIES IN MODERN TIMES—INDEX

| | |
|---|---|
| | Nicaragua, Philippines, Portugal |
| centesimo | Italy, San Marino, Vatican |
| centésimo | Panama, Uruguay |
| centime | Algeria, Belgium, Benin, Burkina, Burundi, Cameroon, Central African Republic, Chad, Comoros, Congo, Côte d'Ivoire, Djibouti, France, French Guiana, French Polynesia, Gabon, Guadeloupe, Haiti, Liechtenstein, Luxembourg, Madagascar, Mali, Martinique, Mayotte, Monaco, Morocco, New Caledonia, Niger, Réunion, Rwanda, St Pierre and Miquelon, Senegal, Switzerland, Togo, Vanuatu, Wallis and Futuna Islands |
| cèntimo | Costa Rica, Paraguay, Peru, São Tomé and Príncipe, Spain, Venezuela |
| chao | (Also spelt hao) Vietnam |
| chetrum | Bhutan |
| chiao | (sometimes spelt jiao) China |
| chon | (Also spelt jun) Korea, North and South |
| colon | Costa Rica, El Salvador |
| córdoba | Nicaragua |
| cruzado | Brazil |
| dalasi | Gambia |
| dinar | Algeria, Bahrain, Iran, Iraq, Jordan, Jugoslavia, Kuwait, Libya, South Yemen, Tunisia |
| dirham | Iraq, Kuwait, Libya, Morocco, Qatar, United Arab Emirates, Western Sahara |
| dobra | São Tomé and Príncipe |
| dollar | American Samoa, Anguilla, Antigua and Barbuda, Australia, Bahamas, Barbados, Belize, Bermuda, Brunei, Canada, Cayman Islands, Christmas Island, Cocos Islands, Cook Islands, Dominica, Ethiopia (until 14.10.1976), Fiji, Grenada, Guam, Guyana, Hongkong, Jamaica, Johnston Island, Kiribati, Liberia, Midway Islands, Montserrat, Nauru, New Zealand, Niue, Norfolk Island, Pacific Islands, Papua New Guinea (until 19.4.1975), Pitcairn, Puerto Rico, St Christopher and Nevis, St Lucia, St Vincent, Singapore, Solomon Islands, Taiwan, Tokelau, Tonga (until 3.4.1967), Trinidad and Tobago, Turks and Caicos Islands, Tuvalu, United States, Virgin Islands, Wake Island, Zimbabwe |
| dong | Vietnam |
| drachma | Greece |
| ekwele | (Plural form is bipkwele) Equatorial Guinea (until 1.1.1985) |
| emalangeni | See lilangeni |
| escudo | Angola (until 10.1.1977), Cape Verde, Chile (until 29.9.1975), Guinea-Bissau (until 2.3.1976), Mozambique (until 16.6.1980), Portugal, São Tomé and Príncipe (until September 1977) |
| eyrir | (Plural form is aurar) Iceland |
| fen | China |
| filler | Hungary |
| fils | Bahrain, Iraq, Jordan, Kuwait, North Yemen, South Yemen, United Arab Emirates |
| florin | Aruba, Netherlands, Netherlands Antilles, Surinam |
| forint | Hungary |
| franc | Andorra, Belgium, Benin, Burkina, Burundi, Cameroon, Central African Republic, Chad, Comoros, Congo, Côte d'Ivoire, Djibouti, Equatorial Guinea, France, French Guiana, French Polynesia, Gabon, Guadeloupe, Liechtenstein, Luxembourg, Madagascar, |

|  |  |
| --- | --- |
| | Mali, Martinique, Mauritania (until 29.6.1973), Mayotte, Monaco, New Caledonia, Niger, Réunion, Rwanda, St Pierre and Miquelon, Senegal, Switzerland, Togo, Wallis and Futuna Islands, Zaire (until 23.6.1967) |
| franken | Liechtenstein, Switzerland |
| gourde | Haiti |
| groschen | Austria |
| grosz | Poland |
| guarani | Paraguay |
| guilder | Netherlands, Netherlands Antilles, Surinam |
| haleř | Czechoslovakia |
| hallala | Saudi Arabia |
| hao | See chao |
| inti | Peru |
| jiao | See chiao |
| jun | See chon |
| khoum | Mauritania |
| kina | Papua New Guinea |
| kip | Laos |
| kobo | Nigeria |
| kopeck | Soviet Union |
| koruna | Czechoslovakia |
| krona | Iceland, Sweden |
| krone | Denmark, Faroes, Norway |
| kurus | Turkey |
| kwacha | Malawi, Zambia |
| kwanza | Angola |
| kyat | Burma |
| laari | Maldives |
| lek | Albania |
| lempira | Honduras |
| leone | Sierra Leone |
| lepton | Greece |
| leu | (The plural form of leu is lei) Romania |
| lev | Bulgaria |
| likuta | (The plural form of likuta is makuta.) Zaïre |
| lilangeni | (The plural form of lilangeni is emalangeni.) Swaziland |
| lira | Italy, Malta, San Marino, Turkey, Vatican |
| loti | (The plural form of loti is maloti). Lesotho |
| lwei | Angola |
| makuta | See likuta |
| maloti | see loti |
| mark | Germany, East and West |
| markka | Finland |
| metical | Mozambique |
| millime | Tunisia |
| millieme | Egypt, Sudan |
| mils | Cyprus, Malta |
| mohur | Nepal |
| mongo | Mongolia |
| naira | Nigeria |
| ngultrum | Bhutan |
| ngwee | Zambia |
| ore | Denmark, Faroes, Iceland, Norway, Sweden |
| ouguiya | Mauritania |
| pa'anga | Tonga |
| paisa | India, Nepal (also spelt pice), Pakistan |
| para | Jugoslavia |
| pataca | Macao |
| penni | Finland |
| penny | (The plural forms of penny are pence and pennies) Falkland Islands, Gibraltar, Guernsey, Ireland, Isle of Man, Jersey, Saint Helena, United Kingdom |
| peseta | Andorra, Equatorial Guinea (until 1973), Spain |
| pesewa | Ghana |
| peso | Argentina, Bolivia, Chile, Colombia, Cuba, Dominican Republic, Guinea-Bissau, Mexico, Philippines, Uruguay |
| pfennig | Germany, East and West |
| piastre | Egypt, Lebanon, Sudan, Syria, Turkey |
| pingin | Ireland |
| poisha | Bangladesh |
| pound | Australia (until 14.2.1966), Cyprus, Egypt, Falkland Islands, Fiji (until 13.1.1969), Gambia (until 1.7.1971), Ghana (until 19.7.1965), Gibraltar, Guernsey, Ireland, Isle of Man, Israel (until 24.2.1980), Jersey, Kenya |

| | |
|---|---|
| | (until 14.9.1966), Lebanon, Libya (until 1.9.1971), Malawi (until 15.2.1971), New Zealand (until 10.7.1967), Nigeria (until 1.1.1973), Saint Helena, South Africa (until 14.2.1961), Sudan, Syria, Tanzania, Uganda (until 15.8.1966), United Kingdom, Western Samoa (until 10.7.1967), Zambia (until 16.1.1968) |
| pul | Afghanistan |
| pula | Botswana |
| punt | Ireland |
| pya | Burma |
| qindar | Albania |
| quetzal | Guatemala |
| qursh | Saudi Arabia |
| rand | Botswana (until 23.8.1976), Lesotho (until 19.1.80), Namibia, South Africa |
| rappen | Liechtenstein, Switzerland |
| rial | Iran, North Yemen, Oman |
| riel | Kampuchea |
| ringgit | Malaysia |
| riyal | Qatar, Saudi Arabia |
| rouble | Soviet Union |
| rufiyaa | Maldives |
| rupee | India, Maldives (until 1.7.1981), Mauritius, Nepal, Pakistan, Seychelles, Sri Lanka |
| rupiah | East Timor, Indonesia |
| satang | Thailand |
| sau | (Also spelt xu) Vietnam |
| schilling | Austria |
| sen | East Timor, Indonesia, Japan, Kampuchea, Malaysia |
| sene | Western Samoa |
| sengi | Zaire |
| seniti | Tonga |
| shekel | Israel |
| shilling | Kenya, Somalia, Tanzania, Uganda, United Kingdom (until 15.2.1971) |

**``**——————————————————

GOLD

*What Nature wants, commodious Gold*
 *bestows,*
*'Tis thus we eat the bread another*
 *sows:*
*But how unequal it bestows observe,*
*'Tis thus we riot, while who sow it,*
 *starve.*
*What Nature wants (a phrase I much*
 *distrust)*
*Extends to luxury, extends to lust:*
*And if we count among the needs of life*
*Another's toil, why not another's wife?*
*Useful, I grant, it serves what life*
 *requires,*
*But dreadful too, the dark assassin*
 *hires:*
*Trade it may help, society extend;*
*But lures the pirate, and corrupts the*
 *friend.*

Alexander Pope *Epistle to Bathurst*

——————————————————**''**

| | |
|---|---|
| sol | Peru (until 31.1.1985) |
| stotinka | Bulgaria |
| sucre | Ecuador |
| syli | Guinea (until 6.1.1986) |
| taka | Bangladesh |
| tala | Western Samoa |
| tambala | Malawi |
| thebe | Botswana |
| toea | Papua New Guinea |
| tugrik | (Also spelt togrog) Mongolia |
| vatu | Vanuatu |
| won | Korea, North and South |
| xu | See sau |
| yen | Japan |
| yuan | China |
| zaire | Zaire |
| złoty | Poland |

# 7
# A YEN FOR CASH

## MONEY BEYOND EUROPE

As already mentioned in Chapter 2, both the Chinese and the Indians are rivals to the title of 'inventor of coins', which today is normally granted to the Lydians of Greece.

Even so, both countries have currencies of ancient origin, with China's colourful paper money attracting much greater attention among collectors, however, than her early coins.

### CHINESE CASH

China's earliest coins differed from western money in that they were cast, rather than struck, by pouring molten metal into a mould, using dies to produce their design. To begin with, Chinese coins evolved out of tools and implements, such as spades and knives, that were themselves used as a means of exchange. Eventually, the distinctive **cash** evolved, and lasted as China's main currency until the second half of the 19th century.

The cash was a coin with a square hole in the centre, the hole being used for stringing and carrying the coins. Strings of coins like this are depicted on early Chinese paper money. The cash was the one-thousandth part of the **tael**, and its name is only coincidentally similar to the modern English word that means 'ready money', 'coins'. (The Chinese cash ultimately derives from Sanskrit *karsa*, 'weight', in gold or silver, while English cash comes from Latin *capsa*, 'chest', and is related to the word 'case'.)

Remaining basically unchanged for 2000 years, apart from minor variations such as inscriptions and mintmarks, the Chinese cash is thus unique among the world's currencies.

The tael, as a term used also for the standard silver weight in the Chinese monetary system, has a name that basically means just 'weight', from Malay *tahil*.

Today, China has the **yuan** as its basic currency, divided into 100 **fen**. The yuan, otherwise known as the 'Chinese dollar', was first struck as a silver-dollar-type piece in the 19th century, but was established as a basic currency unit only in 1914. Its name means simply 'round', and the name is related to that of the Japanese yen. The fen has a name with an equally basic meaning, which is 'part'. In 1948 Communist China introduced the concept of *renminbi* as a term for the country's currency and legal monetary tender. The word means merely 'people's currency'.

## JAPANESE YEN

Japan's sole unit of currency is the **yen**, which as mentioned above means simply 'round'. (The Japanese borrowed the word for the Chinese yuan.) The yen was introduced as a gold coin in 1870, when it was divided into 100 **sen**. The sen itself, now Japan's main copper coin, was introduced as long ago as the 8th century in imitation of the Chinese cash. Like the yen, the name of the sen was borrowed from the Chinese, and means simply 'coin'. By coincidence, the coin's name is very similar to that of the cent, which is also one-hundredth of a larger value.

### SELF-ASSURANCE

The thought may be expressed in curiously out-moded language, but there is much truth in this comment by Anthony Trollope, in his novel *The Small House at Allington*: 'Moneys in possession or in expectation do give a set to the head, and a confidence to the voice, and an assurance to the man, which will help him much in his walk in life—if the owner of them will simply use them, and not abuse them.'

## INDIAN VARIETY

By contrast, the many coins and currencies of India are difficult to categorize systematically, simply because the country itself has such a diffuse and complex history, with most native states issuing their own currencies. This is one reason why India offers promising potential for the numismatist and collector, with a whole range of gold, silver and other coins to be found in many types and varieties.

Today, India's main unit of currency is the **rupee**, divided into 100 **paise**. The rupee was originally struck as a silver coin in the 16th century, and has a name that means simply 'shape', 'beauty', from Sanskrit *rupa*. This name is an additional reminder that many Indian coins are artistically attractive, and collectable on that score alone.

The paisa, although now worth one-hundredth of a rupee, had a former value of one-sixty-fourth of the higher value under British rule, so that it was equal to a quarter of an **anna**. Hence its name,

### THE PIG RUPEE

The so-called pig-rupee was a silver coin issued in India in 1911. It showed Edward VII as King-Emperor wearing what was meant to be an elephant insignia. Unfortunately, the trunk was almost invisible, and many Indians were convinced that a pig, an animal regarded for religious reasons as unclean, had been portrayed on the coinage. The authorities were obliged to withdraw the coin from circulation.

which derives from Sanskrit *pad*, 'quarter'. When introduced in its modern form to India in 1957, it was known for some time as a 'naya paisa', meaning 'new paisa'. (Compare Britain's 'new pence', existing for some years after decimalization in 1971.)

The anna was thus worth one-sixteenth of a rupee. The coin first circulated in the 18th century and was current until the introduction of decimalization in 1957. Its Hindi name was Sanskrit in origin, meaning merely 'small'.

## ORBITING THE ORIENT

The rupee is the main unit of currency in other Asian countries, including Nepal, Pakistan and Sri Lanka. In the latter country, however, it is divided into 100 cents, not paise. In Indonesia, the **rupiah**, introduced in 1950, has a name of the same origin as the rupee, although it is divided into 100 sen, as is the Japanese yen.

Elsewhere in Asia, different currencies and coins are to be found. In Kampuchea the main unit is the **riel**, introduced in 1955 in place of the Indo-Chinese piastre. The name of the riel is of Khmer origin, and of uncertain meaning. It does not, however, appear to be related to the 'royal' family of coin names to which the Spanish real and former English and French rial belong. The riel is divided, like the yen, into 100 sen. Further mention of the piastre will be made when considering the currencies of Middle Eastern countries.

In Malaysia the chief currency is the dollar or **ringgit**, divided into 100 sen. The ringgit gets its name from a Malay word that means 'serrated', referring to the milled edge of the coin, which in turn was based on the design and appearance of the Spanish dollar (the peso). The name of the sen means simply 'coin', like that of the Japanese coin.

The main unit of Mongolia's currency, the **tugrik**, is divided into 100 **mungu**. The first tugriks were struck in 1925 in Leningrad, USSR, as silver coins. The name represents Mongolian *dughurik*, which merely means 'round', hence 'coin', like the Chinese yuan already mentioned. The mungu (in Mongolian, *möngö*) introduced the same year, has a name that rather obviously means what it seems to mean, 'Mongolian'.

In Thailand, the main currency is the **baht**, divided into 100 **satang**. The baht was introduced

**"**

## THE MATRIMONIAL MARKET

'This knowledge I soon learned by experience, viz., that the state of things was altered as to matrimony, that marriages were here the consequence of politic schemes, for forming interests, carrying on business, and that love had no share, or but very little, in the matter.

'That as my sister-in-law at Colchester had said, beauty, wit, manners, sense, good humour, good behaviour, education, virtue, piety, or any other qualification, had no power to recommend; that money only made a woman agreeable; that men chose mistresses indeed by the gust of their affection, but that for a wife, no deformity would shock the fancy, no ill qualities the judgment; the money was the thing; the portion was neither crooked, or monstrous, but the money was always agreeable, whatever the wife was.

'Besides this, I observed that the men made no scruple to set themselves out and to go a-fortune-hunting, as they call it, when they really had no fortune themselves to demand it, or merit to deserve it; and they carried it so high, that a woman was scarce allowed to inquire after the character of estate of the person that pretended to her.'

Daniel Defoe *Moll Flanders* (1722)

**"**

in 1928 to replace the tical, which name is still sometimes used for it. Its name represents Thai *bat*, itself deriving, like the paisa, from Sanskrit *pada*, 'quarter', as it was originally a quarter of a tael, the standard silver weight of eastern Asia already mentioned (above) with regard to the currency of China.

Vietnam's main unit of currency is the **dong**, a coin dating back to the 10th century. It was based on the Chinese cash and had the same central hole. The meaning of the name can be seen in the inscription on the obverse: *thong bun*, 'current coin'. The dong is divided into 10 **hao** or 100 **xu**.

The chief currency unit of Macao, the former Portuguese and future Chinese territory west of Hong Kong, is the **pataca**, divided into 100 **avos**. The name of the pataca at one time applied to the Spanish peso in Brazil, and was also that of a silver coin used in Portuguese colonies. In origin, it may be a corruption of the Arabic name of the peso, which was *abu taka*, literally 'father of a gun' (i.e. as if the coin was called a 'gun'). The name of the avo is simply the Portuguese word for 'fraction'.

Some of the Pacific island states have denominations with interesting names. In 1975 Papua New Guinea introduced the **kina**, divided into 100 **toea**. The kina was equal to the former Australian dollar, and is a native word. 'Toea', on the other hand, appears to be a Pidgin English variant of the word 'dollar' itself. Western Samoa has denominations of similar origin, with the **tala** (from 'dollar') divided into 100 **sene** ('cents'). Tonga's **pa'anga**, a word meaning simply 'money', is worth 100 **seniti** ('cents' likewise). Significantly, Tonga decided against calling its new decimal currency, introduced in 1967, the 'tola', otherwise 'dollar', because this native word also means 'pig's snout'. But many of the smaller Pacific islands still use the Australian dollar of 100 cents as their currency.

Further west, Bangladesh has as a main unit the **taka**, divided into 100 **poisha**, introduced in 1972 instead of the rupee. The taka derives its name from Sanskrit *tanka*, 'coin', while the poisha's name is basically the same as that of the paisa, so similarly means 'quarter'.

For something *really* more exotic, there is the currency of Bhutan, the little Himalayan kingdom between Tibet and India. Its main unit of currency is the **ngultrum**, divided into 100 **chetrum**. The ngultrum was introduced in 1974 to replace the rupee. Its name is based on Tibetan-Burmese *ngul*, 'silver', with *trum* a generic word meaning simply 'money', and probably coming from Hindi. The chetrum's name has a similar origin, with Tibetan-

## MONEY AND STATUS

An occupation may have a status that does not necessarily correspond to how much someone earns from it. Vance Packard reported in *The Status Seekers* on a study carried out in the Chicago area in 1956. Occupations were graded by the informants on a scale of 1 to 7. Some typical results of the grading are shown below:

**Group 1**   Architects, medical consultants, executives of national companies, stock brokers, federal judges, law partners, high ranking military officers, bishops.

**Group 2**   G.P.s, newspaper editors, mechanical engineers, executives of a local company, county judges, downtown lawyers, colonels, naval captains, college professors at prestige institutions.

**Group 3**   Bank cashiers, department store buyers, teachers at small or municipal colleges, advertising copy-writers, junior executives, ministers of religion, office supervisors.

**Group 4**   Bank clerks, small contractors, dental technicians, junior school teachers, factory foremen, insurance salesmen, staff sergeants, secretaries.

**Group 5**   Car mechanics, barbers, bar tenders, carpenters, shop assistants, skilled factory workers, hotel receptionists, corporals, policemen, truck drivers.

**Group 6**   Taxi-drivers, gas-station attendants, plumber's mates, waitresses, watchmen, riveters.

**Group 7**   Dishwashers, hod carriers on building site, domestic servants, gardeners, coal miners, street cleaners.

Another study placed authors somewhere between accountants for large companies and army captains, at about group 3 level.

## MAN'S BEST FRIEND

A dog is traditionally a man's best friend. Dr Crofts, in Trollope's *The Small House at Allington*, thinks otherwise: 'I do care for money very much. I have sometimes broken my heart because I could not get opportunities of earning it. It is the best friend that a man can have, if it be honestly come by.'

Burmese *che*, 'half' followed by the same *trum*. The ngultrum has retained a parity with the Indian rupee, and Indian currency is also legal tender in the country.

Burma's main unit is the **kyat**, divided into 100 **pyas**. The kyat replaced the rupee in 1952, and has a name meaning simply 'weight', 'coin'. The pya, introduced the same year, has a name directly related to that of the paisa, so it also means 'quarter'.

The Burmese kyat has a name that is related to the **tical**, which in modern times was one of the main units of currency in Thailand before being replaced by the baht. Originally, the tical was the so-called 'bullet money' of Siam (modern Thailand), Kampuchea and Burma, as a strangely shaped little coin resembling a small ingot or 'bullet'. It was hammered into a spherical shape and crudely flattened at the side. Its name probably derives from Sanskrit *tarkala*, 'stamped coin', although some numismatists relate it to the word that gave the taka of Bangladesh its name, in which case it means merely 'coin'. Either way, it is quite basically descriptive.

Korea has the **won** as its main currency unit, divided into 100 **jun** in North Korea and 100 **jeon** in South Korea. Both names are perfectly simple in meaning: 'won' means 'round' (like the Chinese yuan), and 'jun' or 'jeon' (essentially the same word) means 'coin'.

The only Far Eastern country to have a thoroughly western-style currency is Taiwan, with the New Taiwan dollar divided into 100 cents. Australia, too, has Australian dollars and cents, while New Zealand, similarly, has New Zealand dollars and cents.

## CADGING AND BLUDGING

To cadge something is to obtain it (for nothing) by asking for it. It could be described as a watered-down form of begging. 'Cadge' theoretically means to borrow, but a cadger usually has no intention of returning what he cadges. In his *Personal Kiwi-Yankee Slanguage Dictionary*, Louis L. Leland says that a similar term in New Zealand is 'bludge'. 'May I bludge a cigarette (or cup of sugar)?' is socially acceptable, though to call someone a 'bludger' is a serious insult. Someone who bludges all the time is a sponger.

The United States is thus far from being the only country where dollars make cents!

### THE MIDDLE EAST

In the Middle East, Iran has the **rial** as its main currency, divided into 100 dinars, while Iraq has the Iraqi dinar, divided into 1000 **fils**. The rial borrowed its name from the Spanish real, so like it means 'royal'. As mentioned, the dinar represents the Roman denarius, while the fils has a name that ultimately comes from Latin *follis*, 'money bag'. (Compare the name of the pul, Afghanistan's lesser currency, below.) The fals, in the same name group, was an early Arabic copper coin. Saudi Arabia's **riyal**, divided into 20 **qursh** or 100 **halala**, has the same name origin as the rial. The qursh, in turn, has a name that ultimately comes from the European Groschen, so means 'large', while the halala, Saudi Arabia's smallest coin, has a name that derives from Arabic *halal*, 'lawful', denoting its legality as currency.

Syria has the Syrian pound as its main unit of currency, with this divided into 100 **piastres**. The piastre is also a small unit of currency in several other Middle Eastern countries, including Egypt, Lebanon, and Sudan, all of which have the pound as their main unit. The name 'piastre' derives from Italian *piastra*, 'plate', representing the full phrase *piastra d'argento*, 'silver plate'.

Jordan, like Iraq, has the dinar, comprising 1000 fils, but Israel has the **shekel**, divided into 100 agorot. The shekel, familiar as the main silver coin of the Jews in biblical times, was originally a unit of weight equal to one three-thousandth of a talent. Its name comes from the Hebrew verb *shaqal*, meaning simply 'to weigh'. Until 1980 the main unit of currency in Israel was the Israeli pound. The agora, appropriately, has a name that means 'small coin', from Hebrew *agorah*.

Oman has the rial Omani as its chief unit of currency, divided into 1000 **baiza**. The latter was formerly a copper coin of Somalia when it was an Italian colony (Italian Somaliland), and was first issued in 1909. Its name, through colloquial Arabic, is the same in origin as that of the paisa, so means 'quarter', from the Sanskrit. North Yemen has the riyal of 100 fils, and South Yemen the Yemeni dinar of 1000 fils, all these being the names of currencies already mentioned for other Middle Eastern countries (above). Bahrain, in turn, has the Bahraini dinar also divided into 1000 fils.

Afghanistan's main unit of currency is the **afghani**, a name of obvious origin. The afghani is divided into 100 **puls**, and was first issued as a silver piece in 1926 to replace the Kabul rupee. The pul ultimately gets its name from Latin *follis*, 'money bag', as does the fils of Iraq and other Middle Eastern countries.

## INTO AFRICA

Moving into Africa, we find Libya likewise with its own dinar as the main unit of currency. Here, however, it is divided into 1000 **dirhams**. The latter coin has a name that is an Arabic version of the Greek drachma, so will also literally mean 'handful'. (In the United Arab Emirates, however, the dirham is the main unit, not the subsidiary, and is divided into 100 fils. It is also the main unit in Morocco, making 100 centimes.)

Algeria's chief currency is the Algerian dinar, divided into 100 centimes, an inheritance from the country's days under French annexation. Egypt, already noted, has the Egyptian pound divided into 100 piastres, but also into 1000 **millimes** (or **milliemes**), whose French name is of obvious origin.

Like Algeria, certain other African countries have retained a colonial currency, in particular the former French franc. The franc is thus the main currency of Benin, Burkina, Cameroon, Central African Republic, Chad, Congo, Côte d'Ivoire, Equatorial Guinea, Gabon, Mali, Niger, Senegal and Togo. In each case the franc involved here is officially the 'Franc de la Communauté financière africaine', or that of the African Currency Union, set up to establish a joint unit of currency for the countries of the West African Currency Union, founded in 1962 as a group of 14 former French colonial countries. The 'Franc CFA' is geared to the French franc in a ratio of 50:1.

Some other African countries have similarly retained the name of the French franc of 100 centimes, including Burundi, Djibouti, Guinea and Madagascar. But Mozambique, as a former Portuguese colony, has retained Portuguese currency names, with the **metical** divided into 100 centavos. 'Metical' is a name ultimately of Arabic origin, meaning merely 'weight'.

Many recently dependent French states have adopted new units of currency, however. Thus Botswana has the **pula** as its main currency, divided into 100 **thebe**. The pula was introduced

**"**━━━━━━━━━━━━━━━━

### FINANCIAL REPORT

*Mr Darcy soon drew the attention of the room by his fine, tall person, handsome features, noble mien, and the report which was in general circulation within five minutes of his entrance, of his having ten thousand a year.*

Jane Austen *Pride and Prejudice*

━━━━━━━━━━━━━━━━**"**

in 1976 and means 'rain', expressing a traditional Tswana greeting or wish. 'Thebe', a similar native word, meaning 'shield', refers to the shield of Botswana that it bears on the reverse. Ghana, similarly, introduced the **cedi** as its main unit in 1965, with this divided into 100 **pesewas**. 'Cedi' means 'shell', a historic harkback to the former type of currency found among coastal tribes here. 'Pesewa' is the native (Fanti) word for 'penny'. Malawi's main unit of currency is the **kwacha**, comprising 100 **tambala**. The name of the larger coin means 'dawn', a symbolic sense for a newly emergent state, while the smaller unit's name means 'cockerel', a bird that crows at dawn. The new currency was introduced in 1971 when the country adopted a decimal system. Zambia also has the kwacha as its larger unit of currency, although here it is divided into 100 **ngwee**. This latter name means 'bright', so is equally symbolic. Zambia's present currency was introduced in 1968.

Zaïre has the **zaïre** as its chief currency, divided into 100 **makuta**. The larger unit takes its name from the country's main river, which is also called the Congo and which gave the name of the country itself when it came into being in 1971. The likuta (singular of makuta) bases its native Nupe name on *kuta*, 'stone', a word that can indicate either a weight or a coin. The new currency was introduced in 1967 to replace the franc in what was then the Democratic Republic of the Congo.

Angola's main unit of currency, introduced in 1977 to replace the former Portuguese escudo, is the **kwanza**, divided into 100 **lwei**. The Kwanza (or Cuanza) is the name of one of Angola's main rivers, as well as of two of its provinces, while the Lwei is a tributary of the Kwanza. Appropriately,

*kwanza* means 'main', so applies equally to river and currency.

Nigeria has the **naira** as its main unit of currency, its name based on that of the country itself. It is divided into 100 **kobo**, a name that is a native rendering of English 'copper', and that was already in use for the penny that it superseded in 1973. The naira replaced the Nigerian pound.

Swaziland has the **lilangeni** as its basic monetary unit, introduced in 1974 and divided into 100 cents. The Bantu name means simply 'money'. The country had the South African rand as its principal unit of currency until 1974, and even now this currency still circulates.

**"**━━━━━━━━━━━━━━━━

### SOUR-GRAPEISM

*'I imagine that a few of the gentlefolks of Cranford were poor, and had some difficulty in making both ends meet; but they were like the Spartans, and concealed their smart under a smiling face. We none of us spoke of money, because that subject savoured of commerce and trade, and though some might be poor, we were all aristocratic. It was considered "vulgar" (a tremendous word in Cranford) to give anything expensive, in the way of eatable or drinkable, at the evening entertainments. Wafer bread-and-butter and sponge-biscuits were all that the Honourable Mrs Jamieson gave, and she was sister-in-law to the late Earl of Glenmire, although she did practise such "elegant economy." "Elegant economy!" How naturally one falls back into the phraseology of Cranford! There, economy was always "elegant", and money-spending always "vulgar and ostentatious"; a sort of sour-grapeism which made us very peaceful and satisfied.'*

Elizabeth Gaskell *Cranford* (1851–53)

━━━━━━━━━━━━━━━━**"**

The South African **rand** was in turn introduced in South Africa in 1961 to replace the South African pound. It takes its name from the popularly abbreviated name of the Witwatersrand, the important gold-mining region of the Transvaal. If 'rand' implies 'gold', then '**krugerrand**' actually *is* gold, as the name of the gold piece first minted in 1967 with a portrait of President Kruger, the Transvaal president who died in 1904. The krugerrand became a popular investment item in the 1970s, when it was smuggled into Britain, and in 1974 its buying price was just under £100, compared with £16 in its year of issue.

The rand is divided into 100 cents, which are also the lesser currency unit in many other African countries, including Ethiopia, Kenya, Sierra Leone, Somalia, Tanzania, Uganda and Zimbabwe. Although the main unit often has a colonial name (the shilling in Kenya, Somalia, Tanzania and Uganda, and the dollar in Zimbabwe), some countries have preserved or introduced a native name. Ethiopia, for example, has the **birr**, from an Amharic word meaning 'silver', and Sierra Leone has the **leone**, of obvious origin.

## ACROSS THE ATLANTIC

Across the Atlantic, Canada has dollars and cents, like its southern neighbour. As with most countries, the history of its currencies is the history of the land itself. Canada first had French currency, then British. The latter was largely in the form of tokens, which were bilingual when issued by the Bank of Montreal from 1837. A decimal coinage, in pounds and cents, was in use by 1858, with a unified currency introduced in 1867, on the formation of the Dominion of Canada, to replace the various provincial issues. No dollar was struck until 1935. It bore the head of George V on the obverse, and a representation of two paddlers in a canoe on the reverse. The latter design lasted, with minor variations, until 1952.

## CENTRAL AND SOUTH AMERICA

In Mexico, Central America and South America, the currencies are in many cases still Spanish or Portuguese in origin. Mexico itself has the peso of 100 centavos, as do Chile, Colombia and Cuba, while Brazil has the **cruzado** of 100 **centavos**. This latter unit is a 'cross' name, referring to the

## CLASS

In his book *The Status Seekers*, Vance Packard comments on the American class system. Describing the 'real upper class' he remarks that 'these people would have you believe that wealth has little bearing on their social pre-eminence. Rather, it is the gracious, leisurely way of life they have achieved as a result of their innate good taste and high breeding.' He quotes, however, a typical member of the real upper class in a small American town on the subject of what it takes to remain a member of that social group: 'First, I'd say money is the most important. In fact, nobody's in this class if he doesn't have money; but it just isn't money alone. You've got to have the right family connections, and you have got to behave yourself or you get popped out. And if you lose your money, you're dropped. If you don't have money, you're just out.'

Another informant, 'an old-family social matron,' told Mr Packard that many of the best families would never have received in their homes the people who now came there. 'But, she sighed, money is money.'

design on the coin.

Honduras has the **lempira**, divided into 100 centavos. The name is that of the 16th-century Indian chief who fought the first Spanish colonists here. El Salvador and Costa Rica have the **colón**, of 100 centavos and céntimos respectively, bearing the name of Christopher Columbus (in Spanish, Cristóbal Colón). The denomination was introduced in 1896 to Costa Rica and in 1919 to El Salvador. In both countries it replaced the

**THE NEVER ENDING THIRST**

*'Wealth is like seawater; the more we drink, the thirstier we become.'*

Arthur Schopenhauer

peso. But Colombia, actually named after Columbus, still has the peso, similarly divided.

Nicaragua has the **córdoba** of 100 centavos, named after the 16th-century Spanish governor of Nicaragua, Hernández de Córdoba, and Panama's currency is the **balboa** of 100 centésimos, named after the 16th-century Spanish explorer who discovered the Pacific, Vasco Nuñez de Balboa. Guatemala, by contrast, has the **quetzal**, of 100 centavos. This name, unlike many of those of its neighbours' denominations, is not that of a national hero but of the country's national emblem, the quetzal (pronounced 'ketsel') being a beautiful bird with a long green tail. The quetzal was introduced in 1924 as a silver coin equal to the American dollar, and shows the bird on both the obverse and reverse.

Venezuela has the **bolívar**, divided into 100 céntimos. The denomination honours Simón Bolívar, the early 19th-century South American revolutionary leader who gave his name to Bolivia. Similarly Bolivia's chief currency is the **boliviano**, of 100 centavos. This is a return of the denomination, which was current in Bolivia from 1864 to 1963, when it was replaced by the peso, divided into 100 centavos. The country's economy deteriorated rapidly from 1977, and in 1987, in an effort to halt inflation, Bolivia reintroduced the boliviano, now with a value of 1 million former pesos.

Ecuador has the **sucre**, of 100 centavos, as its main unit of currency. The name, pronounced 'sookray', is that of the early 19th-century South American liberator and general, Antonio José de Sucre. The coin was introduced as a silver crown-sized piece in 1884.

Like Bolivia, Peru experienced increasing economic problems in the 1980s, and in its own attempt to stem inflation replaced the **sol** in 1985 by the **inti**, with this currency effective from 1986. The sol was named from the Spanish word for 'sun'; the inti has the same meaning, although in the native Quechua language. The inti is divided into 100 céntimos.

Paraguay's main currency is the **guaraní**, of 100 céntimos. The guaraní, which replaced the peso in 1943, borrowed the name of the South American Indian language spoken in Paraguay, along with Spanish.

Other South American countries have kept colonial denominations in the language of the colonists: Uruguay has the peso of 100 centésimos; Guyana's currency is the dollar of 100 cents (as is that of Belize in Central America); Surinam, the former Dutch Guiana, has the guilder of 100 cents and French Guiana the franc of 100 centimes.

## THE WEST INDIES

Cuba, in the West Indies, has already been mentioned. Haiti's main unit of currency is the **gourde**, representing the French version of Spanish *gordo*, 'fat', 'thick', referring to the former peso that circulated in French colonies in the West Indies in the late 18th and early 19th centuries, or to the thick coin that was physically cut out of it. The gourde is divided into 100 centimes.

The rest of the West Indies' denominations are colonial in origin. The Bahamas, Barbados, Dominica, Grenada, Jamaica, Puerto Rico and Trinidad and Tobago all have dollars and cents, while the Dominican Republic has pesos and centavos and Guadeloupe and Martinique have francs and centimes. Further north, too, Bermuda also has dollars and cents.

**"**———————————————

### OILING THE WHEELS

'If the machinery of the Law could be depended on to fathom every case of suspicion, and to conduct every process of inquiry, with moderate assistance only from the lubricating influence of oil of gold, the events which fill these pages might have claimed their share of the public attention in a Court of Justice. But the Law is still, in certain inevitable cases, the pre-engaged servant of the long purse; and the story is left to be told, for the first time, in this place.'

Wilkie Collins *The Woman in White*

——————————————— **"**

 **LINK WORDS**

Sometimes an ordinary English word has an unsuspected connection with money. Here are some examples:

**Case** in its sense of a receptacle, 'case' is closely connected to the word 'cash'. The latter word originally meant the case in which money was kept rather than the money itself.

**Chess** this word, and the associated 'check', came into English from French, where *esches* was the old plural of *eschec* (later *échec*). The French word in turn derived from Persian *shah* 'king'. Saying 'check' to one's opponent when playing chess draws attention to his king. In effect one is saying: your king is being threatened. This meaning led to the more general idea of checking something in order to put it to the test. A financial statement or account is checked in that way, and it was this which gave rise to the idea of a 'check' ('cheque' in British English) being used as a means of payment. It is a payment which can be easily checked or verified.

**East** it used to be commonly said that the excellent reputation of minters who came from the East of Germany, the Easterlings, gave rise to such expressions as 'sterling silver' and the 'pound sterling'. Professor Weekley, in *An Etymological Dictionary of Modern English*, prefers instead to connect 'sterling' with 'star'. He points out that some of the early Norman pennies were marked with a star, and that a star emblem was featured on many other coins.

**Fellow** a 'fellow' was originally a person who laid his money, his 'fee', with that of someone else, in order to become his business partner. He was literally a 'fee-layer'.

**Gazette** originally the name of a small Italian coin, a gazetta. This happened to be the price of an official Italian newspaper, and eventually became the name of the newspaper itself. The word subsequently came to mean any official newspaper.

**Great** this was the meaning of 'groat', the coin familiar to Shakespeare and his contemporaries. It was originally a Dutch coin, called the *groot* in Dutch because it was 'great' in the sense of being thick.

**Operate** the basic meaning of 'operate' is to 'to make work'. The word derives ultimately from Latin *opus* 'work'. It is interesting that the ancients seem to have equated work with the idea of producing wealth, for the Latin words *opus* and *opes*, the latter meaning 'wealth, riches', are closely connected. 'Operate', and words like 'cooperate', 'opera', are therefore cousins of words like 'opulent' and 'opulence'.

**Peculiar** we have mentioned elsewhere (see ZOOLOGICAL MONEY, p. 115) that words like 'pecuniary' and 'impecunious' derive from Latin *pecu*, a word which began by meaning 'cattle', then came to mean 'riches, money'. 'Peculiar' derives from the same source through the word *peculiaris*. This had the original meaning 'the small part of a herd of cattle given to a slave acting as a herdsman as his own private property'. Later the idea of private property seems to have led to the meaning 'standing apart from others' and, eventually, to the modern idea of 'eccentric'.

**Soldier** the Latin word *solidus* meant 'massive, solid, hard', and the phrase *solidus nummus* something like 'hard cash', since *nummus* was the word for 'coin'. Later the *nummus* was dropped, and *solidus* itself took on the meaning of coin. In the reign of Constantine I it became the specific name of a gold coin. *Solidus* was shortened to *soldus*, and in Old French became *soulde*, with the meaning 'pay', especially 'army pay'. The man who accepted such pay became the modern 'soldier'.

**Well** in its sense of being in good health, as opposed to ill, 'well' is closely associated with 'wealth' via Old English *wel*. The original sense of 'wealth' was 'happiness'.

**"**——————————————————

## MONETARY MEDITATIONS

*Where large sums of money are concerned, it is advisable to trust nobody.*
Agatha Christie *Endless Night*

*Some people's money is merited And other people's is inherited.*
Ogden Nash *The Terrible People*

*The rich are the scum of the earth in every country.*
G. K. Chesterton *The Flying Inn*

*All money nowadays seems to be produced with a natural homing instinct for the Treasury.*
Duke of Edinburgh *Observer Sayings* (1963)

*It is not the employer who pays the wages—he only handles the money. It is the product that pays wages.*
Henry Ford

*Money can't buy you friends, but you get a better class of enemy.*
Spike Milligan

*Men who make money rarely saunter; men who save money rarely swagger.*
Lord Lytton *My Novel*

*Honour and money are not found in the same purse.*
Spanish proverb

*When money's taken Freedom's forsaken.*
Old saying

*'Tis sad when you think of her wasted life,*
*For youth cannot mate with age,*
*And her beauty was sold for an old man's gold—*
*She's a bird in a gilded cage.*
Arthur J. Lamb *A Bird in a Gilded Cage*

*Surplus wealth is a sacred trust which its possessor is bound to administer in his lifetime for the good of the community.*
Andrew Carnegie *The Gospel of Wealth*

*The people of this country are not jealous of fortunes, however great, which have been built up by the honest development of great enterprises, which have been actually earned by business energy and sagacity; they are jealous only of speculative wealth, of the wealth which has been piled up by no effort at all, but only by shrewd wits playing on the credulity of others. This is 'predatory wealth', and is found in stock markets.*
Woodrow Wilson, speech made in 1908

*Riches are gotten with pain, kept with care, and lost with grief.*
Thomas Fuller *Gnomologia*

*Knowledge makes one laugh, but wealth makes one dance.*
George Herbert *Jacula Prudentum*

*There are only three ways by which any individual can get wealth—by work, by gift, or by theft. And clearly the reason why the workers get so little is that the beggars and thieves get so much.*
Henry George *Social Problems*

*The most valuable of all human possessions, next to a superior and disdainful air, is the reputation of being well-to-do.*
H. L. Mencken *Prejudices*

*We have heads to get money, and hearts to spend it.*
George Farquhar *The Beaux' Stratagem*

*This bank-note world.*
Fitz-Greene Halleck *Alnwick Castle*

*As I sat at the café, I said to myself,*
*They may talk as they please about*
*    what they call pelf,*
*They may sneer as they like about*
*    eating and drinking,*
*But help it I cannot, I cannot help*
*    thinking*
*How pleasant it is to have money,*
*    heigh-ho!*
*How pleasant it is to have money!*
Arthur Hugh Clough *Spectator ab Extra*

*Sir, money, money, the most charming*
*of all things—money, which will say*
*more in one moment than the most*
*eloquent lover can in years.*
Henry Fielding *The Miser*

*Blessed is the man who hath both mind*
*and money, for he employs the latter*
*well.*
Menander *Demiopylos*

*It is not a custom with me to keep*
*money to look at.*
George Washington letter to J. P. Custis,
January 1780

　　　　　　　　　　　　　　　　　　　　　　”

## AN UNEXPECTED MONETARIST

One tends to think of Samuel Taylor Coleridge in connection with his *Ancient Mariner* and other poems, but he had much to say about money. He contributed many essays to *The Courier* on the subject. On Friday, 2 August 1811, for instance, we find him defining money as 'whatever has a value among men according to what it represents, rather than to what it is. The distinction between money and commodity, the representative and the thing represented, is not verbal or arbitrary, but real and of practical importance. As soon as a commodity becomes money, it ceases to be a commodity; even as a bag of guineas sold by its weight at Paris or Peking loses the nature, as well as name, of money'.

Coleridge went on to promise readers that he would provide them with 'a brief history of the transit from barter to money, then of money in its first form to the complexity of the present circulating medium, and lastly, of the action and reaction of money and barter on each other, and inclusively or by consequence on all the social relations of civilized man'.

**"**

## LAW'S SERIOUS CALL

'But the two things which, of all others, most want to be under a strict rule, and which are the greatest blessings both to ourselves and others, when they are rightly used, are our time and our money. These talents are continual means and opportunities of doing good.

'He that is piously strict, and exact in the wise management of either of these, cannot be long ignorant of the right use of the other. And he that is happy in the religious care and disposal of them both, is already ascended several steps upon the ladder of Christian perfection.

*'The manner of using our money or spending our estate enters so far into the business of every day, and makes so great a part of our common life, that our common life must be much of the same nature as our common ways of spending money.*

*'If a man had eyes, and hands, and feet, that he could give to those that wanted them; if he should either lock them up in a chest, or please himself with some needless or ridiculous use of them, instead of giving them to his brethren that were blind and lame, should we not justly reckon him an inhuman wretch?'*

William Law *Serious Call to a Devout and Holy Life* (1729)

(This was a book which much impressed both Wesley and Dr Johnson. After these general comments on putting one's money to charitable use, Law went on to give a portrait of two maiden sisters, Flavia and Miranda. He wanted to show the difference between those who had religion 'only in their head' and those who had it 'in their heart'.)

*'If any one asks Flavia to do something in charity, if she likes the person who makes the proposal, or happens to be in a right temper, she will toss him half-a-crown, or a crown, and tell him if he knew what a long milliner's bill she had just received, he would think it a great deal for her to give. As for poor people themselves, she will admit of no complaints from them; she is very positive they are all cheats and liars, and will say anything to get relief; and therefore it is a sin to encourage them in their evil ways.'*

Miranda has the same income as her sister, but commits most of it to charitable works, supporting tradesmen in difficulty, educating poor children and finding them employment. *'As soon as any labourer is confined at home with sickness, she sends him, till he recovers, twice the value of his wages, that he may have one part to give to his family as usual, and the other to provide things convenient for his sickness.')*

## THE FINAL AUDIT

The audit, the official examination of accounts, has long been of special interest. Modern auditors might be interested to hear of the special audit ale, formerly brewed at Trinity College Cambridge and several other Oxbridge colleges. Perhaps the idea was that auditors who had been plied with strong ale scrutinized the accounts less keenly.

In the 17th century the word 'audit' was often used to refer to the Day of Judgement, when a man would have to render a solemn account of his life to God. Day of Account was another

name for this occasion. Compt, 'account', occurs in Shakespeare with a similar meaning. In *Othello*, for example, 'meet at compt' means meet at Judgement Day.

A variation on the same theme occurs in William Thackeray's essay *On A Medal of George the Fourth*, which discusses counterfeit money. It ends: 'Ah, friend! may our coin, battered and clipped, and defaced though it be, be proved to be of Sterling Silver on the day of the Great Assay!'

# 8
# STOCKING THE PILE

## BANKS

Where there has been buying and selling and saving of money, there has always been a form of banking, even in ancient times, although not in the form that we think of it today, with cheque books, share dealing and all the other financial functions that modern banks transact.

Clay tablets, for example, have been found in Babylonia and Assyria showing certain financial transactions, such as money-changing and the arrangement of advances. In ancient Greece and Rome, methods of transferring credit from one place to another without the actual involvement of money were also known. The Chinese probably had a form of banking with their early issue of paper money.

Modern banking, however, originated in Italy, where Lombard Jews established a bank in the 9th century. It is known that in 1270 a private bank existed in Venice and that the Bank of St George, was set up in Genoa in 1407. The latter bank had an earlier history as a merchant and financial company, and its customers were the first group of shareholders whose liabilities were limited to their shares. It subsequently became one of the most important banks in Europe, and was active until 1800 when its property was acquired by the French.

### THE FIRST PUBLIC BANK

It is now generally accepted, however, that the first 'proper' **public bank** was the Banco di Rialto, set up in Venice by Acts of the Senate in 1584 and 1587. This was certainly the first public bank in Europe.

## THE RIVER BANK?

Kenneth Grahame (1859–1932), author of one of the most popular children's classics *The Wind in the Willows*, worked for most of his life at the Bank of England. He was Secretary of the Bank from 1898 to 1908, the year in which he published his well-loved book. Grahame had previously published some successful collections of essays about childhood. He created Toad of Toad Hall and his friends Mole, Rat and Badger to amuse his son Alistair, nicknamed Mouse, who died at the age of twenty.

## BANK CUSTOMERS OF EVERY DESCRIPTION

Before someone thought of introducing cheque verification cards, bank clerks had their own system of identifying customers. In *Barclays, A Story of Money and Banking*, we learn that the clerks at a Liverpool bank used to write descriptions of the customers in the bank's signature books. One such book has typical notes about a 'short man; whiskers all round his face; one tooth out in front; looks like a coal heaver' and a 'little pug-faced woman with a squeaky voice'.

In 1619 the Banco del Giro was founded. This subsequently became the only bank in the state and was long famous as the Bank of Venice.

Public banking in Venice developed from the activity of the earlier moneychangers and private banks, and it was the failure of many of the latter that led to the setting up of the Rialto Bank as a public bank by the state.

These early banks were **deposit banks**, that is, they received cash in the form of coins and paid it out on demand, thus taking over the business of the money exchanges.

**Exchange banks** arose not long after. The most famous were the Bank of Amsterdam, founded in 1609 and active until 1820, and the Bank of Hamburg, established in 1619 and operating until 1873. Banks of this type played an important role in the days when there was a large number of clipped and debased coins in circulation. Their purpose was to aid commerce, not by loaning money but by issuing 'bank money' as a kind of international currency. Merchants deposited coins or gold bullion in the bank and were credited with their intrinsic value. Their credit was then available in 'bank money', which they could draw on as necessary to meet their requirements. The exchange banks gained their income from the small charge that they made for negotiating the deals between one merchant and another.

The next big step in banking was the issue of banknotes, as a promise to pay the stated amount in coin. (See Chapter 4, p. 37.)

### BRITISH BANKS

Banking in England is usually dated from 1640, the year in which Charles I seized the gold bullion deposited by London merchants in the Tower of London. When it was returned to them, they deposited it for safe keeping with the goldsmiths, who conducted money-changing, as well as taking charge of rents and money deposited by country gentlemen. Their business developed considerably as a result of the Civil War. The receipts that they gave for money deposited were known as 'goldsmiths' notes', and these were the first form of banknotes in England, circulating even more freely than coins as late as the end of the 17th century.

### THE BANK OF ENGLAND

In 1694 the **Bank of England** was founded to become Britain's central bank, the so-called 'bankers' bank', known simply as 'the Bank' or more jocularly as the 'Old Lady of Threadneedle Street'. Its principal duty is to act as a banker to the government. It also issues banknotes, and aims to regulate conditions in the financial markets. As agent for the government, the Bank of England also arranges government borrowing and manages the National Debt (the amount of money that the government owes). Moreover, the Bank of England can influence money market conditions generally, by its dealing with the discount houses (see Chapter 9, p. 106).

## THE OLD LADY OF THREADNEEDLE STREET

This has long been the nickname of the Bank of England, which is situated in Threadneedle Street in the City of London. Threadneedle Street itself was earlier Three Needle Street, referring to a signboard depicting three needles. This would have indicated a shop which sold needles, or which was the property of the Needle Makers' Company.

The 'Old Lady' reference originated with a cartoon by James Gillray (1757–1815), published during the Napoleonic Wars. A copy of the cartoon is prominently displayed in the Bank. It shows William Pitt the Younger attempting to seize the Bank's gold from an elderly lady seated on a locked chest. The title 'Political Ravishment, or the Old Lady of Threadneedle Street in danger' was possibly suggested by Sheridan. He had spoken of the Bank in the House of Commons as 'an elderly lady in the City of great credit and long standing'.

The Bank is rather proud of its nickname, and has used Old Lady as the title of its house magazine.

## THE RETAIL BANKS

The familiar High Street banks did not emerge until the 19th century as commercial banks, otherwise known as **retail banks** or **clearing banks**, the latter because they run a common centralized system of clearing cheques, that is, processing them to settle the accounts. It was only in 1918 that the 'Big Five' emerged as amalgamations of earlier banks. These were: Barclays Bank, the National Provincial Bank, the Midland Bank, Lloyds Bank and the Westminster Bank.

**Barclays Bank** dates from about 1694, when a London goldsmith, John Freame, set up his business on the site of the Black Spread Eagle (now adopted as the Bank's symbol) in Lombard Street. In 1736 his son and successor, Joseph Freame, then took into partnership his brother-in-law, James Barclay. The concern was subsequently registered as Barclay and Company Limited in 1896, and from that year acquired various other banking businesses.

The **National Provincial Bank** was established more recently. It was founded in London by the banking pioneer Thomas Japlin in 1833, and was originally based on a wide network of country banks. Hence its name. In 1865 it became a fully London-based bank.

The **Midland Bank**, as its name suggests, originated in the Midlands or central counties of England, and was founded in 1836 as the Birmingham and Midland Bank. In 1891 it acquired the Central Bank of London and changed its name to the London and Midland Bank. After further acquisitions, it adopted its present name in 1923.

**Lloyds Bank**, established in 1677, is well known for its symbol of a prancing black horse. This was originally the sign of a London goldsmith, one Humphrey Stokes, goldsmiths being the fore-

## THE BLACK BOOK

A bank which was later absorbed by Barclays had a Black Book in which the directors recorded the misdeeds of their staff. In 1910, for instance, they entered details of a young man who had broken the bank's rule about marrying on an inadequate salary. He was allowed to keep his job only when his father agreed to supplement his income to £150 *per annum*. Another employee incurred debts of £56. He was retained on probation 'provided his mother paid his debts'.

In 1893 the directors recorded the 'reckless spending' of the bank manager at Haverfordwest, though he seems to have been guilty only of professional pride. Instead of the £10 that had been allowed him for the cleaning of his branch, he had spent over £15. The directors ordered him to refund the excess amount to the bank.

## THE BANK OF SCOTLAND

The Bank of Scotland was founded in 1695 by an Act of the Scottish Parliament. Other pieces of legislation which were passed that year included an Act for a Solemn Fast, an Act against Blasphemy, an Act against burying in Scots Linen, an Act in favour of Periwig Makers. There was also an Act for Trading in Africa and India which led to the so-called Darien scheme, the founding of a Scottish colony on the Isthmus of Darien. This was begun in 1698 and abandoned in 1700, ruining the many Scots who had speculated in it wildly.

runners of modern bankers. The founder of the bank was a Welshman, Charles Lloyd, who had settled in Birmingham as an ironmaster and founded his banking business there in the year stated. In its present form, however, the bank was founded in Birmingham by one of his descendants in 1765, as Taylors and Lloyds Bank. It changed its name to Lloyds and Company in 1853 and eventually to Lloyds Bank in 1889, having adopted the Sign of the Black Horse only five years before this.

The **Westminster Bank** was first opened as the London and Westminster Bank in Throgmorton Street, London, in 1834, and its general manager, J. W. Gilbart, became renowned as the leading commercial banker of his day. It adopted the shorter title of Westminster Bank in 1923.

In 1968 the 'Big Five' became the 'Big Four', when the National Provincial and Westminster Banks merged to form the **National Westminster**, or 'NatWest', as it is now commonly known. That same year Barclays absorbed Martin's Bank, which had itself evolved from a goldsmith's business set up in Lombard Street in the second half of the 16th century by Sir Thomas Gresham, founder of the Royal Exchange. (It took its name from the Mayor of London and Master of the Mint, Sir Richard Martin, and was operating as a bank by the early 18th century.)

In 1988 the largest number of **branches** among the 'Big Four' was held by National Westminster, with 3086. Next was Barclays with 2712, then Lloyds with 2189, and the Midland with 2090. About 70 per cent of all adults in Britain have a current account, and more than one third a deposit account.

There are of course other commercial banks in Britain. One of the best known is **Coutts**, founded in about 1690, therefore older than the Bank of England. Its original proprietor was one John Campbell, who was a goldsmith as well as a banker. The connection with the Coutts family dates from 1755, when James Coutts was taken into partnership on his marriage to Mary Peagrim, the niece of George Campbell, John Campbell's son. When George Campbell died in 1760, James Coutts invited his younger brother Thomas to join him, and it is to him that the bank owes its present prestigious status.

Another well known bank is **Williams & Glyn's**, which resulted as a merger in 1969 of Williams Deacon's, founded in 1771, and Glyn, Mills, founded in 1753. The **Royal Bank of Scotland**, founded in 1727, is one more familiar name, as is that of the **Bank of Scotland**, founded in 1695, just one year after the Bank of England. In more recent times, the Trustee Savings Bank and many building societies (see below, p. 100) have come to offer the range of financial services that the 'big boys' provide.

### AMERICAN BANKS

In the United States of America the situation is quite different. There are over 14 000 commercial banks, this large number resulting from laws that prevent banks from operating in more than one state. Most of them are small, and American banking is dominated by about a dozen 'money-centre' banks with household names such as the Chase Manhattan Bank and the Bank of America.

The first US banks arose at the time of the establishment of a national currency (see p. 29). The **First National Bank of Boston**, founded in 1784, describes itself as 'the oldest bank in America' and also as 'the oldest Chartered Bank in the USA'. That same year, the **Bank of New York**, 'New York's first bank', was established. However, there are rival claims as to which exactly is the oldest American bank, and a challenger to the First National Bank of Boston is the **First Pennsylvania Banking and Trust Company**, which

**ENCOUNTER AT THE COUNTER**

Graham Greene makes some humorous comments on the differences between English and American banks in *Our Man In Havana*. His main point is that 'American bankers believe in the personal touch; the teller conveys a sense that he happens to be there accidentally and he is overjoyed at the lucky chance of the encounter.'

dates its foundation, although not under this name, from 1782.

The **Chase Manhattan Bank** was created in 1955 as a merger between the Bank of Manhattan, founded in 1799, originally as the local water company, and the Chase National Bank of the City of New York, founded in 1877 by a 75-year-old former schoolteacher, John Thompson, who named it after the American lawyer and statesman Salmon Portland Chase, the originator of the United States national banking system. This was authorized by Congress both to provide for the financing of the federal government in the Civil War and to correct the chaotic lack of organization that then prevailed among state systems.

The **Bank of America**, formerly but at present no longer the biggest bank in the world, has in recent years had a keen rival in Citicorp as the biggest bank in the United States. It developed out of the Bank of Italy, set up in San Francisco's Italian district in 1904 as a lending bank by the son of Italian immigrants, Amadeo Peter Giannini. It was soon nicknamed 'The Little Fellow's Bank', and began opening branches outside San Francisco. When the Federal Reserve Board ruled in 1921 that no bank belonging to the Federal Reserve System (see below) could open new branches, Giannini circumvented the order by buying the existing Bank of America of Los Angeles, which already had 21 branches. Soon after, his bank adopted this name for its consolidated operations.

**Citicorp**, which in 1989 outstripped its western rival, the 'B of A', as the biggest bank in the United States, was formed in 1812 as the City Bank of New York to back the Anglo-American War that year with war loans. It subsequently adopted its cable address, Citibank, as its name, and in 1955 merged with the First National Bank of the City of New York to become the First National City Bank. In 1968 it created a 'holding company', Citicorp, to take over the ownership of the bank, and it is now usually known by that name.

Although banks in the USA were originally based on the British system, they have since developed distinctive features that make them quite different from most banks in other countries. First, they are chiefly banks of deposit and credit rather than banks that accumulate capital, as they do in Britain. Second, most banks are 'unit' banks, under their own separate ownership and management, and do not have branches, as they do in Britain. (California is the only state where banks are allowed to operate branch offices.)

But both Britain and the United States use that basic feature of banks, cheques, far more than many other countries do, even in continental Europe, and this is the place to say something about them.

 **MISPLACED GENEROSITY**

An American bank employee used some of the bank's money to bet on horses. Amazingly, he won enough to be able to return the money before its loss was discovered. All would have been well if he had not made the foolish mistake of putting back more than he had taken. This led to an investigation which revealed what had occurred. At his trial the judge was not amused when he pleaded that his offence was a minor one. 'All you can say,' said the man, 'was that I was generous to a vault.'

**IT'S ONLY MONEY**

George Washington Carver (1864–1943), an American agricultural researcher, lost his entire life-savings of $70 000 when the Alabama Bank crashed. He may have lost his money, but he certainly didn't lose his cool. He remarked: 'I guess somebody found a use for it. I was not using it myself.'

## CHEQUES

A **cheque** (in the US, **check**) is basically a bill of exchange—a document used by a creditor to pay a sum of money to a debtor. The creditor usually signs the cheque, and names the debtor as the person (or institution) to be paid. But of course he does so through a bank, which has issued blank cheques for this purpose in the first place. This is important, for it means that the creditor has, or should have, money in that bank. If he does not, the cheque 'bounces', and is returned to him unpaid.

In a sense, therefore, a cheque is a logical development from the banknote. Like the note, it is issued by a bank, and also like the note, it guarantees payment. Unlike a note, it is of variable value and relates specifically to two named parties, creditor and debtor. However, the convenience of such a 'money order' was realized once banks had become fully established and begun issuing their own notes. Records show that one Lawrence

 **CHEQUERED CHEQUES**

Millions of cheques are processed by high-street banks every day, the cheques normally being those issued by the banks themselves. Occasionally someone reminds the banks, and the public, that a cheque can legally be written on anything. A donation of ten guineas to the RAF Benevolent Fund, written on the back of a cigarette packet, was honoured by a bank in 1962. In 1970 the writer and humorist A. P. Herbert received a cheque from the editor of *Punch* written on the side of a cow. Sir Alan took the cow to the nearest bank and was given his money.

One of the largest cheques ever drawn on a bank was the one for £853 million presented to the Government of India by the United States in 1974. Another interesting cheque was the one used by the United States to purchase Alaska in 1867. It was cheque 9160 of the United States Treasury, and read: 'Pay His Imperial Majesty The Tsar of all the Russias The Sum of Seven Million Two Hundred Thousand Dollars.'

Childs, an English banker, first printed cheques with his name in about 1761. The use of cheques was slow to catch on at first. But when issues of banknotes were restricted in Britain by the Bank Act of 1844, cheques were immediately utilized as a means of payment by a community that had grown considerably in size and wealth and that needed an ever-larger supply of money. Moreover, banks knew that it was good business on their part to have their money circulating as cheques, rather than coins or notes, so they encouraged their use.

Cheques make good business for a bank because they 'create' money. This is because a bank customer with a cheque book withdraws money from his account, which puts his bank in debt to that amount, but at the same time the identical amount is deposited in someone else's account, which puts *his* bank in credit by that amount. The cheque-sender has thus 'created' that amount of money, a credit against the effective loan that his own bank made him. (For similar reasons, banks like buying shares on the Stock Exchange and paying for them by crediting the seller's account, whether he is a customer of the bank or not. For the seller will deposit the cheque he receives in payment for his shares with his bank, or even have the amount credited direct to his account. Either way, his bank will have increased its deposit, or its 'money'.)

Cheques have traditionally been associated with the payment of larger sums, and in recent years have been drawn for amounts running to millions of pounds. To date, the greatest amount paid by a single cheque is in *billions* of pounds. It was issued on 30 August 1988 and was for the sum of £1 088 524 128.30p, representing the call monies due from clients of the Royal Bank of Scotland in respect of the BP share issue. It was signed by Conrad Milton, the Bank's Assistant General Manager.

A special sort of cheque is the **Eurocheque**. This is a cheque which, when drawn on a bank in the EEC (Common Market), can be cashed in another currency at any bank in the Community participating in the scheme. Eurocheques closely resemble standard cheques, except that the currency is variable and the wording appears in the three main languages of the EEC, English, French and German.

## NO CHEQUE BOOK?

The publisher of the American author Sherwood Anderson (1876–1941) arranged to send him a weekly cheque. He hoped that by relieving Anderson of financial pressure, he would write more. After a few weeks the author returned to the publisher with the latest cheque, saying: 'It's no use. I find it impossible to work with security staring me in the face.'

Just as actual coins and notes have to a large extent been superseded by credit and debit cards (and of course cheques themselves), so the use of cheques, at least in business and commerce, is likely to be replaced by a simpler electronic method of payment in a future 'cashless society'. (For more on this, see Chapter 14, p. 181.)

### THE FEDERAL RESERVE SYSTEM

Although there is no national 'United States Bank' in the way that Britain has the Bank of England and France the Banque de France, there is a counterpart. It is the **Federal Reserve System**.

The 'Fed', as it is popularly known, is the central bank of the United States, its 'bank of banks', having as its clients the commercial banks and the government.

It was created in 1913, and consists of 12 national banks (those granted a federal charter) spread across the country, together with a board of seven governors based in Washington. The members of the board are appointed by the president and confirmed by the Senate, and each serves a term of 14 years.

## FLYING A KITE

The expression 'to kite a check (cheque)' is not used in Britain. In the US it refers to writing a bad cheque. A 'kite' itself is, as *Webster's New Collegiate Dictionary* puts it: 'a check drawn against uncollected funds in a bank account or fraudulently raised before cashing'.

The Fed's most important function is to control the money supply, and it does this by buying and selling government securities and changing reserve requirements. All banks that are members of the Fed, which includes most large banks and a few small ones, are obliged to keep a minimum amount of reserves against their deposits. These reserves are then in turn held as deposits in the Fed. By keeping control of the operation of its banks, the Fed thus keeps control on the loan activities of its banks and therefore on the economy of the country as a whole.

The Fed's most influential activity is the buying and selling of bonds (government securities) through the **Federal Open Market Committee** (FOMC). If the Fed thinks that business is expanding too fast, and inflation is rising steeply, the FOMC will sell bonds to restrict the amount of credit. The buyers of these bonds pay the Fed with cheques written on their banks, and when the Fed presents the cheques to the banks, they pay out of their reserves. The banks thus end up with smaller reserves and less money available to loan. And when they restrict loans, they slow the economy.

The Fed can also control the amount of credit in the economy by setting reserve requirements. It does this by increasing the reserves that it requires its member banks to keep available. With more deposits going into reserve accounts, banks will thus have less money to lend out.

If the member banks become short of cash, they can borrow money from the Fed for a fee, known as the **'discount rate'**. If the Fed wants to encourage bank credit activity, it lowers this rate, making it cheaper for the banks to borrow. If it wants to restrict activity, it raises the rate.

The Fed also issues coins and notes, and through its banks carries out the clearing of cheques and the transference of funds, including foreign exchange operations.

### THE FED v. THE BANK OF ENGLAND

Just as the head of the Fed in America is commonly regarded as the second most powerful person in the country (after the President), so the Governor of the Bank of England is influential in promoting the views of the Bank, and the City as a whole, on economic and financial matters.

## A GUNSMITH?

A bank clerk's life can be far from easy if he happens to work in a troubled city. Steve Smith, an international rugby player as well as bank clerk, was involved in four hold-ups in the space of a single year at his branch of the Bank of Ireland in Belfast. In three of them the robber produced a hand-gun; in the fourth Mr Smith was faced with the twin barrels of a shot-gun.

Steve Smith subsequently gave up banking and took to selling sports equipment.

---

In the same way, too, that the Fed can control the money supply of the USA by altering the discount rate, the Bank of England can alter the interest rate which it charges banks for their credit activity. The rate is also known as its discount rate.

This latter rate should not be confused with what used to be called first **Bank Rate**, then **Minimum Lending Rate**. This was the rate of interest at which the Bank of England would lend money to the discount houses (see p. 112). Minimum Lending Rate, introduced in 1973, was abolished in 1981.

### OTHER BANKS

In France, the **Banque de France** was founded in 1800 by Napoleon as a reorganization of the *Caisse des comptes courants* ('Current Account Fund'). It was initially a private bank formed as an association of leading financiers, but gradually came to be controlled by the state. In 1803 it was granted the sole privilege of issuing banknotes. In 1945 it was nationalized, together with the main credit establishments, the Crédit Lyonnais (founded in Lyon in 1863), Société Générale (founded in 1864), Comptoir national d'escompte, and the Banque nationale pour le commerce et l'industrie (BNCI). The latter two merged in 1966 to form the Banque nationale de Paris (BNP). In 1987 the Société Générale was reprivatized.

'Canada's First Bank' is the **Bank of Montreal**, founded in 1817, and the **Bank of Nova Scotia** in the same country dates from 1832. But the Bank of Montreal was pipped at the post by the **Bank of**

## ADAM AND EVE VISIT A BANK

Nathaniel Hawthorne asks his readers to imagine, in *The New Adam And Eve*, that 'the Day of Doom has burst upon the globe and swept away the whole race of men'. It is a 'universal bankruptcy'. Man's institutions, however, have remained, and a new Adam and Eve explore them.

When they visit a bank 'they take up the bright gold in handfuls and throw it sportively into the air for the sake of seeing the glittering worthlessness descend again in a shower. They know not that each of those small yellow circles was once a magic spell, potent to sway men's hearts and mystify their moral sense. They have discovered the mainspring, the life, the very essence of the system that had wrought itself into the vitals of mankind, and choked their original nature in its deadly gripe. Here, too, are huge packages of bank notes, those talismanic slips of paper which once had the efficacy to build up enchanted palaces like exhalations, and work all kinds of perilous wonders, yet were themselves but the ghost of money, the shadows of a shade.

'Everywhere, my dear Eve,' observes Adam, 'we find heaps of rubbish of one kind or another. Somebody, I am convinced, has taken pains to collect them, but for what purpose? Perhaps, hereafter, we shall be moved to do the like. Can that be our business in the world?'

'O, no, no, Adam!' answers Eve. 'It would be better to sit down quietly and look upward to the sky.'

---

**New South Wales**, in Sydney, Australia, which although also founded in 1817, is almost nine months older.

The 'Wales', as it is known, played an important role in the development of its country, as the **Standard Bank of Johannesburg** did for South Africa. The latter bank calls itself 'the oldest bank in Africa south of the Sahara', and was incorporated in 1862, beginning business the following

## DANIEL DEFOE

Bank records show that Daniel Defoe, author of *Robinson Crusoe*, was a successful, if unscrupulous, self-made man as well as a writer. He began life as the son of a London butcher, but on one occasion in 1729, ten years after the publication of his novel, he paid just over £369 into his account. This was at a time when a labourer thought himself lucky to receive half-a-crown (12½ pence) a day. Defoe persuaded many people to invest heavily in a civet-cat farm, telling them that there was a fortune to be made in perfume. There were no cats: Defoe used the money to ward off his creditors.

year. It did much to influence the growth of the country's diamond and gold fields.

In Japan, the oldest bank is the **Mitsui Bank**, Tokyo, which was established in 1683, and so predates the Bank of England. Its rival for longevity is the **Sanwa Bank**, Osaka, which, although established as the result of a merger in 1933, claims to trace back one of its money-changing operations to 1656. It is Japan, however, that currently boasts the biggest bank in the world. This is the **Dai-Ichi Kangyo Bank**, of Tokyo, formed in 1971 through a merger of the Dai-Ichi Bank (its name means 'number one'), founded 1873, and the Nippon Kangyo Bank, founded 1897.

In pre-revolutionary Russia, the **Bank for the Nobility** was founded in 1754 and the **Astrakhan Bank** in 1764. In 1860 the government set up the **State Bank**, which became the country's most important commercial bank. After the Revolution, all banks were abolished, and even money itself was nearly replaced by 'labour units'. In 1921 the State Bank was re-formed and continues to operate as the sole bank of the USSR today.

In Switzerland, a country still preeminently associated with bankers and money, the oldest bank is that of **Leu & Compagnie**, Zürich, established in 1755 which, unusually, started its operations as a state bank, and subsequently became a private one.

## SAVINGS BANKS AND BUILDING SOCIETIES

Besides the commercial banks, there are other kinds of deposit-taking banks. In Britain, they are the National Savings Bank and the building societies.

The **National Savings Bank** was founded as the Post Office Savings Bank in 1861. It is run by the Department of National Savings (DNS), based in Glasgow, and provides facilities for people to deposit and withdraw their savings at post offices around the country. In 1989 there were about 20 million accounts. Ordinary Accounts were the most common, with interest earned depending on the balance maintained. (Investment Accounts have a higher rate of interest, which is taxable.) In August 1989 the total amount of money invested in National Savings was £36 900 million, all this being part of the National Debt.

The National Savings Bank is distinct from the **National Girobank**, or simply **Girobank**, which is also a banking service operated by the Post Office. It is not a savings bank, but principally a money transfer service, using cheques in the same way as the High Street banks. It also makes loans, however, and offers other standard banking facilities. In 1988 Girobank had over 2000 accounts. Although originally a government bank, in 1990 it was privatized and bought by the Alliance and Leicester Building Society.

**Building societies** are essentially specialized savings banks. Their name is a misnomer, since they do not build houses! They do, however, lend money for people to *buy* their private homes. They

## MUSICAL BANKS

Musical banks are discussed in Samuel Butler's *Erewhon*. They have their ardent supporters, Butler tells us, though many of these are supporters in name only, preferring to go to normal banks themselves. The musical banks have their own currency which is greatly esteemed, but unfortunately it has no commercial value. The reader of *Erewhon* gradually comes to realize that musical banks are a caricature of the Church of England.

do this by using the money of individual savers, who are paid a favourable but variable rate of interest in one of a number of different savings schemes. (If a saver 'ties up' his money in a scheme which does not permit him to make any withdrawals for a fixed period, such as a year, he gets a higher rate of interest.)

Building societies are now increasingly like the High Street banks, and offer more or less the same services, such as issuing cheque books, bank cards, credit cards, regular statements and the like, and providing standing order and direct debit facilities for their clients. They are still closely tied to the buying and selling of houses, however, and offer financial services geared to this, such as the provision of mortgages. They are also often associated with a particular estate agent or life assurance company.

They have developed rapidly since World War I, and there have been many mergers among leading building societies to give a more and more comprehensive service to their members. In 1980 about 70 per cent of all adults in Britain had a building society account.

Although there are still over 100 registered building societies, the three largest ones account for half the total assets of the movement. These are the **Halifax**, founded in the Yorkshire town of this name in 1853, with 8.8 million members in 1988 and assets of over £40 000 million, the **Abbey National**, formed in 1944 as a merger between the Abbey Road (founded in 1849 in the London street of this name) and the National societies, with 8.2 million members and assets of over £31 000 million, and the **Nationwide Anglia**, formed in 1987 as a merger of the Nationwide (founded in 1884) and Anglia (founded in 1848) societies, with 5.6 million members and assets of over £24 000 million.

The oldest British building society is the Chesham, founded in the Buckinghamshire town of this name in 1845.

Of all the British savings banks, the best known has long been the **Trustee Savings Bank**. This was founded as a non-profit-making savings bank opened by a clergyman, the Rev Dr Henry Duncan, at Ruthwell, Dumfriesshire, Scotland, in 1810. It was so named because it came to be controlled in a number of branches on a regional basis

## THE VOICE OF EXPERIENCE

*Kipps*, by H. G. Wells, is the story of a working-class young man who inherits a lot of money. He has ridiculous adventures as he tries to become middle-class and live in the way that his fortune demands. In the course of the story he loses his money, then regains it. He decides to settle down and run a bookshop with his wife Ann—formerly a maid—but indulges in a little philosophy:

'Money—look 'ow it comes and goes! You may kill yourself trying to get it, and then it comes when you aren't looking. Don't seem much sense in it, Ann—'owever you look at it.' He shook his head. 'I know one thing.'
'What?'
'I'm going to put it in jest as many different banks as I can. See? Fifty 'ere, fifty there. 'Posit. I'm not going to 'nvest it—no fear.'
'It's only frowing money away,' said Ann.
'I'm 'arf a mind to bury some of it under the shop. Only I expect one 'ud always be coming down at nights to make sure it was there . . . I don't seem to trust any one—not with money.'

by local managers called 'trustees'. In 1986, however, the TSB altered its functions to become a single commercial bank like the other High Street banks, although still operating a savings facility, as all main banks do. In 1988 it had 1546 branches.

### MERCHANT BANKS
A further type of well-known bank is the **merchant bank**, also known as an **accepting house**. Merchant banks have long had the business of accepting, i.e. guaranteeing, bills of exchange. A bill of exchange is essentially the debt of a company, which the accepting house will buy, as an 'acceptance', by lending the creditor the given amount in the belief that the debtor company will pay up at the end of a fixed period of time, usually three months. Of course, other banks also accept bills of exchange in this way, but the acceptance houses have the special advantage of knowing that the bills they accept will, if necessary, be bought by the Bank of England.

## IF YOU WERE A BANKER...

In his novel *Thanksgiving*, Robert Jordan writes: 'If you were a banker you wouldn't be like those guys in the cushy jobs. You'd be sympathetic to the poor people and the small business man. You could give them loans, help them.'

'Nah. I never met a banker like that. It's impossible to count money and stay nice. You get greedy for more and more.'

---

Merchant banks today carry out a wide range of financial operations besides the acceptance of bills, both nationally and internationally, and they provide specialized advice to companies in the case of a merger, takeover or other corporate reorganization. They also advise on the management of investment holdings, including trusts and pensions. The 'Big Four' all have merchant banking subsidiaries.

Currently the largest merchant bank is S. G. Warburg, which in 1988 had total assets of over £11.5 billion.

### 'THE THRIFTS'
In the United States, the virtual equivalent of building societies are the **Savings and Loan Associations**, known as the **'thrifts'**. They are cooperative associations, with the savers not simply depositors but also owners of the association. Savers buy shares of stock and receive dividends in porportion to the profits of the association, rather than interest. The Savings and Loan Associations actually developed out of British building societies in the second half of the 18th century, which explains their similarity. But there is a distinction between shares in the 'thrifts' and bank deposits in that the investments of the association are long term, meaning that they can less easily be 'liquid' than banks. They therefore write mortgages for longer periods than banks do. Like British building societies, the 'thrifts' issue cheques to their account holders, but unlike them they also provide loans for purchases of goods other than houses.

In 1988, with the collapse of house and land prices in the States, many 'thrifts' ceased to be solvent, so that in 1989 the Bush administration had to bail them out at an estimated cost of $100 billion.

### THE WORLD BANK
The **World Bank** is the short name of the International Bank for Reconstruction and Development (IBRD), a specialized agency of the United Nations. It has its headquarters in Washington, DC, and was set up in 1944 as part of the accord reached among 45 nations at Bretton Woods, New Hampshire. It has the aim of raising the standards of living in developing countries by providing financial resources through loans made to a particular government, or guaranteed by the government concerned.

The funds for the World Bank come from its member countries, with richer countries making the largest contribution, as well as from sales of its own bonds, and from earnings (interest) on its loans.

At present, the bank is owned by the governments of 151 countries. Over the period from its establishment to 1988, it had made loans to 110 of these to the total of $155 048.8 million.

Inevitably, some of the projects that the Bank supports are risky ones, and can result in expensive undertakings that need continued subsidies to operate. In such cases, the Bank can leave the debtor country concerned less able to hold its own in the world economy. On the other hand, the

**"**

### BANKING ON THE FUTURE

'You trust to Providence,' said Sir William.
'Providence or fate,' said Aaron.
'For my own part, I always advise Providence plus a banking account. Providence and no banking account I have observed to be almost invariably fatal.'

D. H. Lawrence *Aaron's Rod*

**"**

World Bank does perform a needed function in providing capital for poor countries to develop, especially those that cannot obtain financial support from private sources.

In 1956 the **International Finance Corporation** (IFC) was formed as an affiliate of the World Bank, and in 1960 the **International Development Association** (IDA) was created similarly. The IFC encourages private enterprise in developing countries, while the IDA supplements the activities of the World Bank by making long-term loans at low rates of interest to the poorer countries.

## THE INTERNATIONAL MONETARY FUND

The **International Monetary Fund** (IMF) was set up after World War II as a way of establishing a fixed exchange rate system. Together with the World Bank (see above) it realized the plan of a world central bank as envisaged by Lord Keynes for Britain and H. D. White for the USA at th Bretton Woods Conference of 1944. It was established two years later in Washington.

In essence, the IMF is a cooperative deposit bank, offering credit to member nations experiencing balance of payment difficulties.

At present it has 151 members, and the Fund itself is made up of money paid in by members, mostly in their own currencies. The size of these dues (called 'quotas') depends on the size of the relevant member nation's economy. In return for their contributions, members have the right to vote on IMF policy and to borrow money. The bigger a country's quota, the greater its power in voting and borrowing. Currently the most powerful member is the United States.

## THE EUROPEAN MONETARY SYSTEM

The **European Monetary System** (EMS) was established in 1979 to promote monetary stability in Europe. It consists of an **Exchange Rate**

**"**

### THE SUBJECT OF EXTRAORDINARY INTEREST

*'Dearest Mother,*
*I am getting on nicely in my work at the bank, and like it . . . I want to find out something about the science of money while I am at it: it is an extraordinarily interesting subject . . .'*

T. S. Eliot A letter written on 11 April, 1917. (Eliot had come to England from America in 1915. He worked for a while as a schoolteacher, then in Lloyd's Bank. *The Waste Land*, which made him famous, was published in 1922).

**"**

Mechanism (ERM), the European Currency Unit, or ECU, used for the financial statements of the European Investment Bank (see p. 68). Although Britain has participated in the EMS from the outset, she does not take part in the ERM, and her involvement in this has long been opposed by Britain's Prime Minister, Margaret Thatcher. She and her Chancellor of the Exchequer, John Major, favour a system of free competition among existing currencies (with each country continuing to use its own currency), these operating interchangeably.

Even so, Britain is committed to participating in the ERM, and 1990/1 will reveal on what terms she does so.

 **RINGING THE CHANGES**

The security operation in large banks is sometimes known as The Guarding of the Change.

## THE WAY TO WEALTH

In his autobiography Benjamin Franklin (1706–90) writes: 'In 1732 I first published an Almanack, under the name of Richard Saunders; it was continued by me about twenty-five years, and commonly called *Poor Richard's Almanack*. I endeavoured to make it both entertaining and useful, and it accordingly came to be in such demand that I reaped considerable profit from it, vending annually near ten thousand. And observing that it was generally read (scarce any neighbourhood in the province being without it), I considered it as a proper vehicle for conveying instruction among the common people, who bought scarcely any other books.

'I therefore filled all the little spaces that occurred between the remarkable days in the calendar with proverbial sentences, chiefly such as inculcated industry and frugality as the means of procuring wealth and thereby securing virtue, it being more difficult for a man in want always to act honestly, as, to use here one of these proverbs, "it is hard for an empty sack to stand upright". These proverbs, which contained the wisdom of many ages and nations, I assembled and formed into a connected discourse prefixed to the *Almanack* of 1757, as the harangue of a wise old man.'

The Preface to which Franklin refers, detached from the *Almanack* and given the title *The Way to Wealth*, was constantly reprinted during his lifetime. Its popularity continued long after his death. By 1900 it had passed through 70 editions in English, 56 in French, 11 in German and 9 in Italian. Translations had also appeared in most of the other European languages and in Chinese.

Franklin says that many clergymen bought copies of *The Way to Wealth* to distribute to their parishioners, but the pamphlet has had its more severe critics. Nathaniel Hawthorne remarked on Poor Richard's obsession with getting money and holding on to it. Herman Melville disliked Franklin's platitudes, obtrusive advice, book-keeper's mind and the fact that he belonged to that race of men who were 'keen observers of the main chance'. Mark Twain pitied boys whose fathers had read Franklin's pernicious works, and devised his own more cynical sayings (see pages 84, 108, 113) for *Pudd'nhead Wilson's Calendar.*

D. H. Lawrence was an especially bitter critic of Franklin: 'The soul of man is a dark vast forest, with wild life in it. Think of Benjamin fencing it off! He made a list of virtues, which he trotted inside like a grey nag in a paddock.' Lawrence was brought up on the sayings of Poor Richard, but was later to write that it had taken 'many years and countless smarts to get out of that barbed wire moral enclosure that Poor Richard had rigged up.'

To allow readers to decide for themselves we give below a selection of the proverbs assembled by Franklin in *The Way to Wealth*. Many will already be familiar; they have certainly been much quoted:

'Taxes are indeed very heavy; and if those laid on by the Government were the only ones we had to pay, we might the more easily discharge them: but we have many others, and much more grievous to some of us. We are taxed twice as much by our IDLENESS, three times as much by our PRIDE, and four times as much by our FOLLY.'

'Dost thou love life? Then do not squander time! for that's the stuff Life is made of.'

'Laziness travels so slowly that Poverty soon overtakes him.'

'Drive thy business! Let not that drive thee!'

'Early to bed, and early to rise,
Makes a man healthy, wealthy and wise.'

'There are no gains without pains.'

'He that hath a trade hath an estate. He that hath a calling hath an office of profit and honour.'

'I never saw an oft removed tree,
Nor yet an oft removed family,
That throve so well, as those that settled be.'

'Diligence is the mother of good luck.'

'Employ thy time well, if thou meanest to gain leisure.'

'Want of care does us more damage than want of knowledge.'

'Not to oversee workmen is to leave them your purse open.'

'If you would have a faithful servant, and one that you like; serve yourself!'

'Many estates are spent in the getting,
Since women, for tea, forsook spinning and knitting;
And men, for punch, forsook hewing and splitting.'

'Women and wine, game and deceit,
Make the wealth small, and the wants great.'

'Who dainties love, shall beggars prove.'

'Buy what thou hast no need of, and ere long thou shalt sell thy necessaries.'

'He that goes a-borrowing goes a-sorrowing.'

'A ploughman on his legs is higher than a gentleman on his knees.'

'A child and a fool imagine twenty shillings and twenty years can never be spent.'

'Creditors have better memories than debtors.'

'Creditors are a superstitious sect, great observers of set days and times.'

'For age and want, save while you may!
No morning sun lasts a whole day.'

'Experience keeps a dear school; but fools will learn in no other, and scarce in that.'

Franklin ended his Preface by saying: 'I was conscious that not a tenth part of the wisdom was my own, but rather the gleanings I had made of the sense of all ages and nations. However, I resolved to be the better for the echo of it; and though I had, at first, determined to buy stuff for a new coat, I went away resolved to wear my old one a little longer. Reader! if thou wilt do the same, thy profit will be as great as mine.'

# 9
# PILING THE STOCK

## THE WORLD OF FINANCE

All of us use money in our everyday lives, earning it, saving it and spending it. There are a number of people who make their living professionally by actually *working* with money.

There is nothing new in this. Money lenders and money changers, for example, have existed for hundreds of years, as have the specialists who deal in the precious metals from which money is made, goldsmiths and silversmiths among them.

But there are particular areas of operation, apart from the homely High Street banks and building societies, where the activity involves not so much basic money as finance.

The following are some of the most familiar such institutions.

### THE STOCK EXCHANGE

There are stock exchanges in all the major capitalist countries of the world, but two of the best known are the London Stock Exchange and the New York Stock Exchange, with their respective share indices, the Financial Times Index and the Dow Jones Index. (For details of these, see p. 110.)

Although there are differences in the way the various stock exchanges are controlled, they basically operate for the same purpose, which is to trade securities, otherwise to buy and sell stocks, shares and bonds.

**Stocks**, as used in this sense (as distinct from stocks of goods in a factory, for example), are the funds allocated by a company or the government from its capital for the purposes of a financial risk.

The funds are issued as 'paper money' in consolidated form, so that they can be transacted in any amount. **Shares**, as their name implies, are the equal parts into which a company's stocks are divided for their purchase by an individual or another company, who then becomes a shareowner and is entitled to a proportion of the company's profits. These are paid to the shareowner in

**"**

## FEMININE FINANCE

*'I think I could be a good woman if I had five thousand a year.'*
Rebecca Sharp in William Thackeray's *Vanity Fair*

*'What female heart can gold despise? What cat's averse to fish?'*
Thomas Gray *On The Death of a Favourite Cat*

*'A gold rush is what happens when a line of chorus girls spot a man with a bank roll.'*
Mae West in *Klondike Annie* (1936)

**"**

the form of a dividend, a term that similarly indicates a division or proportion of a total amount. Shares themselves usually have an individually low value, often simply a few pence. Unlike stocks they cannot be bought or sold in fractional amounts, but only in multiples of the denomination stated.

Ordinary shares, the most common kind, are also known as **equities**. This name refers to the fact that in a typical company its risked capital is roughly equivalent to the value of the shares it issues. (A general term used by the Stock Exchange for stocks and shares taken together is **securities**.)

**Bonds**, also known as fixed interest securities, are the equivalent of shares issued by the government or other financial institution, with the big difference, however, that they usually carry a fixed rate of interest, whereas shares can go up or down in value, making a profit or loss for the shareholder. Moreover, bonds can always be redeemed, or repaid to their purchaser.

In the USA, public bonds are issued by federal, state and local governments.

Bonds are sold to give interest for a stated number of years, at the end of which they mature, and the original amount (which will almost certainly have decreased in actual value) is repayable to the purchaser. Bonds running for a lengthy period are known as **gilts**, short for 'gilt-edged securities',

since they are a relatively safe bet, at least as far as payment of interest and eventual redemption (repayment) are concerned.

Of course, where shares give their purchaser part-ownership of the issuing company, bonds give their holder no such claim on the government or selling corporation.

Buying and selling shares is a relatively simple process. It can be carried out through a local bank, a person's solicitor or accountant, or it can be done through a member of the Stock Exchange itself, who is often referred to as a broker (stockbroker) or a dealer.

## THE LONDON STOCK EXCHANGE

The **London Stock Exchange** developed out of the historic trading companies, with names such as 'The Mysterie and Companie of the Merchant Adventurers for the Discoverie of Regions, Dominions, Islands and Places unknowen'. That was what the Muscovy Company was officially known as when it was founded in 1555, with a monopoly of Anglo-Russian trade.

'Merchant Adventurer' was no misnomer, for trading then *was* an adventure. The different merchants would take 'shares' in an enterprise, and

## UNCOMMON HONESTY

A portrait of a rather exceptional shareholder is given in *Cranford*, by Elizabeth Gaskell. Miss Matty has shares in the Town and County Bank, and is dependent on the interest of £150 a year which she earns from them. In a shop one day she hears an assistant refuse to accept a Town and County banknote; there are rumours that the bank is about to fail. Miss Matty immediately offers the customer five sovereigns for his note. 'I think there is some mistake about it, for I am one of the shareholders, and I'm sure they would have told me if things had not been going on right.' To a friend who queries her action she remarks that it is only 'common honesty in me, as a shareholder'. The bank duly fails, but Miss Matty's friends rally round to contribute between them the income she has lost.

divide up the profits at the end of the voyage. After a while, they realized that an enterprise need not be disbanded, but could continue as a company as long as a way could be found for the original backers to get their money back, by selling their shares to someone else.

Such shares were traded in the coffee houses around the Royal Exchange (see p. 113). In 1773 one of these, 'New Jonathan's', became 'The Stock Exchange', and was the first building to be known by this particular name anywhere in the world. It was not formally constituted, though, until 1802, by which time it had about 550 subscribers and 100 clerks. Other local exchanges then arose in various places round Britain, until finally in March 1973 they amalgamated to form The Stock Exchange of Great Britain and Ireland. Three months later the market floor of the new Stock Exchange in London opened for business in a 100.8-m/*331-foot* tower and dealing premises which replaced the complex of buildings that had stood on the site since the year of constitution.

## THE NEW YORK STOCK EXCHANGE

The London Stock Exchange is an independent organization, even though its biggest user is the government. In this it differs from the **New York Exchange**, which, like other American stock exchanges, is subject to specific legislative regulations, even though the government does not directly participate in its operation.

Securities markets in the United States arose from speculative trading in the issues made by each new government when it came to power. The country's first stock exchange was established in Philadelphia in 1791, then the leading city in domestic and foreign trade. The New York Exchange was set up the following year, when 24 merchants and brokers decided to charge commissions when acting as agents for others and to give one another preference in their dealings. Many of their initial negotiations were conducted under a tree in Wall Street. In 1817 the brokers (now in a building!) decided to organize themselves formally as the New York Stock and Exchange Board, renamed the New York Stock Exchange in 1863.

## BIG BANG

In 1986 the London Stock Exchange underwent a number of radical changes. In March that year it opened its doors for the first time to overseas and corporate membership, so that banks and insurance companies could become members. And on 27 October, the day of **'Big Bang'**, three major reforms were introduced, bringing British practice more in line with overseas exchanges, such as the New York Exchange.

The first big change abolished scales of minimum commissions, so that clients could negotiate freely with their brokers about the charge for their services. The second abolished the long-standing division of members into **brokers** and **jobbers**. Before Big Bang, brokers acted as middlemen (intermediaries) between the public and the jobber, who was the actual dealer, and who had no contact with the public. Now, members of the Stock Exchange are joint brokers and dealers, able to act in either capacity on behalf of their clients. As such, they are frequently referred to simply as market makers.

**''**————————————————

## THE DANGEROUS MONTHS

'*October—this is one of the peculiarly dangerous months to speculate in stocks in. The others are July, January, September, April, November, May, March, June, December, August and February.*'

Mark Twain, *Pudd'nhead Wilson's Calendar*

**''**

## SOME SOUND FINANCIAL ADVICE?

Morton Shulman is the author of *Anyone Can Make A Million*, a book which gives advice about how to make a fortune on the Stock Market. At one point Shulman discusses publications such as his own, which offer advice to investors and speculators: 'Don't subscribe. Don't read them. Don't follow their advice.'

**“**

## SPECULATION MASTERS

'No man is safe from losing every penny he has in the world. How often do I not hear middle-aged women and quiet family men say that they have no speculative tendency; they never had touched, and never would touch, any but the very soundest, best reputed investments, and as for unlimited liability, oh, dear! dear! and they throw up their hands and eyes.

'Whenever a person is heard to talk thus he may be recognized as the easy prey of the first adventurer who comes across him; he will commonly, indeed, wind up his discourse by saying that in spite of all his natural caution, and his well knowing how foolish speculation is, yet there are some investments which are called speculative but in reality are not so, and he will pull out of his pocket the prospectus of a Cornish gold-mine.

'So strongly do I feel on this subject that if I had my way I would have a speculation master attached to every school. The boys would be encouraged to read the Money Market Review, the Railway News, and all the best financial papers, and should establish a Stock Exchange amongst themselves in which pence should stand as pounds. Then let them see how this making haste to get rich moneys out in actual practice. There might be a prize awarded by the headmaster to the most prudent dealer, and the boys who lost their money time after time should be dismissed. Of course if any boy proved to have a genius for speculation and made money—well and good, let him speculate by all means.

'If universities were not the worst teachers in the world I should like to see professorships of speculation established at Oxford and Cambridge. When I reflect, however, that the only things worth doing which Oxford and Cambridge can do well are cooking, rowing and games, of which there is no professorship, I fear the establishment of a professorial chair would end in teaching young men neither how to speculate, nor how not to speculate, but would simply turn them out as bad speculators.'

Samuel Butler The Way of all Flesh

**”**

The third reform was the introduction of a computerized dealing system, known as the Stock Exchange Automated Quotations (SEAQ) system. Instead of dealing face to face, verbally, on the floor of the Exchange, market makers now deal in stocks and shares over the telephone at their own dealing desks, with the various buying and selling prices displayed on a composite screen. The new system provides added security for investors since all deals are now recorded on a database which can be used to resolve any disputes or make any investigations.

Finally, in November 1986, members of the Stock Exchange agreed to merge with members of the international broking community in London, based outside the Exchange, so as to form two new bodies, the **International Stock Exchange of the United Kingdom and Republic of Ireland Ltd** and the **Securities Association Ltd.**

The International Stock Exchange currently has over 7000 securities listed on its books, with an overall value in June 1989 of approximately £2 070 000 million.

When a company enters the stock market for

the first time, it can select one of three possible Stock Exchange markets, depending on its size and requirements.

The first is called the **Listed Market**, that is, securities officially listed on the Stock Exchange, on which the shares of more than 2500 companies are traded. To enter this market, the company must have been trading for at least five years and must place 25 per cent of its shares in public hands.

The second type of market is for smaller, less established companies, and is called the **Unlisted Securities Market** (USM).

In 1986 the International Stock Exchange established a third type of market called simply the **Third Market**. This is for very new and small companies incorporated in the UK or in Ireland.

Apart from the London and New York Stock Exchanges, 136 exchanges are listed elsewhere in the world. The oldest is that of Amsterdam, in the Netherlands, founded in 1602. The largest currently trading is the Tokyo Exchange, with a $1750 billion turnover in 1987, as against the New York trading volume of $1590 billion.

### SHARE INDICES

Anyone who buys shares is advised that the price of shares may go down as well as up. Investors therefore normally follow the movement of their

**"** ─────────────────────────────

### MONEY WORRIES

*Almost every American would sooner get eight per cent from a risky investment than four per cent from a safe one. The consequence is that there are frequent losses of money and continual worry and fret. For my part, the thing that I should wish to obtain from money would be leisure with security. But what the typical modern man desires to get with it is more money, with a view to ostentation, splendour, and the outshining of those who have hitherto been his equals.*

Bertrand Russell *The Conquest of Happiness*

───────────────────────────── **"**

shares in the media, either in the press or through a computerized information service such as Prestel.

On a typical day on the Stock Exchange, some share prices will go up, others will go down, but the majority will probably not move at all. What generally concerns investors is the *overall* movement of the market, because this reflects what investors as a whole think about the prospects for the economy.

This movement of the market is measured on an index. In Britain, this is the **Financial Times Industrial Ordinary Share Index**, started in 1935. It was based on the shares of 30 representative companies, and is calculated to a base of 100. As its name implies, it is published daily in the *Financial Times*. In 1962 a much more sophisticated index, the **All Share Index**, was introduced by the *Financial Times* and the Institute and Faculty of Actuaries. Despite its name, it does not cover all shares, but it does take the size of the companies into account, and has sub-divisions for the different sectors of the market, such as oil companies and gold mines.

The most recent index in Britain is the **Financial Times/Stock Exchange 100 Share Index**, otherwise known as the FT/SE 100, or simply 'Footsie'. This was introduced in 1984 and is based on 100 of the largest companies listed on the Stock Exchange. It operates to a base of 1000. Using computer technology, it calculates share movements on a minute-by-minute basis, as against the hourly calculations of the FT 30 Index or the daily figures of the All Share Index.

In the United States, the **Dow Jones Index** serves as the economic barometer of the New York Stock Exchange. It was instituted in 1896, and, like the London FT 30 index, takes the prices of 30 typical industrial companies and measures their movements. In a sense it is not an actual index at all, since it is calculated by adding the New York closing prices of the 30 shares and adjusting them by a 'current average divisor', a variable figure calculated to preserve the continuity of the index over changes in its component parts. The London FT 30 Index, however, is a true index.

The Dow Jones, or simply 'Dow', is named after the American financial analysts Charles H. Dow (1851–1902) and Edward D. Jones (1856–1920),

**"**

## ON THE STREET

*He bought a little block of stock*
*The day he went to town;*
*And in the nature of such things,*
> *The*
> *Value*
> *Of*
> *The*
> *Stock*
> *Went*
> *Down.*

*He sold a little block of stock:*
*Now sorrow fills his cup,*
*For from the moment that he did,*
> *Up.*
> *Went*
> *Straightaway*
> *Value*
> *Its*

*He bought another block of stock*
*Expecting he would taste of bliss;*
*He can't let go and can't hang on,*

*Its value keeps going down then up again then down like this.*

(Adapted from an anonymous poem quoted
in *A Whimsey Anthology*, a collection of odd
verses compiled by Carolyn Wells, published
in New York by Charles Scribner's Sons,
1906).

**"**

who together set up a business in 1882, publishing financial bulletins and news sheets. Two years later they began compiling the averages of American stock prices. In 1889 they founded the influential *Wall Street Journal*, America's equivalent to the London *Financial Times*.

In Japan, the index on the Tokyo Stock Exchange is known as the **Nikkei Average** (formerly Nikkei Dow), and in Hong Kong the index is the **Hang Seng**. ('Nikkei' is the short title of the Japanese newspaper that publishes the index, the *Nihon Keizei shimbun*, 'Japanese economic newspaper', and Hang Seng is the name of a prominent Hong Kong bank that does the same there.)

The Stock Exchange prices listed in newspapers can look complicated, but are really quite simple to read. Here are a single company's share prices as given in the City pages of the press for 10 November 1989:

| High | Low | Company | Bid | Offer | Change | Yield | P/E |
|------|-----|---------|-----|-------|--------|-------|------|
| 989 | 506 | Reuters | 882 | 888 | −18 | 1.5 | 16.6 |

**High** the company's highest share price (in pence) for 1989.
**Low** its lowest price.
**Company** its name.
**Bid** the price at which a market maker will buy back shares from an investor.
**Offer** the price at which he will sell them.
**Change** the share movement since the previous day, in this case 18p less.

**"**

## SOME INVESTMENT TIPS

*'Never invest your money in anything that eats or needs repainting.'*
(Billy Rose)

*'Put not your trust in money, put your money in trust.'*
(Oliver Wendell Holmes)

*'There is nothing like building our fortunes on the weaknesses of mankind.'*
(Montague Tigg, a character created by Charles Dickens)

**"**

**Yield** a percentage figure which, when converted to pounds and pence, shows in this case that £100 invested in Reuters at £8.88 per share would bring in £1.50, going on the basis of the last dividend to be paid. Clearly, the company will almost certainly not pay exactly this amount next time, but more, or less, or even nothing.

**P/E** 'Price/Earnings Ratio', which compares the market value of the money the company is earning with its profit for the year. The profit is divided by the number of ordinary shares, giving earnings per share, and this is then divided into the market price. The lower the P/E Ratio, the 'better value' the holding, and the higher the P/E Ratio, the greater the prospects for future profitability. The figure quoted here therefore indicates that investors are prepared to pay 16.6 times the current earnings per share. The ratio is frequently lower than this and can be as high as 100 or more. In this particular day's prices, the highest P/E Ratio quoted was 97.4, for News International, showing that investors were buying heavily into that company in the expectation that it would make larger profits.

## MONEY MARKETS AND DISCOUNT HOUSES

Buying and selling shares is a form of financial negotiation (and speculation).

Another form is the dealing carried out in the London **money markets**. Despite the term, there is no actual 'market place', and negotiations are conducted between a series of integrated groups of financial institutions using the telephone, telex and automated dealing systems. All the deals are monitored by the Bank of England to ensure that the codes of conduct are strictly adhered to. Money markets deal chiefly in bills (issued by the Treasury, local authorities or companies), certificates of deposit, and short-term deposits. **Certificates of deposit** (CDs) are ordinary fixed-term interest-bearing deposits that have, however, one special feature: they can be bought and sold like bonds and shares. They are only available in big denominations, but they have grown spectacularly, from 1961, when they were introduced by New York's biggest bank, Citibank, to £8.6 billion in Britain by 1983 and to over $140 billion in America.

> **"**
> ### LEAVING NOTHING TO CHANCE
>
> 'Conrad Lyte was a real-estate speculator. He was a nervous speculator. Before he gambled he consulted bankers, lawyers, architects, contracting builders, and all of their clerks and stenographers who were willing to be cornered and give him advice. He was a bold entrepreneur, and he desired nothing more than complete safety in his investments, freedom from attention to details, and the thirty or forty per cent profit which, according to all authorities, a pioneer deserves for his risks and foresight.'
>
> Sinclair Lewis *Babbitt*
> **"**

An important role in the money markets is played by the **discount houses**. These are an institution that is unique to the City of London, and developed in the 19th century as bill brokers for industrialists. Today discount houses are firms which act as intermediaries between the Bank of England and the rest of the banking world. They arrange an orderly flow of funds between the government and the banks, and they lend funds to the government by guaranteeing to subscribe for the whole of the weekly offer of Treasury bills (bills of exchange issued by the government and repayable in three months). In return for their role as intermediaries, the discount houses have the privilege of knowing that the Bank of England will always act as a 'lender of last resort', that is, it will provide them with the necessary money if they run into difficulties. In 1989 there were ten discount houses, including such well known firms as Alexanders and Smith St Aubyn. The largest is Gerrard & National, with total assets of over £4.3 billion in 1988.

## FUTURES AND OPTIONS

A special form of money market, known as **'futures and options'**, is traded on the floor of the Royal Exchange, London, by the **London**

International Financial Futures Exchange (LIFFE, pronounced 'life'). Both futures and options are a form of so-called forward dealing, where currencies or commodities (such as sugar, wheat, oil or rubber) are traded for future delivery at a particular price. (The 'delivery' is now hypothetical, so that speculators have no actual intention of taking delivery of the stock in which they deal.)

'Futures' refers to forward contracts of this kind generally, while 'options' means that speculators expecting a share price to rise take out an option to buy it at some agreed price on some agreed date in the future. If they are right, and the share price goes above their agreed level, they can immediately resell the share when the time comes to exercise their option. Similarly, if they are expecting the price to fall, they can opt to sell the share at an agreed price on an agreed date.

It can be judged from this that futures and options are a high-risk form of speculation, and are not for the novice or the faint-hearted. (One firm of futures brokers, advertising in 1989, warned its potential clients as follows: 'Futures and option prices can fluctuate wildly and this can lead to losses in excess of monies deposited'. In other words, you could find yourself not only not making a profit, but seriously out of pocket!)

Financial futures were invented in Chicago in the early 1970s, when dealers realized that money could be regarded as a commodity just like cocoa or tin, and in 1972 the International Monetary

## THE FAT OF THE LAND

The American writer Ben Hecht (1894–1957) was paid a large amount to promote Florida real estate in the early 1920s. People remarked at the time that he was becoming rather plump; what was actually happening was that Hecht was carrying around all the money he earned. He was convinced that the property boom would not last, and he had no faith in banks. When the crash finally came he suffered less than most. By that time he had some 30 thousand dollars strapped to his body.

## " THE EGG BASKET

*'Behold the fool saith, "Put not all thine eggs in one basket"—which is but a manner of saying, "Scatter your money and your attention."; but the wise man saith, "Put all your eggs in one basket, and—WATCH THAT BASKET"'.'*

Mark Twain, *Pudd'nhead Wilson's Calendar* "

Market (IMM), part of the Chicago Mercantile Exchange, introduced foreign currency futures, making it the world's first centralized market for this particular kind of financial risk. Other markets followed, with financial futures traded in Canada and Australia, and with the New York Stock Exchange opening a futures market in 1980. It was not until 1982 that LIFFE opened its doors in London.

### THE ROYAL EXCHANGE

The **Royal Exchange**, where LIFFE trades, is the centre of the futures and options markets. It stands on the corner of London's Threadneedle Street, the location of the Bank of England ('The Old Lady of Threadneedle Street'), and Cornhill. The present building was opened by Queen Victoria in 1844, replacing an earlier building of 1667 that was destroyed by fire in 1838.

The first Royal Exchange was inaugurated in 1570, when it was opened by Queen Elizabeth I as a trading centre for merchants. (The building was financed by Sir Richard Gresham, a prominent Merchant Adventurer.) It ceased its original function only in 1939, but after this date continued to serve as the premises for Lloyd's (see below) and as the headquarters of the Guardian Royal Exchange Assurance Company.

Unlike the Stock Exchange, futures and options dealers are not yet automated, and conduct their hectic negotiations by yelling at one another on the floor or 'pit'. Many of them believe that this is still the most effective way. Even so, plans are now in train for screen-based trading, and in late 1989 LIFFE introduced a facility known as **Automated Pit Trading** (APT) as just one stage in the gradual

### BUBBLES

'Bubbly', as champagne is popularly known, is now associated with celebration and success. In the 18th century, especially, 'bubbles' led to the financial ruin of countless speculators. Bubble companies and financial schemes were to be found on all sides, based on wild optimism or deliberate fraud. It seems extraordinary that people were willing to invest in 'importing a large number of jackasses from Spain,' the objective of one such company, or in the proceeds of 'fishing wrecks from the Irish coast,' with which another company concerned itself—but greed can cause people to do strange things. There were even those who invested money in a company which announced that it had been formed 'for an undertaking which shall in due time be revealed'. The promoter disappeared before that due time was reached.

The South Sea Bubble is the name given to the collapse in 1720 of the South Sea Company, which had been given the monopoly of trade with Spanish America. The king and parliament became involved, and shares of £100 temporarily acquired the value of £1000. In France a similar Mississippi Bubble occurred, with shares rising at one time to 40 times their nominal value. This scheme also collapsed in 1720.

At one time men who had lost their money by investing in bubble schemes were themselves referred to as bubbles. There was also a verb, to bubble someone out of something, to cheat him. Thus Wycherley, as early as 1675, has a character in his *Country Wife* say: 'He is to be bubbled out of his mistress as of his money.'

transition to a 'new tech' system. A similar technological advance had earlier been made in 1987 by the London Futures and Options Exchange (Fox) when it brought in an automated screen-based system to trade in white sugar.

In August 1989, when about 190 banks and other financial institutions were members of the market, the average number of futures and options contracts traded daily was about 88 000, with a turnover of some £21 000 million.

### LLOYD'S

Lloyd's of London (nothing to do with Lloyds Bank) is the world's leading insurance market. It arose from the coffee house that Edward Lloyd opened in Tavern Street, London, in 1689, where merchants gathered to discuss their latest 'adventure' and where they consulted the shipping information that Lloyd posted up for the benefit of his patrons. The business subsequently moved several times to different sites and buildings, including the Royal Exchange in 1774, before eventually becoming established in the 1980s in its brand-new designer-built premises in Leadenhall Street.

Lloyd's is an association of over 31 000 private underwriters, or insurers, who provide an interna-

tional market for almost any kind of insurance, although traditionally it has long been associated with marine insurance.

Members operate in groups or syndicates, at present about 400 in number. Together they currently earn a premium income of around £6000 million, with three-quarters of their business coming from outside Britain.

Men and women of any nationality can become members of Lloyd's as long as they meet the stringent financial requirements of the Corporation and provided they can prove that they have assets of up to £250 000. From this, they are required to lodge a deposit, in the form of approved securities, at a rate of 30 per cent of their individual annual premium income.

The syndicates compete with one another for business. In turn they derive their own financial backing from wealthy individuals referred to as 'Names', who accept unlimited liability in support of their particular syndicate. Their money is rarely needed, but in return for sharing the risk, they receive a share of their syndicate's profit.

The world of finance is thus a complex one, and demands specialized knowledge and expertise to make it operate as efficiently as possible.

## ZOOLOGICAL MONEY

G. R. Mitchison, in his *Capital And Investment* (1933), remarks: 'Let us now proceed to Stock Exchange zoology. A "bear" is a person who desires the value of a stock to fall, in order that he may buy it—probably in order to deliver it, when he has sold it beforehand. A "bull" is the opposite—someone who desires the price of a stock to rise, in order that he may make a profit by selling it. A "stag" is someone who subscribes for a new issue, which he does not want and probably cannot pay for, in order to pay the first instalment of the price and then resell the partly paid stock at a profit.'

Mitchison does not say so, but the origin of 'bear' in this sense may have to do with the old proverb: to sell the bearskin before you have caught the bear. In the 18th century people also talked of selling a bear: selling something that one did not actually own.

It is not only in the Stock Exchange that money is linked with animals. In agricultural societies, wealth is likely to be measured in terms of the animals a person owns. The words capital, cattle and chattel (article of moveable property) are closely connected from a historical point of view; the word fee is also from Old English *feoh*, which meant 'cattle' or 'money'. In the Middle Ages a fee-house was either a cattle-shed or a treasury.

## ZOOLOGICAL MONEY QUIZ

Money can be connected with animals in other ways. What is the link between money and: 1) badger, 2) bee, 3) buck, 4) bug, 5) chicken, 6) dog, 7) monkey, 8) pony, 9) rhinoceros, 10) spider? (Answers on p. 116)

## MONEY-OLOGY

Even those who have been professionally concerned with money all their lives might have difficulty defining some of the words given below. They are taken from the book *-Ologies and -Isms*, edited by Laurence Urdang and others.

**agio**   the exchange rate between currencies of different nations

**agiotage**   the business of trading or speculating in foreign exchange

**anatocism**   the act of lending with interest

**aphnology**   the science of wealth

**autarky**   a national policy of economic self-sufficiency

**bimetallism**   the use of two metals jointly as a monetary standard with fixed values in relation to one another

**brassage**   a fee levied for the coining of money

**bullionism**   the doctrine that paper money should at all times be convertible into bullion

**cambism**   the theory and practice of money exchange as an item of commerce, especially in its international features

**chrematist**   a person whose chief goal in life is the gaining of wealth

**chrematistics**   the study of wealth

**chrematomania**   a mania for money

**chrematophobia**   an abnormal fear or dislike of money

**cresomania**   a mania for great wealth

**gombeenism**   the lending of money at usurious interest

**mammonism**   the greedy pursuit of riches

**metallism**   a doctrine advocating metal rather than paper money

**monetarism**   an economic theory maintaining that stability and growth in the economy are dependent on a steady growth rate in the supply of money

**moneyocracy**   government or domination of society by the rich

**nabobism**   leading the lifestyle of a nabob, i.e. one possessing great wealth

**oligopoly**   a market condition characterized by there being few sellers

**oligopsony**   a market condition characterized by there being few buyers

**peniaphobia**   an abnormal fear of poverty

**plutolatry**   an excessive devotion to wealth

**plutology**   the scientific study or theory of wealth

**plutomania**   an abnormal craving for wealth, or a mania characterized by delusions of wealth

**polymetallism**   the use of a number of different metals in coinage

**ptochology**   the scientific study of unemployment, poverty, etc.

**scutage**   a payment made to a lord under the feudal system in lieu of military service

**solatium**   payment for mental suffering or financial loss

**squandermania**   a mania for spending money

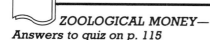

## ZOOLOGICAL MONEY—
*Answers to quiz on p. 115*

**1) Badger**   to overdraw the badger in 19th-century British slang meant to overdraw one's account. Badger was probably a light-hearted variant of banker, especially since a banker was likely to badger you for money. There is also the so-called badger game, a blackmail or extortion trick. A woman entices a man into a compromising situation, then demands money when her 'husband' arrives. The woman is said to be the badger-worker. No doubt this is connected with the verb to badger in the sense of to harrass. There is a good example of the badger game in *Elmer Gantry*, by Sinclair Lewis, though it is not described as such. The hero is trapped by his secretary, whose husband demands $10 000. He manages to escape when her criminal past is uncovered.

**2) Bee**   see p. 13.

**3) Buck**   the common slang term for an American dollar. In use since the end of the 19th century, but no-one has satisfactorily explained the connection with the animal.

**4) Bug**   the dollar bug is a local name in Massachusetts for the whirligig beetle. It is

thought that if you catch one in your hand you will find a dollar there. Also known as the lucky bug.

**5) Chicken**   'What's a thousand dollars?' asked Groucho Marx, in *A Night at the Opera*. 'Mere chicken feed. A poultry matter.' Chicken money is a variant of chicken feed, referring to very small amounts of money. Other possible connections: a chicken was formerly shown on the Irish penny, issued in 1928; in Cockney rhyming slang a 'cock and hen' formerly meant ten (shillings). Perhaps the expression nest egg should also be mentioned. This was originally an egg placed in a nest to induce a hen to lay eggs of her own, though it now refers to a sum of money which has been put aside for future use.

**6) Dog**   another Cockney rhyming slang expression was dog's dinner. The rhyme was (very roughly) with deaner, itself a slang term for a shilling, perhaps from Spanish *dinero*, 'money'. As usual with rhyming slang expressions, the first word was frequently used alone, so that a shilling became simply a dog. A black dog was a counterfeit shilling. The *Oxford English Dictionary* records that dog was once the name of a small copper coin used in the West Indies. A dog-hanging was also a colloquial name for a wedding feast at which money was collected for the bride.

**7) Monkey**   a colloquial term for £500 or $500. Eric Partridge, in his *Dictionary Of Historical Slang*, says that for stockbrokers it means £50 000 of stock. Use of the term has never satisfactorily been explained. In French there is an expression which translates as 'to pay in monkey money'. Brewer's *Dictionary Of Phrase and Fable* says that this means to pay with goods or services rather than coin. It goes on to relate an interesting anecdote about the toll fee that had to be paid in former times by anyone crossing the *Petit Pont*, in Paris, with a monkey, but only if the animal was for sale. If the monkey belonged to a showman, it was allowed to perform its tricks instead. The story is a pleasant one, but the now rather old-fashioned French expression *payer en monnaie de singe* actually means to pay with promises, i.e. not to pay at all.

**8) Pony**   a colloquial term for £25, or £25 000 of stock, according to Eric Partridge. It has been suggested that when the expression was first used, £25 was roughly the price of an average pony.

**9) Rhinoceros**   in the short form rhino, a slang synonym for money. The term is said to be still in use in British prisons, referring to weekly pay. The horn of the rhinoceros was formerly highly valued as an aphrodisiac.

**10) Spider**   in modern usage, a 'money-spinner' is a business venture of some kind which makes a lot of money easily and quickly. In the 19th century the term was applied both to a person who made quick profits, and to the *Aranea scenica*, a small spider which was supposed to bring good luck to anyone it crawled over. The latter is sometimes called the money-spider, though this term has also been applied to the large black and white spider of the genus Salticus. In Jamaica it is a fly rather than a spider which is considered to be lucky. According to popular belief, anyone who sees the money-fly, a bluish wood-boring beetle, flying out of its hole is sure to come into money.

By diligent searching one could probably find other animal connections with money. To shoe one's mule or horse, for instance, at one time meant to embezzle money. The expression alluded to the practice of charging for shoeing that was not done. The American phrase to eat high off the hog refers to living well, since choicer cuts of meat come from high on a hog's side. It's also still possible to say that someone has killed the goose that lays the golden eggs, alluding to Aesop's fable about a greedily impatient man. (See also p. 33, DESIGNING A SET OF COINS, for animal designs on coins.)

# 10
# MONEY WITH A DIFFERENCE

## DIFFERENT KINDS OF MONEY

3 elephants and your gold Rolex and we've got a deal

In this chapter we pause to consider over 70 varieties of money that have attracted descriptive labels. We have restricted ourselves to epithets that contain the word 'money' itself, though some expressions make use of other terms. We always speak of 'petty cash', for instance, rather than 'petty money', using a word that derives from French *petit*, 'little'. The less familiar term **ash cash** is mentioned in *Low Speak*, the dictionary of criminal and sexual slang edited by James Morton. This is used to describe money that is paid to a doctor when he signs the certificate that allows a body to be cremated.

**Bad money** counterfeit money. 'Bad' is used in this way of coins—hence the person who keeps turning up 'like a bad penny'. In normal speech someone describing a job and saying that the money was bad would mean that it was poorly paid. Bad debts are those that cannot be recovered.

**Batta money** in *A Dictionary of Sailors' Slang*, Wilfred Granville says that this is Naval prize money.

He continues: 'After the first World War considerable sums of money were paid to officers and men. When the Second one ended these sums were much smaller and caused great disappoint-

## BALMY MONEY

"

*'Why do people spend more money upon a death, Mrs Gamp, than upon a birth?'*

*'Perhaps it is because an undertaker's charges comes dearer than a nurse's charges, sir,' said Mrs Gamp, tittering. 'No, Mrs Gamp; I'll tell you why it is. It's because the laying out of money with a well-conducted establishment sheds balm upon the wounded spirit. Hearts want binding, and spirits want balming, when people die; not when people are born.'*

Charles Dickens *Martin Chuzzlewit*

"

ment. The word is borrowed from the Army.'

The 'batta' is thought by some authorities to be a form of a Kannadan word, *bhatta*, which means rice in the husk. Europeans may have used the word to describe subsistence money used to buy such rice. It could then have developed the meaning of extra money, added to the pay of British officers when they were on a campaign.

In Indian banking, however, batta is used to mean agio, or exchange rate. The word in this case derives from Bengali or Urdu, where it has the same meaning. The *Oxford English Dictionary* sees this as a separate word, but it seems likely that it led to the Anglo-Indian word meaning 'extra pay'.

**Beer money** originally an allowance of money given to servants instead of providing them with beer. In later use, a gratuity. In modern use, beer money tends to be that part of a husband's wages which is kept for his personal spending. It is a kind of male form of pin money.

**Black money** in modern times applied to money obtained illegally, money which has to be laundered before it can be used. The phrase is also used to describe income which is not reported for tax purposes. Historically, black money was copper coinage or debased silver coinage. It contrasted with white money, standard silver coinage.

**Blood money** the price on someone's head, which will be paid for his betrayal and capture, especially if the wanted person faces execution. The 30 pieces of silver paid to Judas Iscariot for the betrayal of Jesus was blood money.

The term is also used to refer to Anglo-Saxon *weregild*, compensation paid to the kin of a murder victim in an effort to stave off revenge killings.

**Bowed money** a coin which has been bent, then used as a token of love or friendship. Coins were also cut in half and used as love-tokens (see THE OTHER HALF, p. 35).

**Bull money** this is not, as one might think, money used by a Stock Exchange 'bull'. Eric Partridge tells us, in *A Dictionary of Historical Slang*,

## DRINK MONEY

*The Language of Drink*, by Graham and Sue Edwards, lists several money-related entries. There are recipes for three versions of the *Millionaire*, for instance, a cocktail which can be based on brandy, rye whiskey or apricot brandy. The *Million Dollar Cocktail* is composed of gin, sweet vermouth, cream, lemon juice, pineapple juice and egg white. Another cocktail called simply *Million Dollars* is made with gin, Cointreau and Calvados.

Beer has rather humbler associations with money. The 'shilling system', used in Scotland at the end of the 19th century, indicated the gravity level of beer. Higher gravity beers paid higher duty, so a Ninety Shilling Ale was strong, while a Sixty Shilling Ale was a mild, dark beer.

The book also mentions that in the North of England bank-notes are humorously known in slang as 'drinking vouchers'. They are more specifically referred to by colour: a five-pound note becomes a 'blue drinking voucher,' and so on. 'Drink-money' is not listed, though this expression exists in English for a gratuity or tip. It is money theoretically given so that the person who receives it can drink to the health of the donor.

## PLAY MONEY

Philip Henslowe (d. 1616) is remembered today for his theatrical activities, though he was earlier the proprietor of several brothels and had acted as money-lender and pawnbroker. He had come into money by marrying a wealthy widow. In 1587 he rebuilt the Rose Theatre in London, and was later connected with the Swan, Fortune and Hope theatres.

Henslowe used to buy plays from their authors and hire them out at a profit. Before 1600 the highest price he paid for any one play was £6; in later years he sometimes paid as much as £10. Occasionally he paid authors in advance for their work: Ben Jonson received £1 in 1597 for a play which was to be completed by Christmas.

Theatre audiences of the time paid a penny to go into the pit, plus an extra penny for the galleries. (Skilled men at the time earned 12–14 pence a day.) The pennies were dropped into a box which was then locked in a small office, the box office.

that it is 'money extorted from or given by those who in places of public resort have been detected *in flagrante delicto* with a woman, as a bribe to silence'.

**Butter money**   money set aside for the purchase of butter: 'Mrs Hackit declines cream; she has so long abstained from it with an eye to the weekly butter money, that abstinence, wedded to habit, has begotten aversion.' George Eliot *Amos Barton*.

**Channel money**   used variously of money given to men before they land at a home port, and subsistence paid to sailors waiting on a ship that is in dry dock.

**Cheap money**   a modern term for money available plentifully at a low or declining rate of interest. Americans would refer to it as easy money.

**Chicken money**   a variant of chicken feed, i.e. a small amount of money.

**Chief money**   a historical term for capital.

## ABILITY

'Ability' is not today a word which immediately suggests money, but between the 16th and 18th centuries it was often used to mean specifically the ability to provide money. In Shakespeare's *Twelfth Night*, for example, when Antonio asks Viola to return his money, she replies: 'Being prompted by your present trouble, out of my mean and low ability I'll lend you something.' In *The Vicar Of Wakefield*, Oliver Goldsmith writes: 'A draught upon my neighbour was to me the same as money; for I was sufficiently convinced of his ability.'

One of the pleasantest instances of the word's use comes in the letter written by Sir Philip Sidney to his brother Robert, on 18 October, 1580: 'My dear Brother, For the money you have received, assure yourself (for it is true) there is nothing I spend so pleaseth me; as that which is for you. If ever I have ability, you shall find it so: if not, yet shall not any brother living be better beloved than you, of me.'

During the same period 'disability' was used to mean not having the means to provide money, being unable to meet one's liabilities, in other words. 'Liability' looks as if it should be associated with 'ability' and 'disability', but it has in fact a completely different origin.

**Conscience money**   money paid to relieve someone's bad conscience, e.g. by somebody who was a tax-dodger or a thief. Normally paid in the form of anonymous donations to the authorities.

**Counterfeit money**   'counterfeit' was not originally associated automatically with fraud. The word literally means 'made against an original, an imitation'; only later was it assumed that such an imitation would be used in criminal deception.

**Dear money**   money borrowed at a high rate of interest. It is sometimes known as tight money.

**Dirty money**   a special rate of pay given to men doing work of an unpleasant nature in Merchant Navy ships. Also used in the docks for the extra pay given to those who unload an offensive cargo. Money gained by foul means might also be referred to as dirty money.

**Double-bottoms money** an alternative term for dirty money in the British Merchant Navy. 'Double-bottoms' refers to the watertight spaces between the outer plating of the ship's bottom, the tank and margin plates, near the bilges.

**Dwarf's money** a colloquial name in the 16th century for Roman coins found in a field. They were also known as Jew's money, 'and by other foolish names not worthy to be remembered,' as William Harrison expressed it in his *Description of England*.

**Earnest money** money put down as a deposit. 'Money' in this expression is a tautology, since 'earnest' itself meant a sum of money put down as a pledge. The phrase often used in former times was 'earnest-penny' (also 'bargain-penny', 'fastening-penny'). A penny was at one time the actual sum of money used, but the expression was still applied even when the sum was greater.

**Easy money** money which is easily earned, though there may be a catch. In *Look Homeward,*

*Angel*, the novel by Thomas Wolfe, occurs: ' "I've got a job for you, Gant," he said. "Double-time pay. I want you to get in on some of the easy money." ' The job that is being offered is loading a ship with cases of T.N.T. and nitro-glycerine. As another character points out: 'If they ever drop one, they'll bring you home in a bucket.' (See also Cheap money, p. 120.)

**Even money** a betting term used when an equal sum of money is bet on each side. Usually abbreviated to 'evens'.

**Fairy money** money found by chance, and supposedly left by fairies for those who deserve good luck. There was an old tale in which such money reverted to being leaves before it could be used.

**Fall money** money set aside by a criminal to pay his lawyer, should he be arrested.

**False money** counterfeit money.

**Fine money** this is made the subject of *Netty Sargent's Copyhold*, an interesting short story by Thomas Hardy. Netty lives with her uncle, who must pay a small amount of money, called a 'fine', to ensure that the copyhold of his house, garden and field passes to her for her lifetime when he dies. If he does not do so, the property reverts to the lord of the manor.

Jasper Cliff wants to marry Netty, but only if she is sure to inherit the property. Her uncle delays making the payment, even though he is old and ill. 'Jasper could bear it no longer; he produced the fine-money himself and handed it to Netty. 'There's the money. If you let the house and ground slip between ye, I won't marry; hang me if I will!' Netty tells her uncle this and he at last asks for the necessary copyhold documents to be prepared.

Netty's uncle then dies a few hours before the steward calls at the house to witness the signing of the documents. The story relates how Netty fools the steward into thinking that her uncle is still alive. She convinces him that her uncle has signed the documents and thereby gets the property and Jasper as her husband. Years later, disillusioned with Jasper, she tells neighbours what she had to do to win him.

**Folding money** banknotes, especially large quantities of them. In the US also referred to as folding cabbage, green or lettuce.

**Free money** Silvio Gesell (1862–1930), published a book (in German) about what he called 'Free Money' in 1906. It was translated into English as *The Natural Economic Order* in 1929. The characteristic of free money was that it deteriorated in value. It was therefore in nobody's interest to hoard it.

Gesell himself suggested a deterioration rate of 5 per cent. He also suggested a withdrawal of all currency at the end of each year. Old notes (to which a stamp would have to have been fixed to bring them up to value) would then be exchanged for new ones. An economist at the time described Gesell as 'an ingenious amateur, whose theories might be of use during a depression in countries

**❝**———————

**THE NEEDFUL**

*'When I think of all the sorrow and the barrenness that has been wrought in my life by want of a few more pounds per annum than I was able to earn, I stand aghast at money's significance.'*
George Gissing

*'When a man needs money, he needs money, and not a headache tablet or a prayer.'*

William Feather

———————**❞**

**❝**———————

**READY CASH**

*'Let all the learned say what they can, 'Tis ready money makes the man.'*
William Somerville

*'It is only the poor who pay cash, and that not from virtue, but because they are refused credit.'*
Anatole France

*Sign in American shop: 'IN GOD WE TRUST. All others pay cash.'*

———————**❞**

where notes circulate freely. Moreover it is one of the few attempts which have been made to deal with what is undoubtedly one of the intractable elements in industrial fluctuation'.

The magazine *Week* reported in May, 1933 on a practical experiment based on Gesell's theories. The little town of Worgl, Austria had been nearly bankrupt, with its factories closing and unemployment rising daily. 'Nobody did any business, and scarcely anybody paid taxes. Then Unterguggenberger, Burgomaster of Worgl, proposed the following plan, which was adopted. The town authorities issued to the value of 30 000 Austrian schillings notes in denominations of one, five and ten schillings, which were called tickets for services rendered.

'A special feature of these notes was the fact that they decreased in value by one per cent every month. Anyone holding one of the notes at the end of the month had to buy from the local authorities a stamp of sufficient value to bring the note up to face value. This he affixed to the back of the note, and the proceeds of the stamps went to the poor relief fund.

'The result was that the notes circulated with unheard-of rapidity. They were first used for the payment of wages for the building of streets, drainage and other public works by men who would otherwise have been unemployed. On the first day when the new notes were used, eighteen hundred schillings worth was paid out. The recipients immediately hurried with them to the shops, and the shopkeepers and merchants hastened to use them for the payment of their tax arrears to the municipality. The municipality immediately used them to pay the bills. Within twenty four hours of being issued, the greater part of the money had not only come back to the municipality in the form of tax payments, but had already been passed on its way again.

'During the first month, the money had made the complete circle no less than twenty times. There was no possibility of anyone avoiding the one per cent stamp tax on any note he happened to hold at the end of the month, since without a stamp to bring it up to face value, the note lost its entire value.

'Within the first four months after the issue of the new money, the town had accomplished public works to the value of one hundred thousand schillings. A large proportion of tax arrears had already been paid off, and there were even cases of people trying to pay taxes in advance. Receipts of back taxes were eight times greater than in the period before the introduction of the new money. Unemployment was reduced enormously, the shopkeepers were prosperous.'

**Front money**   money put up as an earnest, or deposit, usually a large amount.

**Funny money**   this expression can have several different meanings. To some it means simply counterfeit money. Western visitors to China use

**MONEY IS LIKE . . .**

'Money is like muck, not good unless it be spread.'
Francis Bacon *Of Seditions and Troubles*

'Money is like a sixth sense, without which you cannot make a complete use of the other five.'
Somerset Maugham *Of Human Bondage*

'Money, it turned out, was exactly like sex. You thought of nothing else if you didn't have it and thought of other things if you did.'
James Baldwin *Nobody Knows My Name*

*A SATISFACTORY EXPLANATION*

Two used-car dealers were comparing notes. One attributed his success to a large sign in his showroom: SATISFACTION OR MONEY REFUNDED.
'And how often have you had to make a refund?' said his friend.
'Never,' said the first man. 'So far I've always been satisfied with the money.'

the phrase to refer to the special bank-notes issued to foreigners, which are not the usual Chinese notes.

William Davis, in his *Money Talks*, says that funny money is 'high multiple stock (or, more simply, stock which sells more on faith than on earnings) used by people in a hurry to buy other companies or raise capital . . . There is a very entertaining book on the subject called *The Funny Money Game*, by Andrew Tobias'.

Mr Davis mentions that funny money has more official names. It could be referred to, for instance, as 'six per cent cumulative redeemable partially convertible preference shares with options'. He adds that whatever it is called, investors should treat it with great caution.

**Glove money**   as William Hone says, in his *Everyday Book*: 'Gloves were customary New Year's gifts. They were more expensive than in our times. Occasionally a money present was tendered instead: this was called glove-money. Sir Thomas More, as lord chancellor, decreed in favour of a Mrs Croaker against the lord Arundel. On the following New Year's day, in token of her gratitude, she presented Sir Thomas with a pair of gloves, containing 40 angels. "It would be against good manners," said the chancellor, "To forsake a gentlewoman's New Year's gift, and I accept the gloves; their lining you will be pleased otherwise to bestow." '

The phrase 'glove-money' seems to have taken on the various senses hinted at by Hone. In general terms it was a gratuity given to a servant, or to someone who had otherwise been of service, ostensibly for the purchase of gloves. Sometimes the present was, as Hone suggests, a pair of gloves

*THE DELICATE SUBJECT*

Those people who think it rather vulgar to talk about money are likely to use euphemistic expressions. In *Gideon Planish* Sinclair Lewis remarks: 'the "emolument" (a word used among the loftier teachers and the more amateur editors, and meaning "wages", just as the wages of lecturers are called the "honorarium") would be $4200 a year.'

Dickens makes fun of Mrs General's delicacy in *Little Dorrit*, when Dorrit is interviewing her about a job. 'Might I be excused,' said Mr Dorrit, 'if I inquired what remune—
'Why indeed,' returned Mrs General, stopping the word, 'it is a subject on which I prefer to avoid entering.'

Mrs General suggests that Mr Dorrit inquire of her present employers 'what amount they have been accustomed, at quarterly intervals, to pay to my credit at my bankers'. She also mentions that because Dorrit has two daughters he should increase whatever that amount should prove to be (she pretends not to know) by one third. Dorrit ends up paying her £400 a year.

containing money, and the latter became the 'glove-money'. Some writers suggest that bribes were handed over in this way.
    The *Oxford English Dictionary* says that a special meaning of 'glove-money' was 'extraordinary rewards formerly given to officers of English courts, etc.; especially money given by the sheriff of a county, in which no offenders were left for execution, to the clerk of assize and the judges' officers'.

**Good money**   a speaker who says that he is earning good money is expressing general satisfaction with his rate of pay.

**Gossip money**   this was money paid to a godparent at a christening. 'Gossip' has its earlier sense of 'God-sib', i.e. God-relation.

**Hard money**   coin as opposed to paper money.

**Heavy money**   in modern slang this refers to a large amount of money.

**Honest money**   money earned by legitimate means. The phrase even more frequently found in literature is 'to turn an honest penny (or shilling)'.

**Hot money**   in criminal circles this would mean stolen money, especially money stolen very recently. The expression has another meaning in financial circles. William Davis, in his book *Money Talks*, describes it as 'short-term capital looking for the most profitable—or secure—home'.
    Because it is not invested in plant and equipment, this kind of liquid capital can leave a country just as quickly as it came, responding to a cut in the Bank Rate, a bad set of trade figures, or the emergence of a more attractive home elsewhere. Davis says that from time to time, measures are taken to discourage the flow of hot money. In the past Britain, for instance, has banned the payment of interest on extra deposits by non-residents.

**Housekeeping money**   money given by the wage-earning husband to his dependent wife for normal household expenses. A survey in the 1970s showed that a great many British housewives were unaware of exactly how much their husbands earned. Husbands were also likely to 'forget' to mention that they had received a rise. Studies by the Food Manufacturers' Federation showed that the extra money was often spent on alcohol, cars and electrical goods—traditionally bought by men—rather than passed to wives for supermarket expenses.
    The National Association of Women's Organizations recommended at the time various sanctions to be used against tight-fisted husbands. These included refusing to do his washing and ironing, allowing finance companies to repossess

*"*——————————

*PROVING ONE'S INNOCENCE?*

*There are few ways in which a man can be more innocently employed than in getting money.*

Samuel Johnson

————————— *"*

**TILL MONEY DO US PART**

A recent survey revealed that 54 per cent of married couples argued regularly about money. Where money was tight, that figure rose to 64 per cent.

Principal disagreements were caused by differing attitudes to money—one partner seeing it as something to be used, the other as something to be kept as a form of security. More and more couples were keeping their incomes in separate accounts, especially when the wife earned as much as, or more than, the husband.

Where incomes were pooled, there had been a marked increase in the sharing of financial decisions, compared to the traditional monetary control by the husband. Nevertheless, in marital conflicts of a serious nature, money and sex were the two most commonly used weapons, husbands favouring the former, wives the latter. (See also HOUSEKEEPING MONEY, p. 124.)

the television and feeding him bread and water. The ultimate sanction was, of course, to ban him from the marital bed.

The subject of housekeeping money crops up in *Main Street*, by Sinclair Lewis. The following scene occurs in 1912, Carol Milford having recently married Dr Will Kennicott: 'For the first month it was a honeymoon jest to beg prettily, to confess, "I haven't a cent in the house, dear," and to be told, "You're an extravagant little rabbit." But the budget book made her realize how inexact were her finances.

'She became self-conscious; occasionally she was indignant that she should always have to petition him for the money with which to buy his food. She caught herself criticizing his belief that, since his joke about trying to keep her out of the poorhouse had once been accepted as admirable humor, it should continue to be his daily *bon mot*. But she couldn't "hurt his feelings", she reflected. He liked the lordliness of giving largess.

'She wanted ten pounds of sugar in a hurry, but she had no money. She ran down to the drug store.

**" —**

## THE PEACEMAKER

*'What a charming reconciler and peacemaker money is!'*

William Makepeace Thackeray *Vanity Fair*

**"**

As she entered she heard Mrs Dyer demanding, "Dave, I've got to have some money." Carol saw that her husband was there, and two other men, all listening in amusement. Dave Dyer snapped, "How much do you want? Dollar be enough?" "No, it won't! You got to give me ten dollars—"

'Carol perceived that Mrs Dyer was accustomed to this indignity. She perceived that the men, particularly Dave, regarded it as an excellent jest. She waited—she knew what would come—it did. "Where's that ten dollars I gave you last year?" and he looked to the other men to laugh. They laughed.

'Cold and still, Carol walked up to Kennicott and commanded, "I want to see you upstairs." "Why—something the matter?" "Yes!" '

(See also the Samuel Butler quotation under Pocket Money, p. 127.)

**" —**

## DUE DEFERENCE

*Money! What a curious thing it is! Aaron noticed the deference of all the guests at table: a touch of obsequiousness: before the money! And the host and hostess accepted the deference, nay, expected it, as their due.*

*She seemed to put him just a tiny bit in his place, even in an opinion on music. Money gave her that right, too. Curious—the only authority left. And he deferred to her opinion: that is, to her money. Yes—what did he believe in, besides money? What does any man?*

D. H. Lawrence *Aaron's Rod*

**"**

**Hush money**   money paid to someone to ensure that he will not expose a crime or discreditable action. The expression has been in use since the beginning of the 18th century. *To Gay*, by Jonathan Swift has: 'A dext'rous steward, when his tricks are found, Hush-money sends to all the neighbours round.'

**Idle money**   inactive money, not invested in interest-earning assets or in real goods.

**Jew's money**   see Dwarf's money.

**Mad money**   an informal reference to money carried by a woman in order to pay her fare home should her escort become offensive. It can also be money put aside by a woman for an impulsive or therapeutic purchase. To the economists it is a term for discretionary income.

**Marked money**   banknotes marked in a special way to allow easy identification in the event of theft.

**Marriage money**   money acquired by marriage. Nicholas Udall, in his *Ralph Roister Doister* (1552), has the hero say: 'I hear she is worth a thousand pound and more.' Merygreeke replies:
'Yea, but learn this lesson of me afore:
An hundred pound of marriage-money, doubtless,
Is ever thirty pound sterling, or somewhat less,
So that her thousand pound, if she be thrifty,
Is much near about two hundred and fifty.'

**Merit money**   money awarded at some boarding schools for good work and behaviour; a system whereby the school acted on behalf of the parents in distributing a kind of pocket money. In *The Way of all Flesh* Samuel Butler writes: 'There was

**"**───────────────────

***BEING CAREFUL WITH MONEY***

*Take care of the pence, and the pounds will take care of themselves.*
Old proverb

*'I find it more trouble to take care of money than to get it.'*
Michel Montaigne

───────────────────  **"**

**"**───────────────────

***MATRI-MONEY***

*'When one lives in the world, a man or woman's marrying for money is too common to strike one as it ought.'*

Jane Austen *Persuasion*

───────────────────  **"**

an institution at Roughborough called the monthly merit money; the maximum sum which a boy of Ernest's age could get was four shillings and sixpence; several boys got four shillings and few less than sixpence, but Ernest never got more than half a crown and seldom more than eighteen pence; his average would, I should think, be about one and ninepence, which was just too much for him to rank among the downright bad boys, but too little to put him among the good ones.'

**Military money**   see Paper Money.

**Monkey money**   see Answers to Zoological Money Quiz, p. 117.

**Mortgage money**   money being repaid under a mortgage arrangement. For the origin of *mortgage*, see p. 68.

**Near money**   an asset which can be used in settlement of a debt, e.g. a bill of exchange. Also called quasi-money.

**Old money**   this phrase normally refers to families who have been very rich for many generations, as opposed to the *nouveau riche*, who have only recently acquired their wealth. The distinction is probably a meaningful one. The education and life-style of someone born into an old money family is likely to have been very different from the person who had very little to begin with, but has spent a lifetime acquiring a fortune.

**Paper money**   negotiable documents as opposed to coins. One early form of paper money appeared in the 13th century, when the Mongol emperor Kublai Khan used a wooden printing block to produce 'military money'. He had run out of the usual coin. Unfortunately, too much of the new military money was printed and the notes quickly decreased in value. Kublai had also introduced the concept of inflation.

**"**

### ORGANIC MONEY

*'A man's fortune or material progress is very much the same as his bodily growth. Either he is growing stronger, healthier, wiser, as the youth approaching manhood, or he is growing weaker, older, less incisive mentally, as the man approaching old age. There are no other states. Rich men are, frequently, in these days, saved from this dissolution of their fortune by their ability to hire younger brains. These younger brains look upon the interests of the fortune as their own, and so steady and direct its progress. If each individual were left absolutely to the care of his own interests, and were given time enough in which to grow exceedingly old, his fortune would pass as his strength and will.*

*'A fortune is an organism which draws unto itself other minds and other strength than that inherent in the founder. Beside the young minds drawn to it by salaries, it becomes allied with young forces, which make for its existence even when the strength and wisdom of the founder are fading. It may be conserved by the growth of a community or of a state. It may be involved in providing something for which there is a growing demand. This removes it at once beyond the special care of the founder. It needs not so much foresight now as direction. The man wanes, the need continues or grows, and the fortune, fallen into whose hands it may, continues.'*

Theodore Dreiser *Sister Carrie*

**"**

**Pin money**   pins were an expensive and luxurious item in the 14th century and pin money at that time would have been money allotted annually by a husband to his wife for their purchase. Such money was later used for items associated with pins, such as clothing, and pin money began to take on its modern meaning of a small amount of money used by a woman for any personal expense, especially of a trifling nature. It is now usually money that a woman earns rather than money given to her by her husband.

**Pocket money**   in Britain this refers to the money given to a child each week for spending on sweets, comics and the like. American children would call it their allowance. In *Nicholas Nickleby*, by Charles Dickens, we are told that Ralph Nickleby used to lend money to other children when he was a schoolboy, charging exorbitant rates of interest. He collected his debts on 'pocket-money day', Saturday.

National surveys of how much pocket money children receive are carried out from time to time.

The findings of such surveys are avidly perused by children and used as a weapon against parents who are not providing at least the national average.

In the past wives were often as dependent as children. In *The Way of All Flesh* Samuel Butler ironically describes the marital situation of the odious Theobald Pontifex, a clergyman with a handsome private income, and his wife Christina: 'Theobald made her a quarterly allowance for her dress, pocket money, and little charities and presents. Oh, what a comfort it was to Theobald to reflect that he had a wife on whom he could rely

**"**

### POCKET MONEY

*'Money is always there but the pockets change; it is not in the same pockets after a change, and that is all there is to say about money.'*

Gertrude Stein

**"**

never to cost him a sixpence of unauthorized expenditure! Letting alone her absolute submission, the perfect coincidence of her opinion with his own upon every subject and her constant assurances to him that he was right in everything which he took it into his head to say or do, what a tower of strength to him was her exactness in money matters!

'Even when Christina did outrun her quarterly stipend by some thirty shillings or a couple of pounds, it was always made perfectly clear to Theobald how the deficiency had arisen: the excess of expenditure was always repaid in the following quarter or quarters even though it were only ten shillings at a time.

'I believe, however, that after they had been married some twenty years, Christina had somewhat fallen from her original perfection as regards money. She had got gradually in arrears during many successive quarters, till she had contracted a chronic loan, a sort of domestic national debt, amounting to between seven and eight pounds.

'Theobald at length felt that a remonstrance had become imperative, and took advantage of his silver wedding-day to inform Christina that her indebtedness was cancelled, and at the same time to beg that she would endeavour henceforth to equalize her expenditure and her income. She burst into tears of love and gratitude, assured him that he was the best of and most generous of men, and never during the remainder of her married life was she a single shilling behindhand.'

**Present money**   an expression used in the 17th and 18th centuries for ready money, money in hand.

**Press money,** earlier prest money   money paid to a soldier or sailor on his enlistment, otherwise

**"**————————————————

### THE CURE-ALL

*'At length one of those rich relations died, and to repair the misery he had been instrumental in occasioning, left him his panacea for all griefs—Money.'*

Charles Dickens *Oliver Twist*

————————————————**"**

**"**————————————————

### MONEY TIME

*'Remember that time is money.'*
Benjamin Franklin

*'Time is money—says the vulgarest saw known to any age or people. Turn it round and you get a precious truth—money is time.'*
George Gissing *Ryecroft Papers*

The Swiss naturalist Jean Louis Rodolphe Agassiz (1807–73) was once asked to give a lecture, for which he would receive a handsome fee. Agassiz, who was dedicated to his research work, refused to give the talk, saying that he couldn't afford to waste his time making money.

————————————————**"**

known as the King's or Queen's shilling. In the 15th century the word 'prest' had several meanings connected with an advance of money, a loan. The word derived from Old French *prester*, modern French *prêter*, to lend. A prest could be a loan made to a king in an emergency, or a payment made in advance.

**Prize money**   historically this was always a share of the money or proceeds from any prizes taken from an enemy, a prize being anything taken by force in war, especially a ship. The word derived in this sense from French *prise*, 'taken, captured'. The kind of prize which is awarded as a symbol of success derives from a different French word, *prix*, 'price'. Money associated with such a prize could also be called prize-money.

**Protection money**   money extorted from shopkeepers and others by racketeers posing as a protective association. The phrase tends to recall the American gangsters of the 1920s, but the idea was certainly not new. There was formerly a word 'mail' (surviving in Scotland longer than anywhere else), which was unconnected with either chain-mail or mail in its sense of correspondence. It meant a payment of some kind, such as a tax, tribute or rent.

## PUNISHMENT MONEY

In Royal Navy slang, to be given 'fourteen penn'orth' once meant to be given fourteen days' cell punishment. Money expressions seem to have been used elsewhere for punishment. In his novel *Gorky Park*, Martin Cruz Smith writes: 'In 1946 they were given what was jokingly called at the time 25-ruble notes: twenty-five years' hard labor in the camps.'

In the 16th century the farmers who lived in the border counties of England and Scotland were forced to pay protection money to the gangsters of the time, the freebooters. The common word for such enforced payments was blackmail. The meaning of this word was extended in the 19th century to include any payment extorted by intimidation.

**Quasi money**   see Near money.

**Ready money**   money that can be paid immediately as cash.

**Real money**   an alternative way of talking about ready money.

**Right money**   see Smart money.

**Seed money**   money used to set up a totally new enterprise.

**Single money**   an obsolete expression, but common in the 17th century. It meant small change.

**Slush money**   money from a 'slush fund,' used for dubious political purposes such as buying votes or bribing officials. Slush fund was originally a term used in the American navy for money raised by selling refuse. This 'unofficial' money was used to buy small luxuries or pleasures for the crew of a warship.

**Small money**   loose change.

**Smart money**   money invested or bet by those with inside knowledge. Also known as right money.

**Socket money**   18th-century slang for the fee paid to a woman of pleasure. The term was also used to describe 'money paid for a treat, by a married man caught in an intrigue'. In this sense it seems to have been a kind of hush-money.

**Soft money**   currency which is highly inflated and likely to be devalued. The term is also used in the US of campaign donations not regulated by the Federal Election Commission.

**Spanish money**   18th-century slang for fair words and compliments, rather than actual money.

## RUMMY MONEY

Coleman P. Hyman, in his *Account of the Coins, Coinages, and Currency of Australia* (1893) says: 'It may well be said the rummiest currency known was that initiated here when rum came to be so extensively used as a circulating medium. At first tacitly recognized by the authorities, in a few years this currency became a curse almost ineradicable; Governor Hunter forbade the bartering of spirits for grain, but like many other orders, these were unheeded.'

**"**
## MONEY AND HAPPINESS

*'It is a kind of spiritual snobbery that makes people think they can be happy without money.'*
Albert Camus *Notebooks*

*'I'm tired of love: I'm still more tired of Rhyme. But Money gives me pleasure all the time.'*
Hilaire Belloc *Fatigue*

*'A poor person who is unhappy is in a better position than a rich person who is unhappy. Because the poor person has hope. He thinks money would help.'*
Jean Kerr *Poor Richard*

**"**

**Spending money**  an alternative way of referring to pocket-money.

**Tight money**  used by Americans to describe money that is difficult to obtain. It may well be dear money. A tightwad in the US is a miser or skinflint.

**Trust money**  this would normally refer to money administered by trustees. Turning aside from his usual literary concerns, William Thackeray extended the meaning of the phrase in his indignant essay *On Half A Loaf* to include the money of foreign investors.

A threatened war between England and the US had been averted early in 1862, but Thackeray was commenting on an article which appeared shortly before in the *New York Herald*: 'England cannot afford to go to war with us, for six hundred millions' worth of American stock is owned by British subjects, which, in event of hostilities, would be confiscated; and we now call upon the Companies not to take it off their hands on any terms.

'Let its forfeiture be held over England as a weapon *in terrorem*. British subjects have two or

### MONEY TALKS

O. Henry's short story *The Tale of a Tainted Tenner* begins with the words 'Money talks', then proceeds to interpret that phrase literally. The story is theoretically told in the first person by a ten-dollar note, series of 1901. It discusses various transactions in which it has been involved, and talks to other notes.

The phrase is normally used to mean that money can often influence more than mere words a person whose assistance is needed. In that sense, as Mrs Aphra Behn says in *The Rover*: 'Money speaks sense in a language all nations understand.'

The poet Richard Armour has said:
'That money talks
I'll not deny,
I heard it once:
It said "Goodbye".'

### " WINNERS AND LOSERS

'The power of money is an article of faith in which I profess myself a sceptic. A hundred pounds will with difficulty support you for a year; with somewhat more difficulty you may spend it in a night; and without any difficulty at all you may lose it in five minutes on the Stock Exchange. If you are of that stamp of man that rises, a penny would be as useful; if you belong to those that fall, a penny would be no more useless.'
R. L. Stevenson *St Ives*

"

three hundred millions of dollars invested in shipping and other property in the United States. All this property, together with the stocks, would be seized.

At the time the American Civil War was in progress, Thackeray commented: 'The same politicians who throttle commerce at its neck, and threaten to confiscate trust-money, say that when the war is over, and the South is subdued, then the turn of the old country will come, and a direful retribution shall be taken for our conduct.' The conduct referred to was the non-participation of the British in the Civil War, which caused it to last longer, and cost more, than Northern politicians thought it should.

Thackeray went on to point out that even though war between Britain and the United States had been averted, threats such as those made in the *New York Herald* did a great deal of harm. 'Why have the United States been paying seven, eight, ten per cent for money for years past, when the same commodity can be got elsewhere at half that rate of interest? Why, because though among the richest proprietors in the world, creditors were not sure of them. So the States have had to pay eighty millions yearly for the use of money which would cost other borrowers but thirty. Add up this item of extra interest alone for a dozen years, and see what a prodigious penalty the States have been paying for repudiation here and there, for sharp practice, for doubtful credit. The remembrance of this last threat alone will cost the States millions and millions more.'

The title of Thackeray's essay was explained by his final paragraph: 'Messrs Battery, Broadway & Co of New York, have the kindness to sell my Sainaws for what they will fetch. I shall lose half my loaf very likely; but for the sake of a quiet life, let us give up a certain quantity of farinaceous food; and half a loaf, you know, is better than no bread at all.'

**Universal money**   gold and silver, according to Karl Marx in *Das Kapital*. A passage referring to universal money in the translation by Eden and Cedar Paul begins: 'When money leaves the home sphere of circulation it doffs the local vesture of standard of prices, of coin, of tokens, and of symbols of value, and returns to its original form of bullion. In the world market, commodities display their values in terms recognized as having universal validity. It is only in the world market that money acquires to the fullest extent the character of the commodity whose bodily form is also the direct incarnation of human labour in the abstract. Its mode of existence has become adequate to its concept.'

Much of this famous book is as difficult to follow as the last two sentences given above, though its basic message is, of course, that the poor man gets less than his due, and that the rich man exploits the poor.

The first volume of *Das Kapital* appeared in 1867. In 1868 a series of articles in the British magazine *The Economist* discussed what was called 'international coinage'. These articles, by Walter Bagehot, were published in pamphlet form a year

## WORTHLESS MONEY

E. F. M. Durbin, in his *Money and Prices* (1933), reminds us that 'there is one sense in which money is worthless. No one wants money for its own sake. What we need for our sustenance and pleasure are the real commodities which money will buy—food and clothes and houses. Except for an abnormal minority who want treasures of gold, most people do not want money at all'.

## SUPERLATIVE MONEY

The heaviest money ever used was in the form of aragonite stone discs, still being circulated on the Pacific island of Yap until 1939. Most discs were 30 cm *1 ft* wide, but one denomination had a width of 3.6 m *12 ft*. It was transported on a pole. The lightest money was used in the New Hebrides and consisted of rare feathers. In Borneo until the 19th century human skulls were used as money.

later as *A Practical Plan for Assimilating the English and American Money, as a Step Towards Universal Money*, though the more convenient title *A Universal Money* was generally used.

Bagehot stated that 'no existing coinage is fit as it stands for international uses. And this is really the conclusion which should have been expected. The conditions of an international currency, as we have stated them, are complex, and are very little likely to have been satisfied in rude ages'.

As an instance of what he meant by that last remark, Bagehot pointed out that any international currency would have to be based on a decimal system. 'The Arabic numerals which we use have made ten seem like a law of nature; but in the middle ages, and before these numerals were used, people did not think so much of ten. They thought by halves and quarters; of multiples of two and four. All our present requirements have reference to the modern world, and were not imaginable in the old world. We must not therefore be surprised if we have to invent a new currency, and do not find a fit one ready.'

Bagehot repeated in 1868 that 'we should count all money by tens, just as we reckon on paper all things by tens'. This had been stated previously, and the florin, a tenth of a pound, had been introduced in 1849. It was not until 1971, however, that decimal currency was introduced to Britain.

**Walk-about money**   modern slang for a small sum of money.

**White money**   in the 14th century this meant standard silver coinage. Copper coinage was black money.

## SHAKESPEAREAN MONEY

Shakespeare inevitably refers to money a great deal in his plays and poems. The word 'money' itself occurs over 150 times, and many coins are mentioned by name. Apart from the obvious shilling, penny and the like there are references to angels, deniers, doits, dollars, ducats, groats, marks, nobles, royals, sicles (= shekels) solidares, testers (sixpences). Money becomes 'chinks' in *Romeo and Juliet*.

Other Shakespearean money words:

**ability**   see p. 120
**audit**   see p. 91
**bankrout**   bankrupt
**chuff**   miser
**clipper**   one who clips coins
**coining**   i.e. minting
**compt**   account
**content**   as a verb, to reward or pay
**earnest**   money paid as a deposit
**eight-penny**   something of little value
**escot**   to pay a reckoning for
**exhibition**   allowance of money
**fee**   many meanings in the plays
**gild**   to supply with money
**hundred-pound**   as a contemptuous word for
    a pretender to the title of gentleman, a snob
**jointure**   marriage portion
**meed**   wages, reward
**pitch and pay**   i.e. pay cash
**plate**   silver coin
**putter-out**   one who invests money at interest
**quittance**   discharge from debt
**remuneration**   see p. 53
**sauce**   to overcharge someone
**scot**   payment
**sixpenny**   as an adjective meaning paltry
**sterling**   of full value
**talent**   sum of money
**true penny**   i.e. an honest fellow

Sonnet 87 makes use of the common Elizabethan conceit whereby a person's worth is discussed in monetary terms. It begins:
'Farewell—thou art too dear for my
    possessing,
And like enough thou knowest thy estimate:

The charter of thy worth gives thee releasing;
My bonds in thee are all determinate.
For how do I hold thee but by thy granting?
And for that riches where is my deserving?'
(Estimate = worth; charter = privilege; determine = ended)

There are also references to the marriage market, where potential wives are thought of quite literally in terms of the money they will bring with them for the husband's use. Fenton, however, in *The Merry Wives of Windsor* (3.iv), does have the grace to say:
'I will confess thy father's wealth
Was the first motive that I woo'd thee, Anne,
Yet, wooing thee, I found thee of more value
Than stamps in gold or sums in sealed bags;
And 'tis the very riches of thyself
That now I aim at.'

The following lines, all on the subject of money, are spoken by characters in Shakespeare's plays. How many of them can you identify? (Answers on p. 135.)

1. 'There is either liquor in his pate or money in his purse when he looks so merrily.'
2. 'There's no true drop of blood in him to be truly touch'd with love; if he be sad, he wants money.'
3. 'Hath a dog money?'
4. 'He that wants money, means, and content is without three good friends.'
5. 'I was as virtuously given as a gentleman need to be; virtuous enough: swore little, dic'd not above seven times a week, went to a bawdy house not above once in a quarter—of an hour, paid money that I borrowed—three or four times.'
6. 'I can raise no money by vile means.'
7. 'I think one business does command us all; for mine is money.'
8. 'Mine honest friend,/Will you take eggs for money?'
9. 'They say, if money go before, all ways do lie open.'
10. 'These wise men that give fools money get themselves a good report.'

## DICKENSIAN MONEY

Charles Dickens also has something to say about money in most of his books. The results of either possessing, or wishing to possess, money pervade *Martin Chuzzlewit*. *Great Expectations* shows the effect that wealth can have on a young man. *Little Dorrit* is divided into two parts, called 'Poverty' and 'Riches', and ironically contrasts those states. The well-known 'what is money?' scene in *Dombey and Son* is discussed in the Preface.

Those who know their Dickens may be able to say which characters make the following remarks, in which stories or novels. (The answers are on p. 135.)

1. 'Annual income twenty pounds, annual expenditure nineteen nineteen six, result happiness. Annual income twenty pounds, annual expenditure twenty pounds ought and six, result misery. The blossom is blighted, the leaf is withered, the god of day goes down upon the weary scene, and—in short you are for ever floored, as I am.'

2. 'And yet, Pa, think how terrible the fascination of money is! I see this, and hate this, and dread this, and don't know but that money might make a much worse change in me. And yet I have money always in my thoughts and my desires; and the whole life I place before myself is money, money, money, and what money can make of life!'

3. 'I am constantly being bailed out—like a boat. Or paid off—like a ship's company. Somebody always does it for me. I can't do it, you know, for I never have any money. Let us drink to Somebody. God bless him!'

4. 'The cant of the lying world is, that men like me compass our riches by dissimulation and treachery; by fawning, cringing and stooping. Why, how many lies, what mean evasions, what humbled behaviour from upstarts who, but for my money, would spurn me aside as they do their betters every day, would that ten thousand pounds have brought me in!'

5. 'This is the even-handed dealing of the world! There is nothing on which it is so hard as poverty; and there is nothing it professes to condemn with such severity as the pursuit of wealth!'

6. 'My conscience is my bank. I prize it as a store of value, I assure you.'

7. 'Will you tell me that I oughtn't to go into Society? I, who shower money upon it in this way? I, who might be almost said to—to—to harness myself to a watering-cart full of money, and go about, saturating Society, every day of my life?'

8. 'You are in a counting-house, you know, and you look about you. Then the time comes when you see your opening. And you go in, and you swoop upon it and you make your capital, and then there you are! When you have once made your capital, you have nothing to do but employ it.'

9. 'I didn't take all the money at once. I pretended to put my balance away every night, but I didn't. Now you know all about it.'
   'If a thunderbolt had fallen on me', said the father, 'it would have shocked me less than this!'
   'I don't see why', grumbled the son. 'So many people are employed in situations of trust; so many people, out of so many, will be dishonest. I have heard you talk, a hundred times, of its being a law. How can I help laws?

10. 'I have more money than I can ever need; far more than a man at my age can ever live to spend.'

## MONEY MELODIES

Money would have been a topic of considerable interest to the audiences of the music-hall, the great popular entertainment of the late Victorian period. It sometimes featured as a topic in the songs that were sung there. Miss Bessie Bonehill, for example, used to sing a number called 'Money', written and composed by Arthur West. It asked questions like:

'Why does the little charmer whose age is
    seventeen,
And who to leave her school is very glad,
Get married to a fellow as we've very often
    seen,
Who is really old enough to be her dad?

Why do merchants we admire, their buildings
    set on fire,
Why is bankruptcy no longer a disgrace,
And if lovers do not care for the girl they've
    called 'my fair',
How is it there's a breach of promise case?'

The chorus in each case gave the resounding
    answer.
    'It's for money, ain't it funny!
    How it drives away our sorrow and our
        care?
    If you want honey, you want money!
    Yes it's money, money, money, ev'rywhere.'

Another music-hall song was Sam Torr's M-O-N-E-Y. A typical verse ran:
'The parson preaches in the Church, but does
    not do it free.
The lawyer gives advice, but then he always
    wants his fee.
The Butcher soon will smell a rat if funds are
    getting low.
If you want your meat on credit he will quickly
    answer 'No!'
The Landlord too is so polite if you your rent
    can pay,
But miss a quarter and you'll find the Bailiffs in
    next day.

And Wives seem cold and distant if to stint
    them you should try,
And won't be civil till they get their
    M-O-N-E-Y.'

The chorus was:
'M-O-N-E-Y that is the stuff to bring you joy,
When you've got the L-S-D, everybody seems
    so free,
Folks you never knew before flock around
    you by the score,
Girls to win your love will try, for your
    M-O-N-E-Y.'

Another popular song of the Victorian period contained the lines:
'A guinea it will sink, and a note it will float,
But I'd rather have a guinea than a one-pound
    note.'

Songs continue to be written about money, of course. Abba had considerable success with their 'Money, Money, Money'. The film *Cabaret* made the song 'Money Makes the World Go Around' well-known. It was also, perhaps, the song 'Money is the Root of All Evil', very popular in the late 1940s, which has caused the biblical 'For the love of money is the root of all evil' to be so frequently misquoted ever since. The song was written by Joan Whitney and Alex Kramer and performed by the Stargazers. After repeating the assertion that money is the root of all evil, the lyric goes on: 'Won't contaminate myself with it, Take it away, Take it away, Take it away.'

Those who know their popular music well could no doubt compile an extensive list of musical money allusions. It might range from 'Bad Penny Blues', the jazz number played by Humphrey Lyttleton which got into the British top twenty in 1955, to Noel Coward's 'Poor Little Rich Girl'.

## ANSWERS TO SHAKESPEAREAN MONEY QUIZ *(on p. 132)*

1. Page talking to Ford in *The Merry Wives of Windsor* (2.i) about the host of the Garter Inn.
2. Don Pedro talking about Benedick, the young lord of Padua, in *Much Ado About Nothing* (3.i).
3. Shylock to Antonio, in *The Merchant of Venice* (2.iii). Antonio has in the past called Shylock a dog, but he has now come to borrow money from him.
4. Corin, the old shepherd in *As You Like It* (3.ii), to Touchstone.
5. Sir John Falstaff to Bardolph, in *King Henry The Fourth—Part One* (3.iii).
6. Brutus to Cassius, *Julius Caesar* (4.iii). He continues:

   By heaven, I had rather coin my heart,
   And drop my blood for drachmas, than to wring
   From the hard hands of peasants their vile trash
   By any indirection.

7. The servant of Lucius to Hortensius, in *Timon of Athens* (3.iii). What he actually means is 'We are all here for the same reason, to recover money from Timon.'
8. Leontes to his son Mamillius, *The Winter's Tale* (1.ii). Leontes is distraught with jealousy and is speaking strangely.
9. Ford to Falstaff, *The Merry Wives of Windsor* (2.ii). Falstaff replies 'Money is a good soldier, sir'.
10. The Clown to Sebastian, *Twelfth Night* (4.i).

## ANSWERS TO DICKENSIAN MONEY QUIZ *(on p. 133)*

1. Mr Micawber in *David Copperfield*. He is always desperately short of money, and always expecting 'something to turn up'. His basic honesty eventually stands him in good stead.
2. Bella Wilfer talking to her father in *Our Mutual Friend*. She is adopted by the Boffins, who have inherited a great deal of money.
3. Mr Skimpole, in *Bleak House*, a man in his fifties who is child-like where money is concerned. 'He took a handful of loose silver and halfpence from his pocket. "There's so much money. I have not an idea how much. I have not the power of counting. Call it four and ninepence—call it four pound nine." ' Skimpole sponges on the benevolent Mr Jarndyce.
4. Ralph Nickleby, uncle to the hero of *Nicholas Nickleby*. His father's poverty caused him to learn two great morals— that riches are the true source of happiness and power, and that it is lawful to accomplish their acquisition by all

   means short of felony. When his schemes eventually go wrong he hangs himself.
5. Ebenezer Scrooge in *A Christmas Carol*.
6. This is the arch-hypocrite Mr Pecksniff, in *Martin Chuzzlewit*. Dickens continues: 'The good man's enemies would have divided upon this question between the two parties. One would have asserted without scruple that if Mr Pecksniff's conscience were his bank, and he kept a running account there, he must have overdrawn it beyond all mortal means of computation. The other would have contended that it was a mere fictitious form; a perfectly blank book; or one in which entries were only made with a peculiar kind of invisible ink, to become legible at some indefinite time; and that he never troubled it at all.'
7. Mr Merdle, in *Little Dorrit*, talking to his wife. She is telling him that his manner is not suitable for the social circle in which they move. 'There is a positive vulgarity in carrying your business affairs about with

you as you do.' He answers: 'You supply manner, and I supply money.'

8. Herbert Pocket, explaining to Pip in *Great Expectations* how easy it is to make money.

9. This is young Tom Gradgrind, in *Hard Times*, explaining to his father why he robbed the bank in which he worked to pay his gambling debts. The father has brought Tom up to believe in cold logic and nothing else. Here he demonstrates where that 'system' has led him.

10. Mr Pickwick is talking here to the elder Mr Weller, who has tried to offer him money. The conversation occurs towards the end of *The Pickwick Papers*.
It is difficult to think of Mr Pickwick as anything other than a benevolent old gentleman, but he does say that for most of his life he devoted himself to the pursuit of wealth. Talking to his friends after the dissolution of the Pickwick Club he says: 'I shall never regret having devoted the greater part of two years to mixing with different varieties and shades of human character, frivolous as my pursuit of novelty may have appeared to many. Nearly the whole of my previous life having been devoted to business and the pursuit of wealth, numerous scenes of which I had no previous conception have dawned upon me—I hope to the enlargement of my mind, and the improvement of my understanding.'

# 11
# MADE OF MONEY

## MILLIONAIRES AND MONEY-MAKERS

How much do you earn?

An impertinent question, of course, since your income is a private matter, between you and the tax collector and perhaps your nearest and dearest, or your business partner.

But it is always interesting to discover how much other people earn, especially those household names who are 'in the money'. It is even of interest to discover how the less famous or more mundane among us fare financially. That is what this chapter is about: who makes how much.

Where better to start than at the glittering top, with the millionaires. A millionaire is a person who has a million . . . what? Pounds? Dollars? Francs? It all depends on the currency. Whatever it is, the word describes a very rich person. And a billionaire is a very rich person indeed.

The term is one that fascinates. How did the millionaire make his million(s)? And if 'millionaire' means 'rich person', who is or was the richest person of all? The phrase 'rich as Croesus', meaning 'very rich', gives one familiar answer to this question.

**Croesus** was no mythological character, as sometimes supposed, but a real enough person. He was the last king of Lydia, who ruled in the 6th century BC. He conquered the Greeks of mainland Ionia and was then in turn conquered by the Persians. Stories tell how he used his wealth to become a model of piety by making rich offerings of solid gold to the god Apollo at Delphi.

**"**

### DESERVING CASES

*'There are certainly not so many men of large fortune in the world, as there are pretty women to deserve them.'*

Jane Austen *Mansfield Park*

**"**

It is difficult, if not impossible, to state in modern terms exactly how rich he was. According to legend, he derived his wealth from the gold-bearing sands of the Pactolus River. (This was the river in which the famous King Midas is said to have washed himself, as a result of which it was given the Greek name of Chrysorrhoas, 'gold-flowing'.)

In all probability Croesus gained his wealth from a combination of commercial enterprise and hereditary fortune. The latter derived from his father Alyattes, who had begun the conquest of Ionia and who had taken possession of several Greek cities, which then passed to his son.

Whatever the case, his name soon came to be proverbially equated with riches, and he is mentioned in this respect in the writings of classical authors such as Herodotus, Plutarch and Justinian.

It is significant, of course, that he was king of Lydia, the land where coinage was invented, as mentioned in Chapter 2 (p. 16).

Other rich and wealthy men have become familiar to us from the Bible, where the word 'rich' and 'riches' frequently occurs.

*Genesis* 13:2, for example, tells us that 'Abram was very rich in cattle, and silver, and in gold', and almost half the 22 chapters of *Kings* I are devoted to Solomon, king of Israel, whose name, like that of Croesus, became a byword for wisdom and opulence.

Where Abraham's wealth was represented by his worldly possessions, Solomon's was displayed in his magnificent temple, which was covered in gold and filled with sumptuous ornaments.

In the New Testament, Jesus told more than one parable in which a rich man features. Among them are those of the rich man with the fertile ground (*Luke* 12:16–21), of the rich man and the unjust steward (*Luke* 16:1–8), and, one of the best known, of **Dives** and Lazarus (*Luke* 16:19–31), where Dives is the rich man and Lazarus the beggar. (The name 'Dives', from Latin *dives*, 'rich', does not occur in the Bible itself. It is simply a popular name for this particular man. As such, it has become synonymous with 'rich man', and can be found in this sense in literary references.)

One more legendary rich man is **Plutus**, who in Greek classical mythology was the son of Demeter and the personification of wealth. (His name actually means 'riches', hence English 'plutocrat' and similar words.)

In both legend and real life, riches have traditionally been associated with rulers, of all ages and

## THE BIBLE AND MONEY

Money is mentioned many times in the Bible, but perhaps the two best-known passages are: 'The love of money is the root of all evil,' and 'A feast is made for laughter, and wine maketh merry: but money answereth for all things.'

The first of these is frequently misquoted in modern times, perhaps because of a popular song (see p. 134). The *Revised Standard Version* of the Bible, at *I Timothy* 6.6, now reads: 'There is great gain in godliness with contentment; for we brought nothing into the world, and we cannot take anything out of the world; but if we have food and clothing, with these we shall be content. But those who desire to be rich fall into temptation, into a snare, into many senseless and hurtful desires that plunge men into ruin and destruction. For the love of money is the root of all evils; it is through this craving that some have wandered away from the faith and pierced their hearts with many pangs.'

Mark Twain is usually credited with the alternative version of the original quotation: 'The lack of money is the root of all evil.'

The second passage, from *Ecclesiastes* 10.19, is altogether more worldly. It runs as follows in the modern translation: 'Bread is made for laughter, and wine gladdens life, and money answers everything. Even in your thought, do not curse the king, nor in your bedchamber curse the rich; for a bird of the air will carry your voice, or some winged creature tell the matter.'

in many countries. As with Croesus, however, it is often hard to put a precise value or figure on personal wealth of this kind. One difficulty is that a ruler's fortune may well be expressed in terms of his 'investment' in the country that he rules, and the value of land, property and industrial enterprises can vary from one day to the next. All that can be safely assumed in most such cases is that the wealth, in the form of personal or disposable assets, is hereditary. A ruler thus gains his fortune by virtue of both birth and succession, and so has not earned or 'made' it on his own account.

'Millionaire' is a word that often implies an actual making of money, or the acquisition of a great wealth by commercial or other enterprise.

The word itself is recorded by the *Oxford English Dictionary* no earlier than 1826, when it appeared in Benjamin Disraeli's novel *Vivian Grey*: 'Were I the son of a Millionaire, or a noble, I might have all.'

It must have been current before this for Disraeli to use it, even if he borrowed it from the identical French word, which already existed.

'Billionaire' is first recorded in 1861, in the novel *Elsie Venner* by Oliver Wendell Holmes: 'One would like to give a party now and then, if one could be a billionnaire.'

## AMERICA: MOTHERLAND OF THE MILLIONAIRE

Significantly, Holmes was an American author, and it is with the United States that millionaires and billionaires (and multimillionaires) are still associated today.

Within only the past 200 years, the names of some American millionaires have become legendary and have even become synonymous, like Croesus, with 'rich person'. One such name is **Rockefeller**, which has now found its way into the *Oxford English Dictionary* to be defined in these terms ('The name of John D. Rockefeller (1839–1937), Amer. financier and philanthropist, used as the type of an immensely rich man'). Another is **Rothschild**, which the same dictionary defines similarly ('One who resembles a member of the Rothschild family in being exceptionally rich; a millionaire'). The precise reference here is to Mayer Amschel Rothschild (1744–1812) of

 **MAMMON**

The word 'Mammon' occurs from time to time in literature. The original reference is in the *New Testament* (*Matthew* 6.24; *Luke* 16.13), where we find: 'Ye cannot serve God and mammon.' This is a use of a Semitic word for 'money, riches', but poets such as Spenser and Milton made Mammon the personification of the evils of wealth and miserliness.

The word was picked up by later writers. In his *Sanity of True Genius*, Charles Lamb refers to Mammon as the Money God. Lord Byron, in *Childe Harold*, has: 'Maidens, like moths, are ever caught by glare, And Mammon wins his way, where seraphs might despair.'

In O. Henry's short story *Mammon and the Archer*, the 'archer' refers to Cupid, god of love. In the story a father says to his son: 'You're a gentleman. They say it takes three generations to make one. They're off. Money'll do it as slick as soap grease.'
'There are some things that money can't accomplish', the son replies.
'Now don't say that', says the father. 'I bet my money on money every time. I've been through the encyclopaedia down to Y looking for something you can't buy with it; and I expect to have to take up the appendix next week. I'm for money against the field.'

The father later proves that he can affect the course of true love by means of money. He hires people to cause a traffic jam, which gives his son time to propose to the girl he loves.

Frankfurt, and his descendants, who were proprietors of an international banking firm.

Note the professions of these two millionaires: respectively financier and banker. In other words, 'money makes money'!

Rockefeller and Rothschild were among the earliest millionaires, even billionaires, and their names are linked with others that have come to be popularly associated with great wealth, such as Cornelius **Vanderbilt** (1794–1877), Henry **Ford** (1863–1947) and Andrew W. **Mellon** (1855–1937).

Saying exactly *how* rich such men were is not always easy, however. Many millionaires are reticent about their wealth, and the extent of their wordly possessions apart from any actual reckonable financial assets can often be only approximately stated.

Vanderbilt, who made his fortune through his

transportation enterprise, is generally regarded as having been a centimillionaire, for it is known that on his death in 1877 he left $100 million. Rockefeller made his money through oil, and as a philanthropist gave away more than $500 million to charities and institutions during his lifetime. Ford, the famous automobile manufacturer, built up his company from a nominal capitalization of $100 000 in 1902 to an industrial giant worth over $700 million in 1927. This was all his personal wealth, for his company was the only one of its size that was individually owned. Mellon was one of

## NAMES IN THE MONEY

Many surnames are quite inappropriate for the professions of the people who bear them. We have all heard of the likes of Mr Baker the butcher, Mr Butcher the dentist, and Mr Tooth the solicitor.

Surprisingly, therefore, there are or have been a number of well-known people in the world of finance and commerce who have names of genuine monetary origin.

Among them are:

**James Cash Penney** (1875–1971)   US businessman, founder of one of America's greatest retailing chains.

**The Hon. George Money** (b. 1914)   British banker, former Director, Barclays Bank International Ltd.

**David Money-Coutts** (b. 1931)   British banker, Chairman, Coutts & Co., one of Britain's most exclusive banks.

**James Coyne** (b. 1916)   Canadian banker, financial consultant, former Governor of the Bank of Canada.

**Joseph Stirling Coyne** (1803–1868)   Irish playwright, author of several money-spinning farces, including *How to Settle Accounts with Your Laundress*.

**David Shilling** (b. 1947)   English milliner, nicknamed 'Five New Pence' after decimalization. He designed the unique creations worn at Royal Ascot by his

mother, Mrs Gertrude Shilling, and was a Lloyd's underwriter and merchant banker before turning hatter in 1975. Has written his memoirs, *Twenty to the Pound*.

**Alan Minter** (b. 1956)   British boxer. Made his mint in 1980, when he became World Middleweight Champion.

**Sir Walter Besant** (1836–1901)   English novelist, whose works include *Ready-Money Mortiboy* (1872). (See page 22.)

And although their names are not genuinely monetary in origin, we should perhaps not overlook:

**Eddie Money** (b. 1949)   US rock singer, who changed his original name of Mahoney to bring fame and fortune.

**Robert Dollar** (1844–1932)   Scottish-born US shipping magnate.

In fiction, too, there were:

**Christopher Penny**   'The Coward' in Jerome K. Jerome's *The Passing of the Third Floor Back* (1910).

**Mary Ann Money**   a charwoman in Thomas Hardy's *Far from the Madding Crowd* (1874).

**Miss Moneypenny**   private secretary to 'M' in Ian Fleming's *Thunderball* (1961) and other James Bond stories.

## HUMAN INVESTMENT

Money features strongly in the novels of F. Scott Fitzgerald. 'Her voice is full of money', says Gatsby, referring to Daisy Buchanan in *The Great Gatsby*. Nicole Warren, in *Tender is the Night*, is also extremely wealthy. Some critics see both novels as having the same basic theme—a young man being ruined by his love for a rich woman. Dick Diver, hero of *Tender is the Night*, is not one of the super-rich, but Fitzgerald still saw him in monetary terms. Explaining why Diver was not drafted in World War I, Fitzgerald remarks that at the age of 26 he was 'already too valuable, too much of a capital investment to be shot off in a gun'.

 ## HUSBANDING MONEY

The fact that a man is rich, says Shakespeare in *The Merry Wives of Windsor* 3.iv, may make him seem a decidedly handsome fellow to a prospective father-in-law. Or as Anne expresses it in the play:
'This is my father's choice.
O, what a world of vile ill-favour'd faults
Looks handsome in three hundred pounds a year.'

A fortune could also make a man seem intelligent. In Jane Austen's *Mansfield Park* someone says of Rushworth: 'If this man had not twelve thousand a year, he would be a very stupid fellow.'

the richest men in the United States, if not the world, by the time he became Secretary of the Treasury in 1921. As an art collector he gave his own collection, valued at $25 million, to the US government shortly before his death as well as donating $15 million to build the National Gallery of Art in Washington, DC.

For most of these millionaires, personal wealth is associated with a particular man. With the Rothschilds the wealth became associated with the family as a whole: first with Mayer Amschel's five sons, then with their sons in turn. Even today, almost 200 years after the death of the family founder, who made his initial fortune as a money lender in Frankfurt, the name of Rothschild is still synonymous with immense wealth, and is prominent in banking circles in many countries and cities, notably Paris, London, Vienna and Naples. Again, putting a figure on the Rothschild family fortunes is difficult, and one can only go by individual reports and estimates. In 1989, for example, the wealth of the three British representatives of the family alone—Sir Evelyn Rothschild, chairman of the bank NM Rothschild, Jacob Rothschild, head of an investment company, and the 3rd Baron Rothschild, a distinguished scientist—was put at £200 million (*Sunday Times Magazine*, 2 April 1989). Worldwide and familywide, of course, this figure can be multiplied many times.

Another well-known millionaire name is that of the American businessman Jean Paul **Getty** (1892–1976), who from his oil interests amassed a fortune of over $1000 million—more than a billion. (It was Getty who once said, 'If you can count your millions, you are not a billionaire'.)

So who are the millionaires *now*, and in what countries are they to be found?

From the beginning, as mentioned, America has traditionally been regarded as the land of millionaires, and this is as true today as it ever was. By 1988, there were over a million millionaires in the United States, and more than 20 000 households worth $10 million or more. Indeed, some social commentators, such as Lewis Lapham and Michael Thomas, claim that assets of £20 million are now the minimum criterion for being described as 'rich', and it is not the millionaires who make the headlines in the media but the billionaires.

Every year in the USA, *Forbes* Magazine publishes its list of the 400 richest people in the country, and in its issue for 24 November 1988, it reckoned that the 400 for that year has an average fortune of over half a billion dollars (to be precise, $551 million). American millionaires, are also making money faster than ever, and 33 men of the 400 in 1988 had made most of their fortunes in only 12 years. Of the 800, only 154 were rich

**"**——————————————————

## AN EIGHTEENTH-CENTURY COMMENT ON PERSONAL COMPUTERS

*'I knew three great ministers who could exactly compute and settle the accounts of a kingdom, but were wholly ignorant of their own economy.'*

Jonathan Swift *Thoughts on Various Subjects*

——————————————————**"**

through their inheritance, and there was only one representative of the famous millionaire families of a century earlier. This was David Rockefeller, grandson of John D. Rockefeller.

Whereas previously American millionaires had made their fortunes through oil, railroads and new industries, the multimillionaires of today have mostly acquired their prodigious incomes through non-industrial enterprises, such as real estate, entertainment, and, especially, finance. Exceptions to the rule have been the fortunate few who have gained their wealth from computers, including the billionaire William Gates, of Microsoft, who is still under 40, and the former billionaire Steve Jobs, co-founder of Apple computers, who has now set up his own company, Next.

How does a multimillionaire live? Some, of course, live relatively modest and entirely purposeful and hard-working lives. Others are much more flamboyant and extrovert, and deliberately cultivate an extravagant way of life.

### MODERN MILLIONAIRES

In the late 1980s, one 'new-style' American millionaire of the latter type was the real estate financier in New York, the appropriately named Donald **Trump**.

The son of a wealthy Swedish-American builder in Brooklyn, Trump claimed to be a billionaire by the time he was 41. His showpiece and headquarters is the spectacular Trump Tower, on Manhattan's Fifth Avenue, opened in 1983 and valued at some $700 million by 1987. From this particular highrise and the nearby Trump Parc and 24 000 apartment units in Queens and Brooklyn, Trump extended his empire to at least three casinos in Atlantic City, New Jersey, where his

wife Ivana was chief executive in the grandest, Trump's Castle. His private fortune included a triplex penthouse in Trump Tower, a 15-bedroom house in Connecticut, an $8-million retreat in Palm Beach, Florida, a private Boeing 727 jet, and a French-built 'Puma' helicopter with 'Trump' emblazoned on the side. When the Saudi arms-dealer Adnan Khashoggi faced bankruptcy in 1988, Trump bought his luxury yacht, renaming it the Trump Princess, for the equivalent of £29 million. However, *Forbes* magazine later (30 April 1990) announced the devastating news that Trump's fortune had dramatically slipped to a mere $500 million, making him no longer one of America's 100 richest men.

Another millionaire in the same style as Trump was the owner of **Forbes** magazine himself, Malcolm Forbes, who died in 1990 aged 70, an eccentric rich American with a fortune put somewhere between $400 million and $1000 million. He owned a ranch in Colorado, a palace in Morocco, an island in the Pacific, and a château in France where he held an annual ballooning festival. True to form, he sported a luxury yacht, on which he sailed round the world with two motorbikes and a helicopter, and where he held lunch parties for famous guests, attended by photographers and reporters. In his magazine's head office in Manhattan, too, Forbes had his personal

## SOB STORIES

One of the problems of its being generally known that you are well off, it seems, is that you become the target for begging-letters. Charles Dickens was consistently bothered by them, and eventually wrote an exasperated piece called *The Begging-Letter Writer.* All such letters, he said, were written by idle frauds. 'The poor never write these letters. Nothing could be more unlike their habits. The writers are public robbers; and we who support them are parties to their depredations. There is a plain remedy, and it is in our own hands. We must resolve, at any sacrifice of feeling, to be deaf to such appeals, and crush the trade.'

*THE GREAT CORRUPTER*

*Martin Chuzzlewit*, by Charles Dickens, is largely about a rich man whose money makes him unhappy. He has come to detest the greed which his wealth inspires in everyone he meets. Early in the novel he explains this to his cousin Pecksniff:

'"Sir, I am a rich man. Not so rich as some suppose, perhaps, but yet wealthy. I am not a miser, sir, though even that charge is made against me, as I hear, and currently believed. I have no pleasure in hoarding. I have no pleasure in the possession of money. The devil that we call by that name can give me nothing but unhappiness."

'A thought arose in Mr Pecksniff's mind, which must have instantly mounted to his face, or Martin Chuzzlewit would not have resumed as quickly and as sternly as he did—"You would advise me, for my peace of mind, to get rid of this source of misery, and transfer it to someone who could bear it better. Even you, perhaps, would rid me of a burden under which I suffer so grievously. But that is a main part of my trouble. To what man or woman—to what worthy, honest, incorruptible creature—shall I confide such a talisman, either now or when I die? I have gone, a rich man, among people of all grades and kinds; relatives, friends and strangers; among people in whom, when I was poor, I had confidence. But I have never found one nature in which, being wealthy and alone, I was not forced to detect the latent corruption that lay hid within it, waiting for such as I to bring it forth. Treachery, deceit, and low design; hatred of competitors, real or fancied, for my favour; meanness, falsehood, baseness and servility; or an assumption of honest independence, these are the beauties which my wealth has brought to light."'

museum on the ground floor where he displayed his collection of toy soldiers, toy boats and Fabergé eggs. On his 70th birthday in 1989 he flew 800 guests to his Morocco mansion, including Elizabeth Taylor and Henry Kissinger. In his turn, Forbes was simultaneously fêted by King Hassan of Morocco, who held his own lavish party during the birthday celebrations.

An extrovert and an exhibitionist, therefore. But isn't that what most people expect, even admire, in a millionaire? If the wealthy heroes and heroines of television 'soap operas' attract a huge popular following, how much greater an attraction and more imposing a figure is a real flesh-and-blood millionaire!

## MILLIONAIRE LIFESTYLES

Not all millionaires conform to the archetype. This has been proved by the American writer and social critic Vance Packard, who in his book *The Ultra Rich*, published in 1989, gave his findings on the lives and fortunes of 30 American millionaires and millionairesses, each with an average net wealth of about $350 million.

Packard observes that, in general, millionaires fall into one of three types. They are either entrepreneurs (self-made men or women), inheritors (heirs to family fortunes) or real estate holders (owning land and buildings). He reports that of the 400 richest Americans listed in *Forbes* Magazine in 1985, almost half gained their wealth through inheritance, 59 solely or primarily from real estate, and 100 from commercial chain operations or media empires. Further, he lists five factors that can currently assist a person to make big money and become a millionaire, even if that person lacks conventional entrepreneurial flair. These are as follows:

1. Thanks to swift means of transportation and rapid communications, many new mass markets are opening up, both national and international. Among people who have made fortunes this way are: a manufacturer of teddy bears, a maker of products for pets, a maker of running shoes, the owner of a telephone selling service, and a marketer of greetings cards.

2. A new enterprise tends to grow *quickly*, especially a chain operation in merchandising or media.

### RICH OR WEALTHY?

It has long been known that people of different social classes use different words to describe the same things. One of the differences between upper-class and middle-class speakers, according to sociologist E. Digby Baltzell, of the University of Pennsylvania, is that the former will happily describe someone as 'rich', while the latter tend to use the more genteel expression 'wealthy'.

The term 'filthy rich' was perhaps inspired by 'filthy lucre'. Cole Porter was in the habit of distinguishing between the rich and the rich-rich.

3. Land prices have soared in the last 20 years, so if you are a landowner, you just sit on your land property and watch its value grow. The thinking here is 'There's money in bricks and mortar'.
4. President Reagan has promoted policies favourable to 'fortune builders'. So, one might add, has Prime Minister Margaret Thatcher.
5. Today it is possible to make a lot of money buying and selling shares—as long as one has capital to start with and one is not too faint-hearted!

Vance Packard notes that his entrepreneurs, or self-made people, were usually very energetic and highly motivated, with 14 of the 30 exploiting some new trend or way of life, and that the trends themselves were often peripheral to the invention or manufacture of needed or desired products. Of the 30, at least half were low in social responsibility, and only 10 were 'serious' philanthropists, thus debunking the commonly held theory that many millionaires donate much of their wealth to deserving causes.

Whereas many rich families, such as the Rockefellers, handed down their wealth and particular professional roles to their children, many millionaires' children today are proving successful in quite different fields to those in which their parents made their fortune.

What did the millionaries appreciate about their money? It emerged that the sense of *power* was what appealed the most, although it did not automatically follow that a possessor of wealth actually wielded this power. For some, the power was regarded as their own potential, and several millionaires simply enjoyed the 'accumulating' experience, building up their fortunes as high as they could. Hardly any rich person wanted to 'spend, spend, spend' and derive pleasure that way. One millionaire commented: 'One of the advantages of having money is that you don't have to think about it, you don't have to talk about it'. In other words, there are no worries about paying bills, or losing a job, or being a burden to others when old. Of course, a person need not be an actual millionaire to have such security or peace of mind.

### HOW TO MAKE YOUR MILLIONS
Not all the tales of fortune told by Vance Packard are 'rags to riches' stories, but he does give interesting insights into how some millionaires started on their particular golden roads.

Jack Simplot, 'the potato king of North America', began his career at the age of 15 by renting potato land from his father and feeding pigs a mash of discarded potatoes and barley. Jeno Paulucci, who made the pizza a national dish in America, began by selling vegetables, branching out into the Chinese food business before he was 22. Melvin Simon, famous for his shopping malls, began his working life selling encyclopaedias and then pots and pans. Sarah Korein, possibly the richest self-made woman in America, and now the owner of much valuable real estate, including several prestigious skyscrapers, got into the real estate business by accident. She and her mother acquired a run-

### NO GO

The American film-producer Louis B. Mayer (1885–1957) is reputed to have been unimpressed by charity appeals. When someone tried to persuade him to be generous by pointing out: 'You can't take it with you when you go', Mayer replied: 'If I can't take it with me I won't go.'

## PERIOD OF PROSPERITY

Prosperity Classes seem to have enjoyed a vogue in America in the early part of the century. In *Elmer Gantry*, by Sinclair Lewis, the hero briefly becomes involved in running them: 'To one who had never made more than five thousand a year himself, it was inspiring to explain before dozens of pop-eyed and admiring morons how they could make ten thousand—fifty thousand—a million a year, and all this by the Wonder Power of Suggestion, by Aggressive Personality, by the Divine Rhythm, in fact by merely releasing the Inner Self-shine.

'It was fun, it was an orgy of imagination, for him who had never faced any Titan of Success of larger dimensions than the chairman of a local evangelistic committee to instruct a thirty-a-week book-keeper how to stalk into Morgan's office, fix him with the penetrating eye of the Initiate, and borrow a hundred thousand on the spot.

'His students were school-teachers who wanted to own tea-rooms, clerks who wanted to be sales-managers, clergymen who wanted to be real estate dealers, real estate dealers who wanted to be bishops, and widows who wanted to earn money without loss of elegance.

'He had a number of phrases—all stolen—and he made his disciples repeat them in chorus. Among the more powerful incantations were:
I can be whatever I will to be; I turn my opened eyes on my Self and possess whatever I desire.
I am God's child. God created all good things including wealth, and I will to inherit it.
I am resolute—I am utterly resolute—I fear no man, whether in offices or elsewhere.
Hold fast, O Subconscious, the thought of Prosperity.'

Unfortunately, the Prosperity Classes prove to be of little use to Elmer Gantry. He gets plenty of pupils, but they are by definition rather poor. Gantry himself is obliged to look prosperous at all times, advertise extensively, hire a classroom and stay in expensive hotels. He ends up having to borrow money from an acquaintance to get out of town.

down six-storey apartment block in New York and, with help from its owners, the Prudential Insurance Company, cleaned it out, spruced it up, painted the floors, and by shrewd pricing and careful advertizing turned it into a money-making proposition. Allen Paulson, now chairman of Gulfstream Aerospace Corporation, began his career as an aircraft mechanic. This developed from his interest in the planes at a nearby airport when he was milking cows in California.

## MILLIONAIRES IN BRITAIN

In Britain, the 'enterprise culture' of the 1980s, promoted so vigorously by Prime Minister Margaret Thatcher, saw the rise of several 'million-makers'. Many of them made their fortune by floating their companies on the Stock Market, while others became rich through a management buyout.

An example of the latter was Paul Judge, a divisional managing director at Cadbury Schweppes, the confectionary and soft drinks company. In 1985, in eight frantic days, Judge organized the buyout of the company's food manufacturing business and raised £97 million to fund the deal. The new company, named Premier Brands, prospered with Judge as chairman. In 1989, just four years later, Paul Judge's company was bought by Hillsdown Holdings for £195 million, and he himself walked away with about £40 million in shares.

One of the best-known British entrepreneurs of the 1980s was Anita **Roddick**, of The Body Shop. At the start of the decade she was barely known outside Brighton, where she ran a small herbal cosmetics and toiletries shop. In 1990, six years after her company was floated on the Stock Market, Body Shop soared to a record market value of more than £500 million, making it equal in value to Ratners, Dixons and W. H. Smith, with the shares hitting new highs almost every day in the last two months of 1989, when people were increasingly aware of 'green' issues. Yet in 1984, when first trading, Mrs Roddick's enterprise was worth just £2.3 million.

In the process Anita Roddick has made other people's fortunes as well. In 1977 Ian McGlinn, a Littlehampton garage owner, bought a 30 per cent stake in the Brighton Body Shop for £5000 when the banks refused to back its owner. By 1989, with a world network of more than 250 Body Shops, that same stake was worth £149 million!

The boom in buyouts of this type has resulted in a new type of millionaire in Britain: the one who sells a highly profitable business. The classic example is Fred Walker, who started up a small metal business in Lancashire in the late 1940s. Forty years on he sold the steel stockholding busi-

ness that it had become to British Steel, who paid £330 million for it. Fred's brother Jack, who used to run the company, earmarked some of these colossal proceeds to start up a new airline.

But few *millionaires nouveaux* can hope to match the success of Sir James **Goldsmith**, one of Britain's best-known businessmen. By buying up American companies from 1980, when he had perhaps £100 million to his name, he built up a fortune by the end of the decade of a staggering estimated £870 million.

### MILLIONAIRES WORLDWIDE

Worldwide, the figures relating to the fortunes of individual millionaires are of course subject to constant revision, but in 1989 the facts and figures were the following, as given in *The Guinness Book of Records 1990* and the *HMV Christmas 1989 Magazine*.

**"**─────────────────────────────────────────────

### THE POOR

*We are often told that the poor are grateful for charity. Some of them are, no doubt, but the best among the poor are never grateful. They are ungrateful, discontented, disobedient, and rebellious. They are quite right to be so. Charity they feel to be a ridiculously inadequate mode of partial restitution, or a sentimental dole, usually accompanied by some impertinent attempt on the part of the sentimentalist to tyrannise over their private lives. Why should they be grateful for the crumbs that fall from the rich man's table? They should be seated at the board, and are beginning to know it.*

*As for being discontented, a man who would not be discontented with such surroundings, and such a low mode of life would be a perfect brute. Disobedience, in the eyes of anyone who has read history, is man's original virtue. It is through disobedience that*

*progress has been made, through disobedience and through rebellion. Sometimes the poor are praised for being thrifty. But to recommend thrift to the poor is both grotesque and insulting. It is like advising a man who is starving to eat less. For a town or country labourer to practise thrift would be absolutely immoral. Man should not be ready to show that he can live like a badly fed animal. He should decline to live like that, and should either steal or go on the rates, which is considered by many to be a form of stealing. As for begging, it is safer to beg than to take, but it is finer to take than to beg. No, a poor man who is ungrateful, unthrifty, discontented and rebellious, is probably a real personality, and has much in him.*

Oscar Wilde *The Soul of Man Under Socialism*

─────────────────────────────────────────── **"**

## PRIVATE INCOME

According to Calouste Gulbenkian, 'Mr Five Per Cent' of the oil industry: 'The most precious thing money can buy is privacy'.

The **richest man in the world** is estimated to be Yoshiaki Tsutsumi, Japanese chairman of the Seibu group, with assets of $18 900 million. However, on his own evidence, the world's richest man is the Bahrain-born oil magnate and former United Arab Emirates ambassador to London, Mohamed Mahdi al-Tajir. Despite his boasts to the media, few details are known about al-Tajir's life or the extent of his wealth, and neither *Forbes* nor *Fortune*, the two American magazines that list the world's richest people, has managed to pin him down. He thus appears on no lists of millionaires.

The **richest man in the United States** is Ronald Perelman of New York City, with a personal fortune of $5 billion.

The **richest man in Britain** is reputed to be the 6th Duke of Westminster, whose assets in April 1989 were estimated at £3.2 billion.

The **richest woman in the world** is Her Majesty Queen Elizabeth II, whose fortune from two main sources, land and art treasures, is estimated to be £5300 million. The Crown lands produce approximately £45 million a year, all of which the monarch is entitled to retain. However, the Queen turns every penny of this over to the Exchequer in return for a quarter of that amount for the Civil List expenses (see below).

The **richest woman in Britain** after HM the Queen is landowner Hon. Charlotte Morrison, who became a millionairess at the age of 15 on the death of her father, Viscount Galway. Her fortune is put at £55 million.

The **richest family in the world** is believed to be that of the du Ponts, who originally came to the USA from France in 1800. Their 1500 members may have assets in the order of $150 000 million.

The **highest paid star** in the entertainment world is the singer Michael Jackson, whose income for 1988/89 was £76 million.

The **highest-earning actor in the world** is the American Bill Cosby, who in 1988/89 had an income of £58 million.

The **highest-earning actress in the world** is the American movie star Jane Fonda, who in 1988/89 made £14 million.

The world's **highest-earning rock group** is the British band Pink Floyd, who netted £35 million in 1988/89.

## MAKING THE GRADE

The Lambton-Lufford Report on Love is described in *Room at the Top*, by John Braine. It has little to do with love, being instead a 'grading scheme for women'. Joe Lampton and his friend Charles Lufford profess to have 'noticed that the more money a man had, the better looking was his wife'. A Grade One man, at millionaire level, would theoretically attract a Grade One wife; a Grade Twelve man, earning almost nothing and with no prospects, could only aspire to a Grade Twelve woman in terms of her looks and intelligence.

Braine comments that if a Grade Seven man found himself with a Grade Three wife, he would either lose her to a Grade Three lover or be forced to endure her complaints about their low standard of living for the rest of his life. A man who married a Grade Ten wife, but then became rich later in life to end up as Grade Three or above, would generally get himself a Grade Three mistress.

Braine's novel was published in 1957. If he was subsequently attacked by enraged feminists, he no doubt argued that his grading scheme could be reversed and applied to those men who were the partners or husbands of successful career women.

The **sportsman** with the highest income in the world is the boxer Mike Tyson, who in 1988/89 made £42 million.

The **highest paid novelist in the world** is the American horror story writer Stephen King, who in 1988/89 earned £12 million. In 1988 it was reported that he had scooped a £26 million advance for his next four books.

If profits from dividends (income as interest on stocks and shares held) is counted as 'salary', however, the picture will be different. In 1988/89, for example, Lord Sainsbury, head of the giant supermarket chain, earned £17 million on top of his basic salary of £180 000, making him Britain's highest-paid boss.

Outside industry, wealth can accrue in the world of entertainment. The hit show composer Andrew **Lloyd Webber**, for instance, who in 1987 was estimated to be earning the equivalent of $1 million a *week*, owes his millionaire status to his consistently successful musicals. In 1989 he had no less than four shows running simultaneously, and their accumulated UK box office takings then amounted to over £100 million: *Cats* (opened 1981), £43.7 million; *Starlight Express* (opened 1984), £40 million; *Phantom of the Opera* (opened 1986), £20.3 million; *Aspects of Love* (opened 1989), £5.6 million. This UK total of £109.6 million is modest, however, compared with a world box office total of £533.5 million since 1981: £387 million from *Cats*, £80 million from *Starlight Express*, and £66.5 million from *Phantom of the Opera*.

Apart from 'production figures' like these, statistics can also be produced to show who made his or her fortune in the shortest period of time, or whose income increased the most dramatically,

"

## UTOPIAN PUZZLEMENT

*The Utopians wonder how any man should be so much taken with the glaring doubtful lustre of a jewel or stone, that can look up to a star, or to the sun himself; or how any should value himself, because his cloth is made of a finer thread: for how fine soever that thread may be, it was once no better than the fleece of a sheep, and that sheep was a sheep still for all its wearing it.*

*They wonder much to hear that gold, which is in itself so useless a thing, should be everywhere so much esteemed, that even men for whom it was made, and by whom it has its value, should yet be thought of less value than it is: so that a man of lead, who has no more sense than a log of wood, and is as bad as he is foolish, should have many wise and good men serving him, only because he has a great heap of that metal; and if it should*

*so happen, that by some accident, or trick of law, (which does sometimes produce as great changes as chance itself) all this wealth should pass from the master to the meanest varlet of his whole family, he himself would very soon become one of his servants, as if he were a thing that belonged to his wealth, and so were bound to follow its fortune.*

*But they do much more admire and detest their folly, who when they see a rich man, though they neither owe him anything, nor are in any sort obnoxious to him, yet merely because he is rich, they give him little less than Divine honours; even though they know him to be so covetous and base-minded that notwithstanding all his wealth, he will not part with one farthing of it to them as long as he lives.*

Sir Thomas More *Utopia* (1516)

"

## EUROPE'S RICHEST WOMEN

The following list of the 20 richest women in Europe was published in the January 1990 number of *Harpers & Queen* magazine:

1. Queen Elizabeth II: £5090 million
2. Queen Beatrix of The Netherlands: £2800 million
3. Johanna Quandt, controls 60 per cent of BMW (German car firm): £2100 million
4. Grete Schickedanz, owner of Quelle (German mail order company): £1200 million
5. Liliane Bettencourt, L'Oréal heiress (French cosmetics company): £990 million
6. Madeleine Dassault, owner of 49.7 per cent of Avions Dassault (French military aircraft company)): £630 million
7. Athina Onassis-Roussel, Onassis heiress: £500 million
8. Alicia Koplowitz, ConyCon heiress (property and investment company): £375 million
9. Esther Koplowitz, sister of Alicia (above): £375 million
10. Janni Spies-Kjaer, owner of Spies Rejser (Danish package tours): £330 million
11. Ida Gardini, wife of owner of Ferlin (Europe's biggest grain trader): £310 million
12. Giuliana Benetton, part owner of Benetton (knitwear) chain: £210 million
13. Märtha Philipson: £200 million
14. The Duchess of Alba: £100 million*
15. Eva Larsson, Swedish property heiress: £95 million
16. Odile Recamier, wife of Henri Vuitton (French luggage company): £90 million
17. Hon. Charlotte Morrison, English property heiress: £55 million
18. Isabel Preysier, wife of banker Miguel Boyer: £53 million
19. Lady Anne Cavendish-Bentinck, property heiress: £52 million
20. Lady Shirley Porter, Tesco heiress: £50 million.

*Before her execution (and that of her husband) in December 1989, the 14th place was held by Elena Ceaușescu, wife of former Romanian president Nicolae Ceaușescu.

from the modest to the munificent. One contender for this 'get rich quick' category is the pop singer Madonna. In 1989 she was making the equivalent of £7 million a year from Warner Brother Records. But in 1980 she was earning just £9 an hour as a nude model.

## THE CIVIL LIST

Although a figure for the fortune of HM the Queen, as cited above, is not widely quoted, there are other statistics that are easier to obtain. These are the amounts published every year in the **Civil List**, as the annuity payable not only to the Queen but to individual members of the royal family. The payment, from public funds, is for the maintenance of the royal household and family. Far from being purely a 'personal income', it is intended to cover the salaries of the household staff, as well as travel, entertaining and public engagements at home and abroad.

For 1990 the Civil List was fixed at a total of £6 762 000, allocated as follows:

| | |
|---|---|
| Queen Elizabeth II | £5 090 000 |
| Queen Elizabeth The Queen Mother | £439 500 |
| The Duke of Edinburgh | £245 000 |
| Prince Andrew, Duke of York | £169 000 |
| Prince Edward | £20 000 |
| Princess Anne, The Princess Royal | £154 500 |
| Princess Margaret | £148 500 |
| Princess Alice, Duchess of Gloucester | £60 500 |
| Duke of Gloucester | £119 500 |
| Duke of Kent | £161 500 |
| Princess Alexandra | £154 000 |

The last three members of the royal family are not specifically provided for by Parliament, but since 1976 the Queen has refunded to the Exchequer the sums made available for them out of public funds, paying any shortfall herself. For 1989 she refunded a total of £400 100.

## EARNING POWER

In Britain in 1989, the yearly national average earnings of a man were £14 014; those of a woman £9480. Amongst those earning rather more than the national average, according to a report in the *Observer* newspaper (10.12.89) were Christopher Heath, managing director of Baring Securities (£1 339 000); Lord Hanson, founder and chairman of Hanson, a holding company for many UK and US companies (£1 239 000); Peter Starmonth Darling, chairman of Mercury Assets Management (£1 051 000); Tiny Rowland, chief executive of Lonrho, a holding company (£1 015 000).

The professions were able to offer relatively rich rewards. Senior partners in firms of solicitors and accountants were thought to be earning £500 000, for instance. A high-court judge was on £72 000, a top research scientist in industry on £50 000. The head-master of an exclusive public school was earning £40 000. Amongst the tradesmen, a skilled North Sea oil rig worker could earn £42 000.

Those earning well below the national average included gardeners and groundsmen, hospital porters, barmen, farm workers, hotel workers, library assistants, cleaners, kitchen hands, shop assistants, hairdressers. Those doing such jobs in regions outside London earned even less, especially if they lived in the North of England or Scotland. The lowest-paid workers were earning between £5000–6000 a year.

The comparative earning situation changes slightly each year as annual increases are awarded. Between 1979 and 1989 there had been an average increase in salaries of 165 per cent for those working in the public sector. Teachers in further education, ambulancemen and prison officers were amongst those whose increased earnings during the ten-year period had fallen below the national average. Government ministers and MPs, however, would have been able to point out that their own increases were also well below the national average.

Comparisons between British salaries and those for roughly equivalent jobs in other countries (which perhaps mean relatively little without a full-scale comparison of how much it costs to live in each country), revealed that the average earnings of British businessmen, at all levels, were below those of Belgium, France, The Netherlands, West Germany, Spain and Italy.

## TOP EARNERS

More realistic as true salaries are the annual payments made to politicians and other persons in government service, as well as church dignitaries.

In 1989, the ministerial salaries for the chief British political appointments were as follows:

| | |
|---|---|
| Prime Minister | £34 479 |
| Chancellor of the Exchequer | £34 479 |
| Secretary of State | £34 479 |
| Minister of State (House of Lords) | £37 047 |
| Minister of State (House of Commons) | £24 209 |
| Parliamentary Under Secretary | £18 219 |

The Prime Minister, Margaret Thatcher, is in fact entitled to a salary of £46 109, but since 1980 she has drawn the same salary as a Cabinet Minister.

The regular salary for a Member of Parliament in 1989 was £24 107. (In 1911, when MPs first received payments, the rate was £400.) Cabinet Ministers who were also MPs received a reduced salary of £18 148 in addition to their ministerial salary.

Apart from this basic salary, MPs are also entitled to additional allowances. The most common as are as follows (in brackets, the equivalent rate in the year of introduction):

1. For secretarial and research expenses, now known as the Office Costs Allowance, MPs were receiving £22 588 in 1988 (1969, £500).

## TOP PAID AMERICAN BUSINESS EXECUTIVES IN 1988

The following business executives earned $1 million or more in 1988:

| | |
|---|---|
| Mike Eisner, Chairman, Walt Disney Co. | $40.1 million |
| Ed Horrigan, Vice Chairman, RJR Nabisco | $21.7 million |
| Ross Johnson, Chief Executive Officer, RJR Nabisco | $21.1 million |
| Martin Davis, Chairman, Gulf + Western | $16.3 million |
| Hugh Liedtke, Chairman, Pennzoil | $11.5 million |
| Paul Fireman, Chairman, Reebok International | $11.4 million |
| Ken Olsen, Chairman, Digital Equipment Corp. | $10.0 million |
| Don Petersen, Chairman, Ford Motor Co. | $9.9 million |
| John Sculley, Chairman, Apple Computer Inc. | $9.5 million |
| Phil Rooney, President, Waste Management | $7.5 million |
| Roy Vagelos, Chairman, Merck & Co. | $6.9 million |
| Roger Smith, Chairman, General Motors Corp. | $3.8 million |
| Lee Iacocca, Chairman, Chrysler Corp. | $3.7 million |
| Jack Welch, Chairman, General Electric Co. | $2.4 million |
| Lawrence Rawl, Chairman, Exxon Corp. | $1.4 million |

[Source: *World Almanac and Book of Facts 1990*, quoting *Business Weekly*]

2. For the cost of staying overnight away from their main residence when on parliamentary business, MPs were able to claim a reimbursement of £9298 in 1988, tax free since 1984 (1972, £750).
3. MPs receiving the Office Costs Allowance could claim, in 1989, an additional sum of £24 903 in order to contribute to a pension scheme for the person or persons they employ as secretaries or researchers (1980, £786).
4. For travel by car, rail or air, MPs can claim a further allowance. In 1988/89 MPs' claims were as follows: car mileage £3 954 898, rail travel £632 051, spouse/children travel £395 451, and secretarial travel £205 458. For extended travel within the UK, MPs can make additional claims and in the year stated these totalled £72 949.

So overall, an average MP can earn not far short of £100 000 a year, even though almost half of this will go on the salary and pension contributions of his staff. (Yet in 1990, House of Commons secretaries were claiming salary increases of up to 100 per cent, on the grounds that they were underpaid for their work. Their salary scales varied at the time of the claim from only £7000 a year to £22 500, with 37 per cent earning under £12 000 a year. This compared with Civil Service senior secretaries, their equivalent, who earned £15 953 a year.)

## THE DANGEROUS LUXURY

In *The Innocents Abroad*, Mark Twain humorously discussed the situation of the wealthy in Morocco, which he visited in the 1860s:

'There is no regular system of taxation, but when the Emperor or the Bashaw want money, they levy on some rich man, and he has to furnish the cash or go to prison. Therefore few men in Morocco dare to be rich. It is too dangerous a luxury. Vanity occasionally leads a man to display wealth, but sooner or later the Emperor trumps up a charge against him—any sort of one will do—and confiscates his property. Of course, there are many rich men in the empire, but their money is buried, and they dress in rags and counterfeit poverty. Every now and then the Emperor imprisons a man who is suspected of the crime of being rich, and makes things so uncomfortable for him that he is forced to discover where he has hidden his money.

At the very top of the Civil Service, the Secretary to the Cabinet and Head of the Home Civil Service was earning an annual salary of £95 750 in 1990, with this figure also that of the highest ranks in the armed forces, respectively Field Marshal, Admiral of the Fleet and Marshal of the RAF. The Lord Chief Justice of England, who in this same year was earning £94 870, will move up to the higher scale in 1991.

By comparison, the annual salaries in 1989 for other professional posts and appointments were as follows:

Chairman, British Rail . . . . . . . . . . . . . . £92 691
Lord High Chancellor . . . . . . . . . . . . . . £91 500
Master of the Rolls . . . . . . . . . . . . . . . . £82 750
Clerk of the House of Commons . . . . . . . £72 000
Director-General, British Council . . . . . . £62 750
Speaker of the House of Commons . . . . . £54 357

Commissioner, City of London Police . . . £52 629
HM Chief Inspector of Prisons . . . . . . . . £48 100
Director, Tate Gallery . . . . . . . . . . . . . . £45 400
Director, National Gallery . . . . . . . . . . . £45 100
Chairman, BBC . . . . . . . . . . . . . . . . . . £37 360
Archbishop of Canterbury . . . . . . . . . . . £34 130
Chairman, Broadcasting Standards
 Council . . . . . . . . . . . . . . . . . . . . . . . £30 000
Archbishop of York . . . . . . . . . . . . . . . . £29 800
Bishop of London . . . . . . . . . . . . . . . . . £27 710
Bishop of Durham . . . . . . . . . . . . . . . . . £24 360
Bishop of Winchester . . . . . . . . . . . . . . £20 170

Against this, a consultant in the National Health Service was paid a maximum £43 075 in 1990, and a head teacher at the top of the scale, £36 573. Minimum pay for a student nurse this same year was £5800, and for a teacher, £9000.

 **EPITAPH ON A RICH MAN**

Francis Chartres (1675–1732) was mentioned by Alexander Pope in his *Epistle to Bathurst* and described by the poet in a footnote as follows: 'A man infamous for all manner of vices. After a hundred tricks at the gaming-tables, he took to lending of money at exorbitant interest and on great penalties, accumulating premium, interest, and capital into a new capital, and seizing to a minute when the payments became due; in a word, by a constant attention to the vices, wants, and follies of mankind, he acquired an immense fortune. The populace at his funeral rais'd a great riot, almost tore the body out of the coffin, and cast dead dogs, etc., into the grave along with it.'

Pope's friend, Dr John Arbuthnot, wrote the following epitaph for Chartres:

HERE continueth to rot
The body of FRANCIS CHARTRES,
Who with an inflexible constancy,
and inimitable uniformity of life,
Persisted,
In spite of age and infirmities,
In the practice of every human vice;
Excepting prodigality and hypocrisy:
His insatiable avarice exempted him from the
first,
His matchless impudence from the second.
Nor was he more singular
in the undeviating pravity of his manners
Than successful
In accumulating wealth.
For, without trade or profession,
Without trust of public money,
And without bribe-worthy service,
He acquired, or more properly created,
A ministerial estate.
He was the only person of his time,
Who cou'd cheat without the mask of honesty,
Retain his primeval meanness
When possess'd of ten thousand a year.
Oh, indignant reader!
Think not his life was useless to mankind!
Providence conniv'd at his execrable designs,
To give to after-ages
A conspicuous proof and example,
Of how small estimation is exorbitant wealth
in the sight of God,
By his bestowing it on the most unworthy of
All mortals.

## MRS McMAMMON

*Modern Types* (1955), by Geoffrey Gorer and Ronald Searle, wittily described some of the types of people one might encounter socially and professionally. Mrs McMammon was the name given to the woman whose husband 'suddenly made all that money during and immediately after the war'. The McMammons decided to swap their small terraced house for a 'really posh residence standing in its own grounds in a very nice neighbourhood', but their new neighbours treat them as if they 'were something the cat brought in'.

The Mrs McMammon sketch highlights the very real problems that can be faced by a working-class family who acquire enough money to live in a decidedly middle-class area. Such a family may be unable, or may not wish, to ape the behaviour of their new neighbours. If their children are young enough to adapt while the parents are not, problems may arise within the family.

The theme of the social problems that can accompany sudden wealth, when the recipient is working-class, was also explored amusingly by H. G. Wells in *Kipps* (1905).

## SUDDEN MONEY

There are obviously several ways in which an ordinary person can suddenly find himself or herself 'in the money' and so become a millionaire.

A popular ambition is to win a vast sum of money by gambling or betting, for example on the football pools, in a state lottery or in horse racing. there is even the 'jackpot' in a 'fruit machine'.

The biggest **pools winner** in Britain to date is a Witney, Oxfordshire man, a plumber earning £300 a week, who in January 1990 hit the jackpot and won £1 505 443 from Littlewoods Pools. This compares with the winning dividend of £2 12s 0d which the same firm paid out in their first week in February 1923. On the state-run Italian pools, however, two unnamed individuals won the equi-

valent of about £1.5 million each as long ago as November 1972.

The biggest individual **gambling win** is that of $40 million, which Mike Wittkowski netted in the Illinois State Lottery in 1984. He and his family had bought just $35 worth of 'Lotto' tickets, and his winning six numbers brought him $2 million for the next 20 years.

The greatest **horse-racing payout** to date is $1 627 084.40c, won in April 1987 on a $64 nine-horse accumulator at Santa Anita Racecourse, California, by two Britons, Anthony A. Speelman and Nicholas John Cowan. This sum, moreover, was the amount that remained *after* federal income tax of $406 760.00c had been withheld.

The biggest **slot machine or 'one-armed bandit' win** so far is $6 814 823.48c, which went to Cammie Brewer at the Club Cal-Neva, Reno, Nevada, on 14 February 1988, a real 'Valentine' Day Massacre' of a victory by man over machine.

Gambling is hazardous, however, and a big win could just as easily be a huge loss. Sometimes one person's inadvertent loss can mean another person's fortuitous gain. This happened in January 1990 to a young London surveyor, Martin Ritchie, who walking in the City of London one day found

## EL DORADO

El Dorado, or Eldorado as it is sometimes written, now refers to any place where money is easily acquired. Originally the phrase was applied to the reputed king of Manoa, supposedly a city of enormous wealth which existed somewhere in the northern part of South America. This king was said to be periodically smeared with oil or balsam, then covered with gold dust so that he became 'the gilded one' (*El Dorado* in Spanish).

The epithet was transferred to the city which he ruled, and many expeditions set out from Spain and England in the 16th century, intent on finding it. Two of them were led by Sir Walter Raleigh. The explorers penetrated into vast tracts of unknown territory, but the fabled city of El Dorado was never found.

bonds worth £4 million lying in the gutter outside the Stock Exchange. The bonds, in the form of four certificates of deposit worth £1 million each, had fallen from the briefcase of a messenger employed by a merchant banker. With commendable honesty, Mr Ritchie contacted the company to tell them of his find. When a messenger arrived to collect the precious documents, he handed Mr Ritchie a magnum of champagne as a token of gratitude. For half an hour, Martin Ritchie had been a multimillionaire, able to forget about his trifling £2500 overdraft.

Another way in which a person may suddenly gain a large sum of money is by a legal award, notably one of damages.

The highest award of **damages for personal injury** is $78 million, made in September 1987 to a 26-year-old model, Maria Hanson, whose face had been slashed with razors in Manhattan three months earlier.

The highest award of **damages for defamation** is $16 800 000, made in November 1972 to Dr John J. Wild at the Hennepin district Court, Minnesota, against the Minnesota Foundation and others. In Britain, the greatest **damages for libel** is £1.5 million, awarded in the High Court, London, in 1989 to Lord Aldington, a former Conservative Party chairman, against Count Nikolai Tolstoy and Nigel Watts, who had accused him of war crimes. *The Times*, disapprovingly, described the award as 'so manifestly extravagant that it has brought the law into disrepute'.

Tragic instances of **damages for negligence** have also been made in record sums. In 1989 a 10-year-old British girl was awarded £1 002 799 by the High Court for brain damage caused by an error on the part of hospital doctors during an operation.

## MONEY IN ART

The buying power of millionaires is often breathtakingly revealed in the art world, where works by famous painters are sold at auction for millions of pounds (or dollars). The auction record to date is the $53.9 million paid in November 1987 for Van Gogh's *Irises*, the unidentified buyer bidding by telephone from Europe to Sotheby's in New York. This record was equalled in 1989, when Picasso's *Les Noces de Pierrette* was sold for

the same amount in Paris. Meanwhile, 1987 was something of a 'millionaire's year' in the world's auction rooms, for in April Sotheby's in Geneva sold the Duchess of Windsor's jewels for £31 380 197, approximately five times their ordinary retail value as jewels.

Increasingly, bids for works of art of this type are made by telephone, the calls being taken by a bidder who, sitting in the actual auction room, may pass on bids of £1 million a time. But the bidder's own salary does not rise in proportion to the bids executed: it stays at a fixed £150 a week!

The art saleroom operates in a rarefied atmosphere, dominated by wealthy connoisseurs. Once in a while the sale of an unsuspected 'treasure' by an ordinary person can result in overnight riches and the status of 'instant millionaire'. It is, after all, many people's dream to find a priceless painting hidden away in the attic, or a unique manuscript tucked between the pages of a shabby secondhand book.

One example of the dream come true occurred in 1989. A statue of a dancing faun which had stood in an elderly couple's garden for 40 years, having been bought by them for about £100 in the 1950s, was recognized by an art expert as a bronze original by the 16th-century Dutch-born sculptor Adrien de Vries. It was auctioned by Sotheby's in London, and fetched a staggering £6.8 million, breaking all records for sculpture.

For the changing values of works of art sold at auction in the 1980s, see Chapter 13, p. 168.

There is thus a popular common equation, working both for the connoisseur and (as we shall see in the next chapter) the criminal, that 'Art means Money'.

 **COUNTING IT OUT**

If a millionaire had nothing better to do, he could amuse himself by counting out his money. At the rate of one pound or dollar a second, it would take him 277 hours to count his million, or nearly seven normal five-day weeks, working non-stop, eight hours a day.

## IMAGINARY MILLIONAIRES

Many countries have a state lottery, by means of which an individual may become a millionaire overnight. Britain has its Premium Bond scheme, where investors are gambling with the interest their money might otherwise earn, but are not risking the principal.

In his *Everyday Book* (1826–7), William Hone discussed lotteries and raffles at some length. Of the 18th century he said that 'the rage for lotteries reigned uncontrolled'. The prizes were either money or goods. Hone even quotes an advertisement which appeared in a Calcutta newspaper on 8 September, 1818: 'Be it known, that six fair pretty young ladies, with two sweet and engaging young children, lately imported from Europe, having roses of health blooming on their cheeks, and joy sparkling in their eyes, are to be raffled for next door to the British gallery . . .'

Hone's collection of lottery anecdotes includes the tale of a footman in the reign of George II who invested his life-savings in two lottery tickets. Because of a dream, he was convinced that he would win the £5000 prize:

'As soon as I have received the money, I will marry Grace Towers; but, as she has been cross and coy, I will use her as a servant. Every morning she shall get me a mug of strong beer, with a toast, nutmeg, and sugar in it; then I will sleep till ten. My dinner shall be on table by one, and never without a good pudding. I will have a stock of wine and brandy laid in. About five in the afternoon I will have tarts and jellies, and a gallon bowl of punch; at ten, a hot supper of two dishes. If I am in a good humour, and Grace behaves herself, she shall sit down with me. To bed about twelve.'

Unfortunately for the footman, he drew two blank tickets. Hone reports that 'after a few melancholy days, he put an end to his life'. His plan for disposing of his winnings was found in his room.

Lotteries were popular at all levels of society,

and were permitted at the great public schools. In *Tom Brown's Schooldays*, published in 1857 but describing school life at an earlier period, Thomas Hughes comments at one point: 'The next morning was Saturday, the day on which the allowances of one shilling a week were paid, an important event to spendthrift youngsters; and great was the disgust amongst the small fry to hear that the allowances had been impounded for the Derby lottery. That great event in the English year, the Derby, was celebrated at Rugby in those days by many lotteries. It was not an improving custom, I own, gentle reader, and led to making books and betting and other objectionable results; but when our great Houses of Palaver think it right to stop the nation's business on that day, and many of them bet heavily themselves, can you blame us boys for following the example of our betters?'

The reference to the 'Houses of Palaver' is to the British Houses of Parliament, which until 1891 used to suspend business on Derby Day to allow members to go to the races.

Hone quotes from Henry Fielding's farce *The Lottery*, produced at the Drury Lane theatre in 1731, and prints a poem which appeared anonymously in 1761. The latter includes the verses:

> With hope to gain TEN THOUSAND
>   POUND,
> How many post to ruin,
> And for an empty, airy sound
> Contrive their own undoing.
>
> Unmoved by Fortune's fickle wheel,
> The wise man chance despises;
> And Prudence courts with fervent zeal—
> She gives the highest prizes.

Against this plea for prudence one should perhaps put the remark of Doolittle in G. B. Shaw's *Pygmalion*: 'Ten pounds is a lot of money: it makes a man feel prudent like; and then goodbye to happiness.'

Charles Lamb, commenting on the last State Lottery in England, held in 1826, showed that he understood the lottery's appeal: 'The true mental epicure always purchased his ticket early, and postponed enquiry into its fate to the last possible moment, during the whole of which intervening period he had an imaginary twenty thousand locked up in his desk—and was not this well worth all the money?' The millions of people who hold Premium Bonds, or complete their Football Pools coupons every week—the imaginary millionaires of the present day—would no doubt answer Lamb's question with a resounding 'Yes'.

## MONEY IS . . .

'Money is better than poverty, if only for financial reasons.'
Woody Allen

'Money is always on the brain so long as there is a brain in reasonable order.'
Samuel Butler

'Money is a terrible master but an excellent servant.'
P. T. Barnum

'Money is what you'd get on beautifully without if only other people weren't so crazy about it.'
Margaret Case Harriman

'Money is flat and meant to be piled up.'
Scottish proverb

'Money is round and meant to roll.'
English proverb

'Money is honey, my little sonny, And a rich man's joke is always funny.'
T. E. Brown

'Money is indeed the most important thing in the world. Every teacher or twaddler who denies it or suppresses it, is an enemy of life. Money controls morality.'
G. B. Shaw

'Money is a good thing to have. It frees you from doing things you dislike. Since I dislike doing nearly everything, money is handy.'
Groucho Marx

'One can do nothing—be nothing, without money, not even in the White House. Money is power.'
G. B. Means

## THE BOOBY PRIZE?

*It is impossible to ignore the role of women throughout the past of mankind as prizes, incentives and rewards. They have always fallen into that role with extreme readiness, accepted the jewels and dresses and played the hostess queen to the triumphant robber.*

*Through the long ages of insufficiency, women have always been the demure receivers of the captured joys and displays of life.*

H. G. Wells *The Work, Wealth and Happiness of Mankind* (1932)

# 12

# FILTHY LUCRE

## FRAUDS AND FIDDLES

Just as there are certain ways, by good luck or good management, in which money can be made, so there are several ways in which it can be lost. One can be robbed, for example, or be declared bankrupt. One can be cheated or conned into parting with ones money, even a whole life's savings.

People who steal money or engage in some ingenious financial deception or 'fiddle' are frequently exposed and brought to justice, so that they subsequently pay the price. Others evade justice, and escape with their robbery or fraud. Either way, enormous sums of money can be involved.

Here are some examples of noteworthy cases in the different categories.

### ROBBERIES

**Robberies** involving large sums of money never fail to hit the headlines. The greatest robbery on record, however, dates from over 40 years ago, and involved the theft from the German Reichsbank in 1945 of a sum which today would have a value of some £2500 million. The robbery, which took place following the collapse of Germany at the end of World War II, is described in detail in Ian Sayer and Douglas Botting's book *Nazi Gold*, published in 1984.

Recent robberies have been more modest, but in some cases more spectacular. In May 1990, a robber snatched a briefcase containing nearly

**"**

### THE WORST EVIL

'Of evils current upon earth,
The worst is money. Money 'tis that sacks
Cities, and drives men forth from hearth and home:
Warps and seduces native innocence,
And breeds a habit of dishonesty.'

Sophocles *Antigone* (translated by F. Storr)

**"**

**"**————————————————————————————

### THE GREATEST LOSS?

'A man can stand being told that he must submit to a severe surgical operation, or that he has some disease which will shortly kill him, or that he will be a cripple or blind for the rest of his life; dreadful as such tidings must be, we do not find that they unnerve the greater number of mankind; most men, indeed, go coolly enough even to be hanged, but the strongest quail before financial ruin, and the better men they are, the more complete, as a general rule, is their prostration.

'Suicide is a common consequence of money losses; it is rarely sought as a means of escape from bodily suffering. If we feel that we can die warm and quietly in our beds, with no need to worry about expense, we live our lives out to the dregs, no matter how excrutiating our torments.

'Loss of money indeed is not only the worst pain in itself, but it is the parent of all others. Let a man's money be suddenly taken from him, and how long is his health likely to survive the change in all his little ways which loss of money will entail? How long is the esteem and sympathy of friends likely to survive ruin? People may be very sorry for us, but their attitude towards us hitherto has been based upon the supposition that we were situated thus or thus in money matters; when this breaks down there must be a restatement of the social problem so far as we are concerned; we have been obtaining esteem under false pretences. The three most serious losses which a man can suffer are those affecting money, health, and reputation. Loss of money is far the worst.'

Samuel Butler *The Way of all Flesh*

————————————————————————**"**

£292 million in negotiable bonds from a City of London messenger. However, the opportunist had small chance of making anything from his crime, once the Bank of England had warned City dealers. Even so, the mugger's action instantly wiped almost £300 million from the City's money market liquidity. This obliged the Bank of England to step in with £300 million of aid to help the market avoid problems for the owners of the bonds, as well as eliminate any risk that the shortage would increase overnight lending rates in the money markets.

The biggest recorded **train robbery** took place in 1963, when in the early morning of 8 August a mail train from Glasgow to London was ambushed near Mentmore, Buckinghamshire, and mailbags containing over £2.6 million worth of bank notes were stolen. The notes were on their way to London for destruction. Of this huge haul, only £343 448 has ever been recovered.

### RANSOMS

**Ransoms** also make the news. The largest sum demanded by ransom in modern times is the 1500 million pesos for the release of the brothers Jorge and Juan Born, of Bunge and Born, paid to the guerrilla group Montoneros in Buenos Aires, Argentina, in June 1975. The largest **hijack ransom** actually paid is the $6 million demanded from the Japanese government by the hijackers of a Japanese Airlines DC-8 aircraft at Dacca Airport in 1977. The payment gained the release of 38 hostages and the exchange of six convicted criminals.

### ART THEFTS

There have been some notable thefts of world-famous paintings. Undoubtedly the art theft with the highest value was that of the *Mona Lisa* from the Louvre, Paris, in 1911. It was recovered two years later. It is impossible to put a figure on the robbery because the well-known portrait has never been valued. It was, however, assessed for insurance purposes at $100 million when it was taken from the Louvre to Washington, D.C. and New York for exhibition there in 1962.

On the other hand it is possible to put a value on the three paintings by Van Gogh that were stolen in 1988 from a museum in Otterlo, Netherlands. They were estimated to be worth between 100 and 150 million Dutch florins, or approximately £28 to £42 million sterling.

Jewels, too, are a traditional 'haul' for thieves. The greatest recorded **jewel theft** took place in 1980, when jewels valued at $16 million were stolen from the bedroom of the supposedly secure villa owned by Prince Abdul Aziz bin Ahmed Al-Thani near Cannes, France. In Britain, £6 million worth of jewels were stolen from a Conduit Street, London, jewellers in 1983.

## BANKRUPTCIES

To have money or valuables stolen is a real misfortune. Another is to lose any fortune made by becoming **bankrupt.**

Over the years, more than one famous person has become bankrupt.

One of the earliest bankrupts was Edward III, King of England in the 14th century. Not content with the English crown, Edward yearned to rule France, too. His overriding ambition led to the Hundred Years' War, and the only result of his endeavours to invade France from the north in 1339 and 1340 was to reduce him to bankruptcy for a total of £30 000, a huge amount in those days. Edward III was the first national ruler to go bankrupt in this way.

In the 19th century, one noted bankrupt was the American inventor Charles Goodyear, who discovered how to vulcanize rubber. He repeatedly engaged in patent litigation with his rivals, lost patents in England and France due to technicalities, and suffered heavy infringement in the United States. When he died, he left his family $200 000 in debt.

The well-known writer Mark Twain, author of such classics as *Tom Sawyer* and *Huckleberry Finn*, spent, and lost, around $500 000 on a wide range of inventions that included steam generators and marine telegraphs. His fatal decision, however,

## BEYOND THE GRAVE

Debt-collectors were even more persistent in former times than they are now. Mrs Henry Wood writes, in her novel *East Lynne* (1861): ' "There are those two men upstairs, in possession of—of him: I could not get rid of them." The peer looked at him. "I do not understand you." "Did you not know that they have seized the corpse?" asked Mr Carlyle, dropping his voice. "Two men have been posted over it, like sentinels, since yesterday morning. And there's a third in the house, I hear, who relieves each in turn, that they may go down to the hall and take their meals." ' "Mr Carlyle, do I understand you aright—that the body of the late earl has been seized for debt?" demanded the peer, solemnly. "Seize a dead body! Am I awake or dreaming?" '

Samuel Lover, in his *Handy Andy* (1842), has: 'Superadded to the dismay which the death of the head of a family produces was the terrible fear which existed that O'Grady's body would be seized for debt—a barbarous practice which, shame to say, is still permitted.'

was to invest in the Paige typesetting machine rather than Alexander Graham Bell's telephone company. Twain backed the machine with $250 000, but the device actually complicated the printing process, rather than making it easier. In 1894 Twain's losses obliged him to declare bankruptcy.

Artists have often had to endure poverty and extreme financial insecurity. The 19th-century American painter James Abbott McNeill Whistler was no exception. He frequently had to borrow money or pawn his paintings to pay his debts. Eccentrically, when a debt collector came to sequester an item of furniture in lieu of payment, Whistler would simply paint a picture of the missing item and place it where the piece of furniture had stood. Such devices could not indefinitely postpone the inevitable, and in 1879 Whistler became bankrupt with debts of $10 000.

Phineas Taylor Barnum, the famous American showman, initially made millions exhibiting the

## BUSINESS INTERESTS

Ralph Salerno, an authority on American crime, once remarked that of all illegal activities, those of the loan-shark (or Shylock) are the most profitable. Unlike a legitimate banker he has no expensive premises to maintain, his record-keeping (in code, to make his transactions untraceable) is minimal, and he pays no taxes. His interest rates are probably ten times higher than those of the normal banker, so that his profits are enormous. His main business expense is the hiring of thugs to punish defaulters. He runs few risks and is rarely brought to court, since his customers are well aware of what is likely to happen to anyone who testifies against him.

dwarf Tom Thumb as well as other human freaks and wild animals. He frequently made unwise investments, however, and his poor financial sense resulted in a final humiliation in 1855, when he invested over $500 000 in the Jerome Clock Company, only to find himself the victim of a massive swindle. The loss plunged him into bankruptcy, and even caused him to consider suicide. He recovered, to open 'The Greatest Show on Earth' in Brooklyn in 1871 and to found Barnum and Bailey's Circus ten years later. Instructively, it was Barnum who allegedly said 'There's a sucker born every minute'.

In the 20th century, bankruptcies continued apace. In 1921, Walt Disney founded the Laugh-O-Gram Corporation in Kansas City with $15 000 from investors. Two years later he was forced to file for bankruptcy when his backers pulled out, and Disney left for Hollywood with all his worldly goods: a pair of trousers, a coat, a shirt, two sets of underwear, two pairs of socks, and a few salvaged drawing materials. The rest is history!

One other famous entertainer who 'went bust' was the popular American singer Eddie Fisher. In 1972, exactly 30 years after his career began in a Philadelphia radio show, Fisher was declared bankrupt in a federal court in San Juan, Puerto Rico, with debts totalling almost $1 million.

## OFFICIAL FORGERY

Counterfeiting has always been looked upon as a major crime. Individuals who forged bank notes were punished by hanging in Britain until 1821, yet the British government had earlier sanctioned forgery on a large scale. It deliberately brought into existence large quantities of counterfeit assignats, the paper money issued by the revolutionary government of France, in an attempt to undermine the Revolution. The American Revolution, for its part, is said to have begun with the official forgery of British banknotes.

During World War II a massive amount of official forgery occurred. The Germans produced British notes to the value of 140 million pounds, and probably as much again in US dollars. Britain and the USA were meanwhile printing vast amounts of counterfeit German marks.

In peacetime the US Secret Service published a book called *Know Your Money*. It gave precise details of how to detect a counterfeit banknote, listing the mistakes that forgers make. Mike Landress, a well-known counterfeiter, said that no forger should be without it. He added that a free copy could be obtained by writing to Washington.

Million-dollar debts are no joke, but Eddie Fisher's bankruptcy pales into insignificance beside that of Rajendra Sethia. An Indian-born British businessman, 35-year-old Sethia was arrested in New Delhi in 1985 on charges that included criminal conspiracy and forgery. He had been declared bankrupt by the High Court in London earlier that year when Esal Commodities was stated to be in debt for a record £170 million. Sethia's personal debts were estimated at £140 million, and his bankruptcy is to date the largest ever.

Not far behind Sethia is William G. Stern, a Hungarian-born American citizen who, at the same age of 35, set up the Wilstar Group Holding Company in the London property market in 1971.

In 1979 Stern was declared bankrupt for over £104 million, a figure that by 1983 had risen to nearly £143 million. He was discharged in the latter year for £500 000, suspended for 2½ years.

## FRAUD

**Fraud** is a financial crime that has an infamous record. Several instances involve the setting up of a bogus company with the aim of attracting wealthy investors and 'pocketing' their money.

One such case that came to light in the United States in 1984 was that of the firm of J. David & Co., who promised investors up to 40 per cent annual return on their money, tax free, and with complete confidentiality. The ostensible aim of the company was that of currency trading. Most of the money, however, went on the various personal activities of the company's founder, J. David Dominelli, who owned six houses, three jet aircraft, and over two dozen luxury cars. When investors began to get suspicious in 1983 and asked for their investments back, Dominelli's

## LOVE OFFERINGS

The American writer Sinclair Lewis clearly detested religious hypocrisy, which he attacked in several of his novels. In *Elmer Gantry* (1927) a professional discussion takes place between two successful evangelical preachers, Sharon Falconer and Dr Howard Bancock Binch. They talk of some of the tricks of the trade, and soon get round to a specific exchange of ideas about raising money.

'We tried a stunt that was new for us. We opened up on some of the worst dives and blind tigers by name. We even gave street numbers. The attack created a howling sensation; people just jammed in, hoping we'd attack other places. I believe that's a good policy.'

'There's a danger in that sort of thing, though,' said Dr Binch. 'I don't advise it. Trouble is, in such an attack you're liable to offend some of the leading church-members—the very folks who contribute the most cash to a revival. They're often the owners of buildings that get used by unscrupulous persons for immoral purposes, and while they of course regret such unfortunate use of their property, if you attack such places by name, you're likely to lose their support. Why, you might lose thousands of dollars! It seems to me wiser and more Christian to just attack vice in general.'

'How much orchestra do you use, Dr Binch?' asked Sharon. 'All I can get hold of. I find that

a good tune, sort of a nice, artistic, slow, sad one, puts folks into a mood where they'll come across both with their hearts and their contributions. By the way, speaking of that, what luck have you folks had recently in raising money? And what method do you use?'

'It's been pretty good with us', said Sharon. 'We're sticking to the idea of the free-will offering the last day. We can get more money than any town would be willing to guarantee beforehand. If the appeal for the free-will offering is made strong enough, we usually have pretty fair results.'

'Yes, I use the same method. But I don't like the term "free-will offering", or "thank-offering". It's been used so much by merely second-rate evangelists, who, and I grieve to say there are such people, put their own gain before the service of the Kingdom, that it's got a commercial sound. In making my own appeal for contributions, I use "love-offering".'

'That's worth thinking over, Dr Binch', sighed Sharon, 'but oh, how tragic it is that we, with our message of salvation, have to be practical and raise money for our expenses and charities. Oh, the world doesn't appreciate evangelists. Think what we can do for a resident minister! Those preachers who talk about conducting their own revivals make me sick! They don't know the right technique. Conducting revivals is a profession. One must know all the tricks.'

cheques bounced with increasing regularity. It was discovered that he had only $600000 in liquid assets to cover over $150 million in liabilities.

A particularly unpleasant type of fraud is one that involves deliberate murder. A life policy is taken out on a selected relation or business colleague, who is then 'disposed of' so that the beneficiary can claim the cash from the insurance company. Expensive policies of $100000 to $500000 are now common for this purpose in the United States, whereas in 1980 the norm was nearer $15000.

A case of this type occurred in 1982, when Craig Young, president and sole stockholder of a Montana finance company, was found shot dead on a road near Houston. The company was actually just a 'shell', controlled by a friend, Jack Dickie, who had offered Young the presidency on incorporation, and who through the company had purchased mining claims for $2.5 million on promissory notes signed by Young. Dickie advised Young to take out insurance to cover this liability, which he duly did. It turned out that the company from which the claims had been bought was another 'shell' set-up owned by Dickie. So when Young died, the $3 million insurance proceeds paid to his estate were required to pay off the promissory notes, thus filling the coffers of Dickie's second company. In 1987 Dickie was found guilty of procuring Young's murder in order to collect the insurance.

A similar plot with a domestic rather than a business background was the case of Linda Von Bergen, a Florida savings bank manager. She was covered by life insurance for $5.2 million, with her husband as beneficiary. In 1986, she drowned while on a fishing trip with her husband off the coast of Puerto Rico. The captain had been instructed to take the boat far out to sea, even though he had advised that the fishing there was poor. A passenger on the boat testified that Mrs Von Bergen had stumbled into him and that they had both fallen overboard. He had tried to save her, but had failed, he claimed. However, another witness stated in probate court that he had been offered $100000 by Mr Von Bergen to kill his wife on a cruise trip in a way that would make the death seem accidental. In the event, the suit was dropped before a judge could rule, and by way of settlement Mr Von Bergen transferred his rights as beneficiary to Mrs Von Bergen's father.

Both these cases were reported in the *Wall Street Journal* (Stanley Penn, 'Deadly Policies', 4 January 1988). Despite their recent occurrence the life policies and payouts mentioned here are not the largest that have been recorded. (See Chapter 13, p. 175.)

One recent fraud that affected hundreds of people was the £190 million collapse of the investment company Barlow Clowes International in May 1988. The firm's chairman, Peter Clowes, was arrested by City of London Fraud Squad officers in June that year on a charge of diverting up to £100 million of investors' money to finance his own personal business empire. Yet despite continuous pressure on the British government to recognize its moral responsibility towards the estimated 18000 investors who lost their savings, in many cases their life savings, only in December 1989 did it announce compensation, when it undertook to repay 90 per cent to those (the majority), who had invested up to £50000.

## GREENMAIL

Greenmail is less familiar than blackmail to the general public, but the term seems to have established itself in the financial world. *Chambers English Dictionary* defines it as: 'a form of business blackmail whereby a company buys a strategically significant block of shares in another company, sufficient to threaten takeover and thus to force the parent company to buy back the shares at a premium'.

### SECRET MONEY

Many people are secretive about the money they own, especially if the sum is sizeable and if it has been 'stashed' in some tax haven or quietly exported. There are several reasons why people should choose not to reveal information about their money, from the wealthy businessman fleeing creditors to the husband fleeing his wife to the politician fleeing unwelcome publicity. Although some such circumstances can be perfectly legal and

## " MAN'S ESTATE

'The education of Mr Jonas had been conducted from his cradle on the strictest principles of the main chance. The very first word he learned to spell was "gain", and the second (when he got into two syllables), "money". From his early habits of considering everything as a question of property, he had gradually come to look, with impatience, on his parent as a certain amount of personal estate, which had no right whatever to be going at large, but ought to be secured in that particular description of iron safe which is commonly called a coffin, and banked in the grave.'

Charles Dickens *Martin Chuzzlewit*

"

 THE STINKING RICH?

Lewis H. Lapham's book, *Money and Class in America: notes on the civil religion*, has some unkind things to say about the American rich. Mr Lapham thinks they are 'as sympathetic as lizards, as petulant as children and as rational as dervishes'. There are also too many of them, he says—over 70 000 Americans acknowledge to the taxman that they are dollar millionaires. The nastiest of all, it seems, are the old rich. They see themselves as perpetually under siege, which is why they have to stick closely together to protect themselves.

In a conversation with Mr Lapham (who himself came from an American old rich family but failed to inherit) for the *Observer* in May, 1989, Peter York made the point that Britain is becoming quite good 'at growing its own hordes of new rich people' who are rather nasty.

above board, there are others that involve a grey and murky world of tax evasion, slush funds and money laundering.

It is a well-known fact that many dictators, especially of developing countries, have long held secret assets abroad. Anastasio Somosa, the former dictator of Nicaragua, is reported to have exported at least $500 million before he was overthrown by the Sandinistas in 1979. Most of his money ended up in foreign accounts. Similarly, Emperor Haile Selassie was said to have more than $15 billion in foreign assets at the time of his death in 1975, including annual deposits in Switzerland of 500 kg 1102 lb of gold bullion, an amount that must have seriously strained the physical storage resources of the bank concerned.

When Jean-Claude ('Baby Doc') Duvalier and his family fled Haiti in 1986, sources reported that he had salted away in foreign accounts somewhere between $200 million and $500 million of his poor country's wealth, this being funds that he had accumulated since coming to office in 1971. He and his family simply treated Haiti and its public funds as if they were private, personal property.

A truly breathtaking example of this type is that of Ferdinand and Imelda **Marcos**, the former president of the Philippines and his wife. The Marcoses were flown out of the Philippines to Hawaii in 1986, when Mrs Cory Aquino's government came to power, travelling in two United states Air Force C-141 aircraft, the first transporting themselves, and the second their baggage, consisting of 22 crates of goods.

Customs authorities in Hawaii immediately impounded the goods and the US State Department subsequently released full details of their loot. It included $1.2 million in crisp new Philippine peso notes, two Philippine bank certificates of deposit valued at $1.8 million, $7.7 million in cash and valuables, including jewellery worth over $4 million, and papers listing assets held elsewhere. The latter included $88.7 million held in banks in the United States, Switzerland and the Cayman Islands, plus a further $35 million deposited but not yet credited. Later, back in the Marcoses' royal palace in the Philippines, further papers were found which indicated numerous other holdings, including 15 trusts, two with bond portfolios worth more than $15 million, two with cash of over $115 million, and one with stocks and shares worth more than some $65.5 million.

It was estimated that the total salted away by the Marcoses was probably in the order of $5 billion to $10 billion, figures which represented several times the Philippine national budget, which for 1985, for example, was $3.1 billion. Ironically, the official salary of Ferdinand Marcos as president was fixed at just $4700, and at the time when he and his wife fled the country, 70 per cent of Filipinos were living below the poverty standard, as opposed to 48 per cent when Marcos became president in 1965.

How did the Marcoses amass such a colossal fortune? The short answer is 'corruption', but a closer examination of events showed that Marcos had declared martial law and ruled by decree, enabling him to grant his friends monopolies to handle the country's traditional income-earning exports, such as coconuts, bananas and sugar.

## THE TWOPENNY GAME

Avarice, an inordinate greed for wealth, is one of the seven deadly sins, but Lord Byron once said: 'For a good old gentlemanly vice, I think I shall put up with avarice.' William Thackeray quoted this with seeming approval in one of his essays (*Autour de Mon Chapeau*), though he went on to equate avarice with saving small amounts of money by various means. 'If you play this game all through life it is wonderful what daily interest it has, and amusing occupation. For instance, my wife goes to sleep after dinner. As soon as the dear soul is sound asleep, I advance softly and puff out her candle. Her pure dreams will be all the happier without that light; and, say she sleeps an hour, there is a penny gained.' Thackeray's warning comes later in the essay: 'In this delightful, wholesome, ever-novel twopenny game, there is danger of excess, as there is in every other pastime or occupation of life. If you grow too eager for your twopence, the acquisition or the loss of it may affect your peace of mind, and peace of mind is better than any amount of twopences.'

## THE PHILANTHROPIC INDUSTRY

In *Gideon Planish*, Sinclair Lewis portrays a hypocritical character called Deacon Wheyfish who is a skilled money-raiser. His philosophy is that people need to be trained to give generously to charities in order 'to expand their own miserable, narrow peanut souls by the divine habit of giving'.

He tells a group of friends: 'Philanthropy, in hard dollars and cents, already ranks eighth among the major industries of America. But it ought to rank first. The philanthropic industry has been steadily increasing, but not because of any improving generosity or imagination among the great body of givers—not on your life! It's only because they've been scientifically coaxed to give—scientifically, mind you. The raising of funds must be a separate calling, with an infallible technique.'

Marcos was thus able to take a sizeable proportion of the profits for his personal account. He also benefited from the willingness of foreign banks to lend to the Philippines, resulting in the debts of the country rising from $2 billion to $25 billion in the 1970s.

Mrs Aquino's government has had an uphill task to make good the tremendous financial loss, and by mid-1988 had managed to recover only about $161.9 million of the country's exported wealth—nothing at all from the Marcos family. This same year, Marcos's associates denied reports that he had offered to return $5 billion acquired during his presidency if he was allowed to live in the Philippines. Marcos was still in exile in Hawaii when he died in 1989, aged 72.

### BRIBERY

**'Bribery'** is a word commonly linked to 'corruption', and there have been several instances of bribes being offered or made in commercial connections. One such bribery was the so called 'Bofors case' of 1986, when the Swedish arms manufacturer of this name was said to have bribed Indian officials to win a major weapons contract. To this end, up to $47 million was paid into secret

Swiss bank accounts in order to persuade Indian middlemen to procure for the company a $1.13 billion order for a field artillery system. This was not the first occasion when Bofors had engaged in questionable financial transactions. It is even suggested that one such affair led directly or indirectly to the murder of the Swedish prime minister, Olaf Palme, in 1986.

## SMUGGLING

**Smuggling** is a word still ringed with romanticism. But in the cold light of the late 20th century it implies tax evasion, the black market and, in particular, the illegal shipment of drugs. Certain countries, especially in Central and South America, have gained a notorious reputation in connection with their smuggling activities. Bangladesh is another country with such a reputation. It is estimated that smuggling there costs the government about $350 million a year in lost import duties alone. The illegally imported goods are not so much drugs as a miscellany of products and goods, from cigarettes to gold, sugar to cotton.

## CHEATING THE TAXMAN

Cases of **tax fraud** are fairly common, and to some people the taxman almost seems 'fair game' as a legitimate challenge for a financial fiddle. After all, taxes for many of us place a considerable strain on the annual domestic or business budget. In return for the large tax bills we pay, the standard utilities or services that are provided are not always necessarily what we need or want.

An area of taxable income that sometimes

## VOLUNTARY TAXATION

In an essay entitled *More Taxes Please*, Robert Lynd once argued ironically that the Chancellor of the Exchequer, by taxing such things as tobacco and alcohol, had 'given us some excellent reasons for spending the money that he has left us on the things we like best.' Public-spirited people, he said, could now smoke and drink with a feeling of pride, knowing that they were making a substantial contribution to the national income. He compared the situation with the voluntary system of taxation in ancient Greece.

He congratulated the Chancellor for imposing the taxes, but thought that 'he had made a mistake in not appealing to his listeners to devote as much of their expenditure as possible to the articles that are taxed most highly'. Lynd himself said that he leaned towards being a non-smoker and tee-totaller, but wondered whether he had the right to evade taxes that were voluntary any more than those which were compulsory.

appears to yield promising returns is that of 'expenses'. The finer points of what is or is not a legitimate tax-deductible expense are usually matters for the experts.

Sometimes, however, this very area is one that causes the greatest downfall. This was the case with the New York billionairess and hotel owner Mrs Leona **Helmsley**, reviled as the 'queen of mean' for her lavish personal lifestyle and niggardly payments to staff and taxman alike. In 1989 she was jailed for four years and fined $7.1 million for evading taxes on a whole range of expenses, from clothing to a new swimming pool. Sentencing her, Judge John Walker denounced her 'naked greed' and ordered her to pay the $1.2 million she owed in taxes and to work in a New York centre for the homeless. The jail term was demanded by the prosecutor, who claimed that Mrs Helmsley should be punished for her lack of remorse.

Love of money may not be the root of *all* evil, but it certainly appears to be the motive for much that is corrupt and fraudulent in the western world.

## INCENTIVE SCHEME

The late James Agate, the British theatre critic, is said to have made a New Year's resolution one year to spend more money. He explained that only by doing so would he force himself to earn more money.

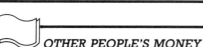

## OTHER PEOPLE'S MONEY

Some people find it easier to tell others how to spend their money than to spend their own. Probably most of us have met a character like Mrs Norris, in Jane Austen's *Mansfield Park*: 'Nobody knew better how to dictate liberality to others; but her love of money was equal to her love of directing, and she knew quite as well how to save her own as to spend that of her friends.'

It is this same lady who suffers a reduction of income when her husband dies, though Jane Austen remarks that she nevertheless 'consoled herself for the loss of her husband by considering that she could do very well without him'.

## WHERE THE MONEY GOES

A mid-seventies survey into the spending habits of the average American family showed that they were likely to dispose of their income as follows:

| | |
|---|---|
| Food, alcohol and tobacco | 22.3% |
| Housing | 14.5% |
| Household operation | 14.4% |
| Transportation | 13.6% |
| Clothing | 10.1% |
| Medical care | 7.7% |
| Recreation | 6.5% |
| Personal business | 5.6% |
| Private education | 1.7% |
| Personal care | 1.5% |
| Religious/welfare activities | 1.4% |
| Foreign travel | 0.7% |

## SPEND!

*Those of them who have money should start spending it at once—spending quiets the nerves—and should spend it as if civilization is permanent; buy books, go to concerts and plays. It is childish to save; thrift was only a virtue so long as it paid, which it has ceased to do.*

E. M. Forster *Two Cheers For Democracy*

## NOT MUCH TO ASK

*I only ask that Fortune send
A little more than I shall spend.*

Oliver Wendell Holmes

## THE SPENDING MACHINE

*The middle-class woman of England, as of America . . . think of her in bulk . . . is potentially the greatest money-spending machine in the world.*

Granville Barker *The Madras House*

## THE OTHER TALENT

*'To tell you the truth, Bertie, you'll never make a penny by any profession.' 'That's what I often think myself', he said, not in the least offended. 'Some men have a great gift of making money, but they can't spend it. Others can't put two shillings together, but they have a great talent in all sorts of outlay. I begin to think that my genius is wholly in the latter line.'*

Anthony Trollope *Barchester Towers*

*EXPRESSIVE COMMENTS*

Some of the colloquial expressions in English which relate to money are fairly vivid. Some examples:

**To bite someone's ear**  to borrow money from someone

**To blow one's money**  to spend it all

**Golden handshake**  the large amount of money given to somebody who is forced to leave a company

**To have the Midas touch**  to appear to be able to make money easily; a reference to the legend of the king who asked the gods to make everything he touched turn to gold.

**To make one's pile**  make one's fortune

**That ain't hay**  that's a lot of money

**Cash on the barrel (head), or in Britain, cash on the nail**  to pay in full at the time of purchase. The American expression no doubt dates from the time when perishable goods were packed in barrels to keep them fresh. Paying on the nail was originally connected with drinking, according to Professor Ernest Weekley. The reference was to the finger-nail, and to draining a glass so that only one drop of wine fell on to the thumbnail. German has *auf den Nagel trinken*; French *boire rubis sur l'ongle*. Pay on the nail therefore means to pay every last drop of what is owing.

**A County Clare payment**  no payment

**Foot the bill**  sign one's name at the bottom of the bill to indicate acceptance of payment

**Fork out**  pay for something, presumably from resemblance of the hand to a fork

**Buy something on tick**  ie, on the ticket, in small instalments

**Peanuts**  a small amount of money

**To shell out**  to pay for something. To take money from your pocket like peas from a pod?

**To be hard up**  to be short of money. This may have had a nautical origin. Hard-up was a command given to a helmsman when it was necessary to turn a ship's head away from the wind. Charles Dickens comments on the phrase as a recent one in *The Chimes* (1844).

**To have money to burn**  to have plenty of money, though no one is likely to be in this position if money burns a hole in his pocket.

**To launder money**  to transfer it in such a way that its illegal source is concealed

**Not worth a rap**  worthless; a 'rap' was a counterfeit Irish halfpenny in the 18th century

**gold-digger**  used literally of a man, but metaphorically of a woman who thinks of a man mainly as a monetary source

**Have a good run for one's money**  an expression of satisfaction that time and money have been reasonably well-spent, even if success did not come in the end

**To run into debt**  no one ever walks into debt, or walks out of money. Such things always happen quickly enough to justify the 'run'.

**Money for jam, or old rope**  money easily acquired. The 'jam' reference has been linked to its common use in the British army during World War I.

**Put one's money where one's mouth is**  prove that one has enough confidence in what one is saying to risk money on it

**Money-grubber**  someone prepared to grub about in the dirt, if necessary, in order to get money

**Moneybags**  a rich person, one with bags of money

**Money player**  an American expression for a player who can be counted on to perform well under pressure. In the 1930s the term seems to have been applied to one who was only interested in making money from sport, but had no real fighting spirit. He is now a player who can be relied upon at difficult moments.

# 13
# WHAT'S IT WORTH?

## VALUE JUDGEMENT

If he puts on any more weight the treasury is in big trouble

Putting a price on something can be a complicated matter. A painting signed by the artist is worth much more than an unsigned picture, and certainly much more than a copy of the original, even though all three may be virtually indistinguishable to the viewer. A book signed by its author is similarly worth more than one that is unsigned, and a secondhand book, signed or not, can be worth much more than a modern reprint. Indeed, it can have torn and stained pages and be almost falling apart at its stitching, yet still be worth more than a brand new unread edition.

In both these examples—the painting and the book—the 'value factor' is not simply the artistic or literary worth of the object, but equally its rarity. 'Rare' is a word that usually implies 'costly', 'very valuable'. If a work of art is unique, as for example the *Mona Lisa*, it cannot readily be assigned a monetary value at all. (See Chapter 11, p. 137.)

Scarcity and, supremely, uniqueness, are qualities that confer a high price on an object—and indeed on a human being. If you are one of just a few people who can offer a necessary special-

## " INNER RICHES

'Most of the luxuries, and many of the so-called comforts of life, are not only not indispensable, but positive hindrances to the elevation of mankind. With respect to luxuries and comforts, the wisest have ever lived a more simple and meagre life than the poor. The ancient philosophers were a class than which none has been poorer in outward riches, none so rich in inward.'

Henry David Thoreau *Walden*

"

### THE BABY BUSINESS

In Daniel Defoe's *Moll Flanders* (1722) a midwife offers a complete delivery service to women who are unable to have their child at home. The service is of three grades, according to the means of the woman concerned. The heroine of the novel is in straitened circumstances at the time, and is therefore obliged to accept the grade three service. It is detailed as follows:

|   |   | £ | s. | d. |
|---|---|---|----|----|
| 1. | For three months' lodging in her house, including my diet, at 10s. a week | 6 | 0 | 0 |
| 2. | For a nurse for the month, and use of child-bed linen | 1 | 10 | 0 |
| 3. | For a minister to christen the child, and to the god-fathers and clerk | 1 | 10 | 0 |
| 4. | For a supper at the christening if I had five friends at it | 1 | 0 | 0 |
| 5. | For her fees as a midwife, and the taking off the trouble of the parish | 3 | 3 | 0 |
| 6. | To her maidservant attending | 0 | 10 | 0 |
|   |   | £13 | 13 | 0 |

Moll later pays a countrywoman £10 a year to look after the son that is born to her.

ized service, you can demand, and get, high fees. Hence the top payments made to such diverse categories of specialists as brain surgeons, 'head hunters', financial advisers, defence experts, and the different kinds of key executives found in business and industry throughout the world.

Conversely, hence the *low* 'value factor' normally assigned to everyday objects and to people who perform unskilled work or routine jobs.

The actual content or composition of an object can of course affect its purchase price, even if the object itself is a familiar and common one. The cost of manufacturing it, too, has to be taken into account. This is why a pint of water costs less than a pint of milk, or a bottle of wine costs less than a bottle of spirits.

Sometimes, especially with objects of highly variable prices, such as secondhand books, an individual purchaser can get a genuine bargain, real 'value for money'. If I am looking for a copy of a particular novel to make up the nearly complete set by my favourite author, I may one day come across it priced at £5 in a bookshop and eagerly snap it up. I have got a real bargain: a book that, to me, was actually worth much more than this, for it now completes my collection. But to the bookseller, it was just one of a number of novels by that particular author.

### VALUE VARIATIONS

On the whole, things we basically need to keep going from one day to the next are normally much cheaper than rarities or 'luxuries'. We can have champagne and caviar for breakfast every day, at a price, but we do not need to. So our bread, milk, tea and butter, which can serve very well for breakfast, are items that can still be bought in pence (or cents), rather than pounds (or dollars).

The fact that goods and services today are

### " COMPARATIVE VALUES

'Of so little value are silver and gold in comparison to love, that gift in every one's power to bestow.'

Elizabeth Gaskell *Mary Barton*

"

apparently much more expensive than they used to be, is something that baffles many people. We look in an old magazine, and see an electric cooker advertised for £50, for example, or a house for sale at just £700, and wonder why their prices have increased so much. The answer is that they have not. Prices vary and fluctuate, of course, but overall the value of money itself has fallen over the years. This means that the cost of things we buy appears to have gone up; but in reality the 'pound in our pocket' has gradually come to be worth less and less.

As long as this 'shrinking pound' effect is borne in mind, the differences in prices between now and 'then', whenever it was, can be more meaningfully appreciated. It is not that a bar of soap actually cost less 20 years ago, but that pounds and pence were worth more, so fewer pennies were needed to buy the bar of soap.

One practical effect of the constant devaluing process is the way in which lower-value coins eventually go out of circulation (like the farthing and halfpenny in Britain) while higher-value banknotes come in and lower-value notes (like the £1 note) are replaced by a coin, which is more durable. If it had not been for the decimalization of British currency in 1971, it is very likely that the pre-decimal penny would have similarly been withdrawn. Even now, after decimalization, the

## THE MONEY ILLUSION

This term in economics relates to a response to increased income which ignores a corresponding rise in the price of essential goods. You may, for example, be earning twice as much now as you were ten years ago. But if it now costs twice as much as it did then to buy food and other necessities, it is clear that your standard of living has not actually changed. Your higher income nevertheless makes you feel richer. You may therefore start to buy luxury goods, thinking that you can now afford them. What is really happening is that you are suffering from the Money Illusion.

## VALUE JUDGMENTS

The 17th-century English writer Nicholas Barbon said: 'Nothing can have an intrinsic value'. What he meant was that nothing can have a fixed intrinsic value; the value of any object will vary according to the circumstances of the time. At any one moment, as Samuel Butler was later to express it:

> 'The value of a thing
> Is just as much as it will bring.'

penny is worth very little, and might go the way of the decimal halfpenny, leaving prices to be rounded to the nearest 2p.

When 'then and now' prices are compared, there are other factors to be taken into account. Some goods, especially electrical or electronic, are relatively 'cheaper' now than they originally were. This is because they were harder to manufacture 'then', and can be more easily mass-produced 'now'. This is partly in response to public demand for them. But some mechanical goods, for one reason or another, are much 'dearer'. Refrigerators, for instance, have virtually only doubled in price over the past 30 years, while cars now cost almost ten times as much!

Factors such as the availability of parts (which may have to be imported now, whereas before they were made in this country), automation, manufacturing costs, levels of supply and demand, and the perennial 'trade cycle' ('booms' and 'slumps'), to say nothing of the general economy and employment situation, add to the complexity of the overall picture.

### THAT WAS THEN, THIS IS NOW

With this background in mind, a 'then' and 'now' table of comparative costs and prices is much more meaningful. The one below, quoted in *TV Times*, 28 January–3 February 1989, shows what certain common household items or goods cost in 1955, as compared to 1988, 33 years later. The 1955 prices were of course pre-decimal, but here their approximate decimal equivalent has been added in brackets.

| Object or service | 1955 | | | | 1988 |
|---|---|---|---|---|---|
| | £ | s | d | | £ |
| Single rail fare London to Leeds | 1 | 9 | 2 | (£1.46) | 32.00 |
| Middle-of-range saloon car | 850 | 0 | 0 | | 9842.00 |
| Gallon of 4-star petrol | | 4 | 7 | (£0.23) | 1.70 |
| Sports bicycle | 19 | 6 | 6 | (£19.32) | 130.00 |
| 17-inch screen TV | 85 | 7 | 0 | (£85.35) | 329.99 |
| Washing machine | 83 | 14 | 0 | (£83.70) | 299.99 |
| Electric cooker | 40 | 0 | 0 | | 299.99 |
| Refrigerator | 59 | 7 | 0 | (£59.35) | 119.99 |
| 15-denier nylons | | 13 | 11 | (£0.70) | 1.29 |
| Made-to-measure man's suit | 10 | 0 | 0 | | 250.00 |
| Pint of milk | | | 7 | (£0.03) | 0.27 |
| Cotton bra | | 6 | 7 | (£0.33) | 2.90 |
| Loaf of bread | | | 6 | (£0.02½) | 0.48 |
| Bottle of table wine | | 6 | 0 | (£0.30) | 2.20 |
| Half-pound of margarine | | 1 | 1 | (£0.05) | 0.19 |
| Large size washing powder | | 1 | 8 | (£0.08) | 1.88 |
| Large tube of toothpaste | | 2 | 5 | (£0.12) | 0.49 |
| Average terraced house | 2280 | 0 | 0 | | 54 785.00 |
| Average annual salary | 690 | 0 | 0 | | 12 432.00 |

## PUTTING A PRICE ON ART

It is not just in household goods that prices have changed and increased. In the specialized world of art, the prices paid for paintings in auction sales rooms have shot up dramatically over the past few years. Tastes, too, have altered, with the prices of objects owned by popular celebrities, such as pop stars, now fetching millions of pounds.

As a general yardstick for the 1980s, the record price paid for a work of art at the beginning of the decade can be compared with that paid at its close. In 1980, the record sum paid for a painting was £2.7 million, for Turner's *Juliet and her Nurse*. In 1989 it was a staggering £30.7 million, paid for Picasso's *Les Noces de Pierrette* (see also Chapter 11, p. 137). This represents a tenfold increase.

Other works by individual artists fetched prices that increased similarly over the nine-year period, as shown in these figures quoted in *The Times* for 14 December 1989:

| | 1980 | 1989 |
|---|---|---|
| Highest prices for a Benin bronze | £200 000 | £1.32 million |
| Average price for a Utrillo painting | £12 500 | £150 000 |
| Stanley Spencer painting sold at auction | £16 000 | £429 000 |
| Highest price for English furniture | £131 818 | £565 714 |

Not surprisingly, the turnover of noted art sales companies has shown a similar increase: Christie's turnover leaped from £49 million in 1980 to £1.04 billion in 1989.

'Pop memorabilia' is a phenomenon of the late 1980s, largely resulting from a deliberate change in sales strategy by art auctioneers, who found that traditional works of art such as 'Old Master' paint-

### IN THE ABSTRACT

It is said that an American who was visiting Pablo Picasso in his studio stopped in front of one of his abstract paintings and asked: 'What does this represent?' 'Two hundred thousand dollars', said Picasso. On another occasion friends asked him why he had none of his own paintings on the walls of his house. This time his reply was: 'I can't afford them.'

ings and furniture were attracting less interest. Thus in 1988, Elton John's 'Art Nouveau' and platform boots fetched £4.8 million at auction, Liberace's pianos £1.2 million, and Andy Warhol's cookie jars £13.5 million.

When auctioning works of art, sales rooms will usually give an estimate of the price each will fetch. Sometimes the estimates are accurate. Sometimes they are way out. In 1989, for example, Sotheby's estimated that a Dictaphone recording of Agatha Christie's last novel, made by the author herself, would fetch about £3500 pounds. In fact it was sold to an anonymous Frenchman for £7480. Similarly, a silver pocket watch owned by Lewis Carroll went at the same sale for £9350, also twice its estimated value. On the other hand, Ian Fleming's nine carat Zenith wristwatch fetched just £880, much lower than its estimated price of £1500, and an autographed draft letter from Ronald Reagan to a Californian girls' school, valued at £6000, failed to sell at all. Book dealers can also under- or over-estimate the books they sell. One firm of London

**“**

## THE PROBLEMS OF POSSESSIONS

*Property is really a nuisance. Property not merely has duties, but has so many duties that its possession to any large extent is a bore. It involves endless claims upon one, endless attention to business, endless bother. If property had simply pleasures, we could stand it; but its duties make it unbearable. In the interest of the rich we must get rid of it.*

*So completely has man's personality been absorbed by his possessions that the English law has always treated offences against a man's property with far more severity than offences against his person, and property is still the test of complete citizenship.*

*The industry necessary for the making of money is also very demoralizing. In a community like ours, where property confers immense distinction, social position, honour, respect, titles, and other pleasant things of the kind, man, being naturally ambitious, makes it his aim to accumulate this property, and goes on wearily and tediously accumulating it long after he has got far more than he wants, or can use, or enjoy, or perhaps even know of. Man will kill himself by*

*overwork in order to secure property, and really, considering the enormous advantages that property brings, one is hardly surprised. One's regret is that society should be constructed on such a basis that man has been forced into a groove in which he cannot freely develop what is wonderful, and fascinating, and delightful in him—in which, in fact, he misses the true pleasure and joy of living.*

*He is also, under existing conditions, very insecure. An enormously wealthy merchant may be—often is—at every moment of his life at the mercy of things that are not under his control. If the wind blows an extra point or so, or the weather suddenly changes, or some trivial thing happens, his ship may go down, his speculations may go wrong, and he finds himself a poor man, with his social position quite gone.*

*Now nothing should be able to harm a man except himself. Nothing should be able to rob a man at all. What a man really has, is what is in him. What is outside of him should be a matter of no importance.*

Oscar Wilde *The Soul of Man Under Socialism*

**”**

book auctioneers sold a first edition of Virginia Woolf's novel *Jacob's Room* in 1989 for £1960, more than ten times the original estimate.

### 'ONE FAMOUS OWNER . . .'

As is obvious from these examples, the 'ownership factor' of an auctioned article is significant in determining its value and selling price. For historic possessions, the importance or international renown of the owner is the important criterion, with monarchs, for example, rating higher than musicians. For modern objects, the greater the celebrity status of the owner, the greater the value, with actors and actresses, and entertainers generally, worth more than, say, archbishops. The nuptial bed of the world-famous actress Marilyn Monroe and her husband, the American baseball player Joe DiMaggio, was sold at a New Jersey auction in 1989 to a Japanese furniture manufacturer for $60 300 (about £38 000). This high price was determined both by the fame of the bed's owner and the event associated with it, its literal 'Marilyn slept here' cachet.

Similarly, the actress Mae West's costume jewellery was sold at Christie's, London, also in 1989 for prices several times higher than those estimated by the auctioneers. Her white necklace and matching earrings, for example, went for £880 (estimated price, £200 to £400), two bracelets went for £385 (estimate, £200 to £300), another necklace made £770 (estimate, £200 to £300), and a third necklace fetched £880 (estimate, £250 to £450). At the same sale, the first love letter written by the romantic film actor Errol Flynn when he was in London as a 13-year-old schoolboy made £2860, as against the estimated price of £800 to £1200.

The fact that the experts frequently find it hard to give an accurate estimate of the value or selling price of an object illustrates all too well the difficulty in pricing a unique item, or of estimating what a buyer will be prepared to pay for it.

In recent years, the previously sophisticated world of art collecting has changed from the cool pursuit of the demanding aesthete to a hectic financial activity, resembling that of dealers in a stock exchange or even gamblers at a casino. The comparison is appropriate enough, for many dealers take out bank loans to back their high-flying

## RELATIVE VALUES

The 1990 edition of *Social Trends*, the annual report on British life issued by the Central Statistical Office, contained some interesting data on the cost of living 'then' and 'now'. Among its many facts and figures, it notes the following:

In 1971, the richest 1 per cent of the population owned 31 per cent of the country's wealth, compared to 18 per cent in 1987.

In 1971, the average man had to do 22 minutes' work to pay for a dozen medium-sized eggs, compared with just 13 minutes to buy the equivalent in 1988.

In 1988, it took £1 to buy goods that would have cost the pre-decimal equivalent of 9p in 1951.

In 1971, it took 9 minutes to earn enough to buy a loaf of bread, compared with 6 minutes in 1988.

In 1988, 11 minutes' work were needed to buy a pint of beer, as against 14 minutes in 1971.

bids, and some auctioneers, such as Sotheby's, now offer resources in this respect, so acquiring a joint-purpose function.

On the basis of figures like those quoted above, it looks as if the most sought-after works of art may be fetching as much as £200 million by the end of the century.

### CAR NUMBERS AND VALUES

An interesting 'valuation area' is that of car number plates, in particular those that 'spell' words or names or that are a status symbol of the owner, with combinations of single letters and figures rated the highest. The area is significant since clearly the sale or purchase price is not that of simply the number plate alone, but of its prestige value. The more 'rarefied' the number, the more it is seen to be unique and so the more it is worth. A plate bearing a number such as OTF 381V is clearly unremarkable. But a plate proudly bearing A1 is the ultimate in self-promotion, with the

**"**

## SELLING ONESELF

'The "wages" of every noble work do yet lie in Heaven or else nowhere. Not in Bank-of-England bills, in Owen's Labour-bank, or any of the most improved establishment of banking and money-changing, needest thou, heroic soul, present thy account of earnings. Human banks and labour banks know thee not.

'My brother, the brave man has to give his life away. Give it, I advise thee;— thou dost not expect to sell thy life in an adequate manner? What price, for example, would content thee? Thou wilt never sell thy life, or any part of thy life, in a satisfactory manner. Give it, like a royal heart; let the price be Nothing: thou hast then, in a certain sense, got All for it!

'The heroic man,—and is not every man, God be thanked, a potential hero?—has to do so, in all times and circumstances. In the most heroic age, as in the most unheroic, he will have to say, as Burns said proudly and humbly of his little Scottish songs, little dewdrops of celestial melody in an age when so much was unmelodious: "By heaven, they shall either be invaluable or of no value; I do not need your guineas for them!" '

Thomas Carlyle *Past and Present*
(The remark of Burns to which Carlyle refers was made in a letter of 16 September, 1792.)

**"**

implication that both the car and its owner are first class, or in excellent condition.

In 1989, the Driver and Vehicle Licensing Centre was authorized by the government to sell off the cream of its hitherto unissued collection of registration numbers. The sale was held by auction at Christie's and overall fetched £1.54 million, double the estimate for what the numbers would fetch. The proceeds went to the Department of Transport.

The actual number A1 is already in use, owned by the construction and energy company BTR plc. But Christie's had 1A to auction, and after keen bidding starting at £25 000 the unique plate went to an undisclosed buyer for £176 000, so smashing the previous record of £98 000, paid at an earlier auction for the number 1 VIP.

Other numbers also went for thousand-pound bids, including:

| | |
|---|---|
| MUS 1C | £65 000 |
| JUL 1E | £43 000 |
| B1 LLY | £36 000 |
| BUY 1T | £29 700 |
| 1 OU | £24 200 |

| | |
|---|---|
| G1 LTS | £13 200 |
| F1 GHT | £10 000 |
| 100 UFO | £5500 |
| B10 PSY | £4950 |
| 10 LBW | £2400 |

At values like these, what price GL0 RY?

## HUMAN VALUES

If manmade objects such as paintings and car number plates can fetch astronomical prices, what is the value of a human being? Put another way, what is a human life worth?

As with manufactured objects, it depends on the person. How special or 'unique' is the human being? How irreplaceable?

The insurance companies are the best guide in such cases. But even life insurance premiums and payouts can vary, depending on the degree of risk involved in the person's life. The higher the risk, the lower the premium and the lower the payout. A deep-sea diver is more likely to suffer a fatal accident than a deacon, and so is a greater insurance risk. Similarly an old person is statistically more likely to die, in the very nature of things,

## SELLING ONE'S WIFE

*The Mayor of Casterbridge*, by Thomas Hardy, begins with a scene where a drunken Michael Henchard offers his wife and child for sale. A sailor called Newson offers five guineas, which Henchard accepts. The wife reacts by saying: 'Mike, I've lived with thee a couple of years, and had nothing but temper! Now I'm no more to 'ee; I'll try my luck elsewhere. 'Twill be better for me and Elizabeth-Jane, both. So good-bye!'

Hardy based this scene on two reports in the *Dorset County Chronicle*, both of which he copied into his Commonplace Book. On 25 May 1826, a man had offered his wife for sale in the market place at Brighton. The couple had two children, 'one of whom the husband consents to keep, the other he throws in as a make-weight to the bargain'.

On 6 December, 1827, at Buckland Dinham, near Frome, a labourer named Charles Pearce sold his wife to a shoemaker for five pounds. Pearce brought his wife in a halter and publicly handed her over to her purchaser, but Hardy noted that she was quite happy with the transaction.

Such wife-sales had, of course, no legal validity, but as in Hardy's novel, those concerned seem to have acted as if they were the equivalent of a remarriage.

---

than a young one. He or she, too, will be a greater insurance risk.

At the end of the 1980s, a typical average **life insurance payout** for an ordinary person who died accidentally was something in the order of £20 000, or about one and a half times the national average salary.

However, the record payout to date on a single life was that of some $14 million made for Mrs Linda Mullendore, a wife of an Oklahoma rancher. She died in 1970, the year after her murdered husband had paid $300 000 in premiums.

This in turn pales into insignificance against the life assurance policy of $44 million taken out in 1982 for Victor T. Uy, a Calgary land developer. The previous record had been held by James D. Slater, a London investment banker, who in 1971, at the age of 42, was reported as having taken out a life policy of £10 million.

Payments in millions of pounds have also been made for human beings in a specialized type of deal: that of the **football transfer fee**. A talented player can be worth a fortune to his club, and a rival club or team may well be prepared to offer a near astronomical sum to win him over to their side. In 1968, for instance, a transfer fee equivalent to more than £400 000 was paid by Juventus, of Turin, Italy, for the Varese centre forward Pietro Anastasi, and in 1971 the Everton player Alan Ball was 'bought' by Arsenal for £220 000, then the highest British transfer fee. Both these values have subsequently been upped. In 1984, Napoli paid 15 895 million lire for Diego Maradona of Argentina, a sum that exceeded the fee equivalent to approximately £5 million which Barcelona had earlier paid for Maradona in 1982. In British foot-

## " _____

### MY DEBT TO YOU

*My debt to you, Beloved,*
*Is one I cannot pay*
*In any coin of any realm*
*On any reckoning day.*

*For where is he shall figure*
*The debt, when all is said,*
*To one who makes you dream again*
*When all the dreams are dead?*

*Or where is the appraiser*
*Who shall the claim compute*
*Of one who makes you sing again*
*When all the songs were mute?*

Jessie Rittenhouse (Former Secretary of the Poetry Society of America.)

_____ "

## THE VALUE OF EDUCATION

*Elmer Gantry*, by Sinclair Lewis, is a novel about a man who ends up as a hypocritical preacher. Gantry's thoughts as a young student are described thus: 'When he had come to college, he had supposed he would pick up learnings of cash-value to a lawyer or doctor or insurance man—he had not known which he would become. But this belief he found fallacious. What good would it be in the court-room, or at the operating table, to understand trigonometry, or to know (as last spring, up to the examination in European History, he remembered having known) the date of Charlemagne? How much cash would it bring in to quote all that stuff—what the dickens was it now?—all that rot about 'The world is too much around us, early and soon' from that old fool Wordsworth? Punk, that's what it was. Better to be out in business.'

ball, clubs are now also talking in millions. In 1988 Tottenham Hotspur paid £2 million for Paul Gascoigne of Newcastle United, and the same amount was paid that same year by Everton to West Ham for Tony Cottee. These are simply fees between British clubs. Internationally, an estimated equivalent of £3.2 million was paid in 1986 by Juventus of Italy for Ian Rush of Liverpool.

Transfer fees in other sports have generally been much more modest. In **rugby league**, for example, the record fee to date was £155 000 paid by Leeds to Hull in 1987 for centre Gary Schofield, while in **rugby union**, Widnes reportedly paid a fee of around £200 000 to Llanelli in 1989 for Jonathan Davies.

Even so, to rate a sportsman in thousands or millions of pounds is an impressive evaluation, by any standard.

### ANIMAL MILLIONAIRES

Similar values have been put on animals. **Racehorses**, in particular, have been bought and sold for record sums, and a potentially promising stallion can change hands for literally millions (pounds or dollars). To date, the highest amount paid for a yearling is $13.1 million. This was the sum that *Seattle Dancer* fetched in 1983 when he was sold to Robert Sangster and partners at Keeneland, Kentucky.

Racehorses fetch such colossal sums because they are themselves great money-makers, with potential to win one important high-staked race after another—and in due course to sire further money-spinning racers.

In a real sense, therefore, a racehorse's winnings are a considered estimate of its true value and its ability to turn its owners, trainers and jockeys into millionaires. To date, the record winning career is held by the 1987 Kentucky Derby winner *Alysheba*. He has brought in a total of over $6.6 million, with half this the 'income' of seven wins out of nine races in a single year, 1988. In his final race, the Breeders' Cup Classic, run in November that year, he won over $1.3 million.

The single race record is held by the appropriately named *Spend a Buck*, who in the Jersey Derby run in May 1985 netted his owners $2.6 million. Of this, $2 million was a bonus for having previously won the Kentucky Derby and two preparatory races at Garden State park, the New Jersey course where the Jersey Derby is run.

Nor is it just the horses that are worth the big money. Dogs, too, have their day and their high values, especially **show dogs**. The 'top dog', moneywise, is the Pekingese 'Ch. Ch'êrh of Alderbourne', owned by the famous dog breeder Mrs Clarice Ashton Cross of Ascot in the early years of the present century. In 1907 she actually turned down an offer of £32 000 from the American millionaire financier J. Pierpont Morgan. Mr Morgan then made another approach with a 'blank cheque', but again the dog's owner turned the offer down.

No doubt the little dog laughed to see such fun.

*LITTLE TREASURES*

It is almost commonplace to compare a child with money and riches of a more conventional kind. Pet names sometimes make the point— my precious, my treasure. Hester Prynne, in Hawthorne's *The Scarlet Letter*, goes a step further in naming her daughter Pearl, 'as being of great price—purchased with all she had—her mother's only treasure'.

George Eliot's story *Silas Marner* has much to say on this theme. The hero is a weaver who leads a solitary life and becomes a miser. At night he takes out his money and bathes his hands in the coins, as Eliot expresses it. We are also told that he 'thought fondly of the guineas that were only half-earned by the work in his loom, as if they had been unborn children'.

Marner's money is stolen, but he adopts a real child, an orphaned baby girl whom he calls Eppie. In a lyrical passage George Eliot writes: 'Unlike the gold which needed nothing, and must be worshipped in close-locked solitude—which was hidden away from the daylight, was deaf to the song of birds, and started to no human tones—Eppie was a creature of endless claims and ever-growing desires, seeking and loving sunshine, and living sounds, and living movements; making trial of everything, with trust in new joy, and stirring the human kindness in all eyes that looked on her. The gold had kept his thoughts in an ever-repeated circle, leading to nothing beyond itself; but Eppie was an object compacted of changes and hopes that forced his thoughts onward—carried them away to the new things that would come with the coming years. The gold had asked that he should sit weaving longer and longer, deafened and blinded more and more to all things except the monotony of his loom and the repetition of his web; but Eppie called him away from his weaving, and made him think all pauses a holiday.'

Silas Marner is completely won over by the child, who becomes far more important to him than money. A more cynical view is given in *The Way of All Flesh*, by Samuel Butler, where the hero has both money and children: 'Money came pouring in upon him, and the faster it came the fonder he became of it, though, as he frequently said, he valued it not for its own sake, but only as a means of providing for his dear children.

'Yet when a man is very fond of his money it is not easy for him at all times to be very fond of his children also. The two are like god and Mammon. George Pontifex felt this as regards his children and his money. His money was never naughty; his money never made noise or litter, and did not spill things on the tablecloth at mealtimes, or leave the door open when it went out. His dividends did not quarrel among themselves, nor was he under any uneasiness lest his mortgages should become extravagant on reaching manhood and run him up debts which sooner or later he should have to pay.

'His children might, perhaps, have answered that he did not knock his money about as he not infrequently knocked his children. He never dealt hastily or pettishly with his money, and that was perhaps why he and it got on so well together.'

## THE GREAT RACE

Charles Lamb wrote an essay, *The Two Races of Men*, about those who borrow money and those who lend it. The man he refers to as Ralph Bigod in the abridged version below was actually John Fenwick, editor of the *Albion*.

'The human species, according to the best theory I can form of it, is composed of two distinct races, *the men who borrow*, and *the men who lend*. The infinite superiority of the former, which I choose to designate as the *great race*, is discernible in their figure, port, and a certain instinctive sovereignty. The latter are born degraded. There is something in the air of one of this cast, lean and suspicious; contrasting with the open, generous manner of the other.

'What a careless, even deportment hath your borrower! What rosy gills! What a beautiful reliance on Providence doth he manifest! What contempt for money—accounting it (yours and mine especially) no better than dross! His exactions, too, have such a cheerful, voluntary air! So far removed from your sour parochial or state-gatherers, those ink-horn varlets, who carry their want of welcome in their faces! He cometh to you with a smile, and troubleth you with no receipt; confining himself to no set season.

'Reflections like the foregoing were forced upon my mind by the death of my old friend, Ralph Bigod, Esq., who departed this life on Wednesday evening; dying, as he had lived, without much trouble. Having had the honour of accompanying my friend, divers times, in his perambulations about this vast city, I own I was greatly struck at first with the prodigious number of faces we met, who claimed a sort of respectful acquaintance with us. He was one day so obliging as to explain the phenomenon. It seems these were his tributaries; feeders of his exchequer; gentlemen, his good friends, to whom he had occasionally been beholden for a loan. Their multitudes did in no way disconcert him. He rather took a pride in numbering them.

'With such sources, it was a wonder how he contrived to keep his treasury always empty. He did it by force of an aphorism which he had often in his mouth, that 'money kept longer than three days stinks.' So he made use of it while it was fresh. A good part he drank away, some he gave away, the rest he threw away. When new supplies became necessary, the first person that had the felicity to fall in with him, friend or stranger, was sure to contribute to the deficiency. For Bigod had an undeniable way with him. He had a cheerful, open exterior, a quick jovial eye, a bald forehead, just touched with grey. He anticipated no excuse, and found none.

'When I think of this man; his fiery glow of heart; his swell of feeling; and when I compare with him the companions with whom I have associated since, I grudge the saving of a few idle ducats, and think that I am fallen into the society of *lenders*, and *little men*.'

## THE WOMAN WITH THE GOLDEN LEG

Long before Ian Fleming thought of his *Goldfinger*, Thomas Hood had written his poem *Miss Kilmanegg and her Precious Leg*. The poem is full of Hood's usual clever puns and humour. Of the heroine's father, for instance, he writes:

'He had roll'd in money like pigs in mud,
Till it seem'd to have enter'd into his blood
By some occult projection:
And his cheeks, instead of a healthy hue,
As yellow as any guinea grew,
Making the common phrase seem true
About a rich complexion.'

Miss Kilmanegg duly learns her L.S.D. before her A.B.C. and her teachers make sure she understands the value of money:

'The very metal of merit they told,
And prais'd her for being as "good as gold"
Till she grew as a peacock haughty;
Of money they talk'd the whole day round,
And weigh'd desert like grapes by the pound,
Till she had an idea from the very sound
That people with naught were naughty.'

Miss Kilmanegg later has an accident when her horse Banker (by Bullion out of Ingot) bolts. Told that she needs an artificial leg she announces her wishes:

A Leg of Gold—solid gold throughout,
Nothing else, whether slim or stout,
Should ever support her, God willing!
She must—she could—she would have her
  whim,
Her father, she turned a deaf ear to him—
He might kill her—she didn't mind killing!
He was welcome to cut off her other limb—
He might cut her off with a shilling!'

Miss Kilmanegg is duly given her golden leg, which becomes famous. Society worships her 'Golden Calf'. She is courted by old men and young, but inevitably, says Hood, chooses the wrong man:

'But, alas! alas! for the Woman's fate,
Who has from a mob to choose a mate
'Tis a strange and painful mystery!
But the more the eggs, the worse the hatch;
The more the fish, the worse the catch;
The more the sparks, the worse the match;
Is a fact in Woman's history.'

The so-called Count that she marries is a gambler and drunkard who ill-treats her and dissipates her fortune. He eventually needs even her golden leg, which he wants to melt down. After a quarrel he creeps into her bedroom, intending to steal it. She wakes and he uses the leg to batter her to death. Hood tells us the moral of his story:

'Gold! Gold! Gold! Gold!
Bright and yellow, hard and cold,
Molten, graven, hammer'd, and roll'd
Heavy to get, and light to hold;
Hoarded, barter'd, bought, and sold,
Stolen, borrow'd, squander'd, doled:
Spurned by the young, but hugg'd by the old
To the very verge of the graveyard mould;
Price of many a crime untold;
Gold! Gold! Gold! Gold!:
Good or bad a thousand fold!
How widely its agencies vary—
To save—to ruin—to curse—to bless—
As even its minted coins express,
Now stamp'd with the image of Good Queen
  Bess,
And now of a bloody Mary!'

 **BRITISH MONEY MILESTONES OVER THE LAST 75 YEARS**

**1915** Stonehenge sold by auction for £6600
**1916** Loaf of bread goes up to 10d, then its highest price ever
**1917** Bankers and Chambers of Commerce call for decimalization
**1918** Penny Post abolished
**1919** National Debt rises to £473 645 000
**1920** Pound falls from $3.50 to $3.46 after miners' strike
**1921** Lloyds Bank takes over Fox, Fowler & Co., the last provincial bank to issue its own banknotes

**1922** Budget cuts 1s off Income Tax
**1923** £1 is worth 183 000 000 marks in Germany
**1924** Petrol rises 4½d to about 2s a gallon
**1925** Income Tax reduced to 4s in the pound
**1926** Coal strike loses the industry £300 million
**1927** Price of 4 lb loaf drops to 9d, petrol to 1s 4½d a gallon
**1928** First £1 and 10s notes issued
**1929** Coal up by 1s 2d a ton, with best coal at 53s a ton

1930  New Morris Minor sells at £215
1931  Britain forced off Gold Standard
1932  Report recommends £30 annual pay rise for first-year nurses
1933  Sainsbury's sell butter at 1s per pound
1934  Butter falls to 10d per pound, then its cheapest ever
1935  Petrol now 1s 6d per gallon
1936  Sirloin costs 1s 7d, salmon 3s 3d per pound
1937  Millionaires rise in number from 775 to 824
1938  Whisky up to £1 15s per bottle; peaches 1d each, oranges ½d
1939  Government plans to spend £580 million on defence, up £175 million
1940  London woman fined £75 for buying sugar for 140 weeks' rations
1941  Average working class family is living on less than £5 a week
1942  UK war spending is over £9050 million, more than whole of World War I
1943  100 per cent tax imposed on luxury goods
1944  PAYE ('Pay As You Earn') taxation introduced
1945  Income Tax cut from 10s to 9s in the pound
1946  Wages are now 80 per cent higher than in 1938
1947  In austerity crisis, meat ration reduced to 1s-worth a week
1948  National Insurance introduced
1949  Pound devalued from $4.3 to $2.90
1950  Civil Servants' pay frozen
1951  Austin raise the price of their A40 model by £31 to £685
1952  Commons vote for equal pay for women
1953  Trees worth over £3 million destroyed by storms in Scotland
1954  TV licence raised from £2 to £3
1955  Petrol goes up to 4s 6d a gallon
1956  £1 Premium Bonds introduced
1957  Bank Rate raised to 7 per cent as counter inflationary measure
1958  Bank Rate cut from 5 to 4 per cent
1959  Picasso painting sold for £55 000, world record for a living artist

1960  New £1 note introduced
1961  Cigarettes go up ½d to an average of 1s 9d for 10
1962  10 per cent cut in Purchase Tax brings Mini down to £495 19s 3d
1963  American Express card introduced in UK
1964  Average weekly wage is £16 14s 11d
1965  Corporation Tax on company profits introduced
1966  Barclaycard introduced
1967  Bank rate cut from 7 per cent to 6.5 per cent, ending a sterling crisis
1968  First decimal coins in circulation
1969  50p coin introduced
1970  Government lends Rolls Royce £20 million
1971  Decimal currency introduced
1972  Access card introduced
1973  Crisis budget cuts £1200 million from public spending
1974  Inflation soars to 14 per cent, a post-war record
1975  Record number of bankruptcies, with 1875 winding-up orders
1976  Sterling at new low of $1.71
1977  Inflation down to 11 per cent
1978  Britain says she will not join EEC's new European Monetary System
1979  Building societies put mortgage rate up 3.5 per cent to record 15 per cent
1980  Sixpenny pieces (= 2½p) cease to be legal tender
1981  Stock market has second worse fall in its history
1982  20p coin introduced
1983  £1 coin introduced
1984  No more £1 notes to be issued
1985  FT Index goes through 1000 barrier for first time
1986  'Big Bang' (see p. 108)
1987  'Broom cupboard' house 5 ft 6 in wide, 11 ft long, for sale in London for £36 500
1988  Record trade gap (balance of payments deficit) of £2.2 million
1989  Record libel payment of £1.5 million awarded to Lord Aldington
1990  GUINNESS BOOK OF MONEY out

# 14
# FLEXIBLE
# FRIENDS

## THE CASHLESS SOCIETY

Sure I'll give you the price of a cup of tea – do you take plastic?

Most of us now use cheques, credit cards, personal accounts, and similar convenient devices. Some people use 'real' money only for the smallest purchases, paying larger sums by one of the many cashless methods now available.

The first cashless method of payment in modern times was undoubtedly credit itself. A person well known to a second party, from whom he wishes to buy something, will have been trusted to settle up at a future date. 'Tick' then gave way to cheque, as outlined in Chapter 4.

### THE RAPID RISE OF THE CREDIT CARD
Many of us hold that handy but also potentially harmful invention, the **credit card**.

Our present 'pieces of plastic' are essentially the modern equivalent of the traditional letters of credit and bills of exchange used in historic times by merchants. They are different in one important respect, however. They cannot, indeed must not, be passed on to another person.

A prophetic mention of credit cards was made over a hundred years ago by the American writer Edward Bellamy. In his Utopian romance *Looking Backward*, published in 1888, he wrote: 'An American credit card is just as good in Europe as American gold used to be, and on the same condition, namely, that it be exchanged into the currency of the country you are travelling in.'

Today's real credit cards also originated in America, but in the 1920s, when various firms such as oil companies and hotel chains began issuing them to credit-worthy and trustworthy cus-

## CREDIT ACCOUNT

'He lived comfortably on credit. He had a large capital of debts, which, laid out judiciously, will carry a man along for many years, and on which certain men about town contrive to live a hundred times better than even men with ready money can do.'

This sounds reasonably modern, but it occurs in William Thackeray's *Vanity Fair* (1847–48). Thackeray has two chapters in the novel called 'How to live well on nothing a year'. In passing he describes the social game which is still widely played, in which one speculates about the income of one's neighbours and friends, trying to work out how they can afford to live as they do.

A more recent commentator on the social scene has said that the worst credit risks are the middle-class 'upward-strivers'. They are usually spending more than they can afford on houses, cars, club-memberships and other things that confer the status they desperately seek. The problem is that their aspirations are always ahead of their actual earnings.

tomers for purchases made at retail outlets. The holder of such a card could buy petrol or pay for a hotel room without tendering any actual currency: he was invoiced by the company in due course.

After World War II, the credit card was much more widely and generally adopted. The first modern card was issued by the **Diners Club** in 1950. The system then was essentially what it is now—the credit card company charged its cardholders an annual fee and invoiced them on a monthly or yearly basis. Retailers and other participating firms and organizations paid a low percentage fee in the order of 4 to 7 per cent of total invoicing.

The next major credit card to appear in the USA was that of **American Express**, which was first issued in 1958. The American Express Company was itself set up as long ago as 1835, when it arose as a small New York freight company. It later grew into the banking giant that it is today.

A year later America saw the nationwide **Bank-Americard**, issued by the Bank of America in California and licensed in other states in 1966. This was the first credit card to be issued by a bank.

In Britain, the American Express credit card was introduced in 1963. It was available to 'members' earning at least £2000 a year, and cardholders were invoiced monthly. The fee for joining was then £3 12s 0d (£3.60). (There is now no enrolment fee, but the annual subscription is £32.50.)

The first all-purpose British credit card was the **Barclaycard**, introduced by Barclays Bank in 1966. Its main 'rival', the **Access card**, did not follow until 1972.

Barclays Bank installed their first cash dispenser in 1967, thus introducing a paradoxical situation: whereas credit cards enabled the holder to purchase goods without actual currency, they made it much easier for him to withdraw cash from banks!

Cardholders usually pay interest on their credit card accounts, although in many cases they can avoid interest if they settle their account in full before a specified date, normally 25 days after the date of billing.

**❝**

### LOVE AND DEBT

*This one request I make to him that sits the clouds above;*
*That I were freely out of debt, as I am out of love.*
*Then for to dance, to drink, and sing, I should be very willing;*
*I should not owe one lass a kiss, nor ne'er a knave a shilling.*

*'Tis only being in love and debt, that breaks us of our rest;*
*And he that is quite out of both, of all the world is blessed.*
*He sees the golden age, wherein all things were free and common;*
*He eats, he drinks, he takes his rest, he fears no man or woman.*

Sir John Suckling (1609–1642)

**❞**

## THE NEVER-NEVER

What the British call hire-purchase and the Americans the instalment plan is known colloquially in Britain as 'the never-never', since the payments appear never to come to an end.

The broadcaster Gilbert Harding was once asked what he thought of hire-purchase. He replied: 'I would like to quote what a judge said not long ago—that all his experience both as Counsel and Judge had been spent in sorting out the difficulties of people who, upon the recommendation of people they did not know, signed documents which they did not read, to buy goods they did not need, with money they had not got.'

## CHEQUE CARDS, CASH CARDS AND SMART CARDS

Complementary to credit cards in the cashless society are **cheque cards** and **cash cards**. Cheque cards, also known as **bank cards** or **banker's cards**, are cards that guarantee a cheque up to a specified sum, usually £50, although £100 cheque cards now exist. Cash cards are cards issued by banks and other organizations to enable the holder to draw cash from a cash dispenser. They cannot be used for any other purpose. A well-known example of a cash card is the Link card, which can be used at a wide range of dispensers belonging to different banks and building societies.

Some banks, such as the National Westminster, now issue a multi-purpose card (called a Servicecard by NatWest), which is a combined cash card, cheque card and **debit card**. A debit card is a development of the credit card. When its holder makes a purchase at a recognized outlet, such as a store or petrol station, the card is 'swiped' through a machine so that the amount due is instantly drawn from his current account at the bank.

A development in turn of the credit or debit card is the **smart card**. This is a card containing a single chip microcomputer which keeps a record of all transactions conducted with the card. Smart cards avoid the need to refer back to the bank's central computer to check every occasion of use, such as when the holder withdraws cash from a dispenser. The card thus remembers how much the holder has in his account, and so speeds transactions up considerably.

There are even **supersmart cards**, which have a keyboard and a display panel, enabling the holder to find out how much is in his account. (A smart card knows how much there is, but cannot tell its holder.)

## TOKEN PAYMENTS

A special substitute for cash, especially for small payments, is the **token**, and there are a number of unofficial tokens that can be used for certain specified purposes and that may or may not have a particular value. Examples are video game tokens, night club tokens, gambling tokens (in casinos), transport tokens, cable TV tokens and telephone tokens. Understandably, within the premises of the Royal Mint (see Chapter 3, p. 27), payments are made with plastic tokens rather than coins for security reasons.

In Italy, there are not only telephone tokens (*gettoni telefonichi*) when cash is not to hand, but sweets are used instead of small change. A similar substitute existed formerly in Britain in pre-decimal days, when many stores would give a small item such as a packet of needles to represent a farthing when the coins themselves were not available. The shortage of farthings was frequently

**GAINING TIME?**

*The rich man does not know what to do with leisure. As he gets richer and richer it becomes easier and easier to make money, until at last five minutes a day will bring him more than he knows how to spend. The poor man is thus left at a loose end as a result of his success. This must inevitably be the case so long as success itself is represented as the purpose of life.*

Bertrand Russell *The Conquest of Happiness*

## GETTING THE PUSH

A friend of one of the authors remarked that when he was a child he had a nanny who was paid to take him for walks in a push chair. He added ruefully that he'd been pushed for money ever since.

caused by the pricing of many goods as one far-thing short of a round total, for example 19s11¾d instead of £1 0s 0d. (Such prices are still found today, for example 'ONLY 99p', and are favoured by manufacturers and retailers on the rather suspect supposition that a price expressed in pence, however high, is psychologically regarded as considerably lower than one expressed in pounds.)

Whereas tokens of the coin type are found mainly in specialized situations, however, there are cash substitutes that are much more generally used.

### BOOK TOKENS AND RECORD TOKENS

One obvious token is the **Book Token**, often given as a prize or a present, enabling the holder to select a book to the stated value (or more, if conventional payment is added). Book Tokens were invented in 1926 by Harold Raymond, future chairman of the publishers Chatto & Windus, although it took him another six years before he could convince booksellers to cooperate in his scheme. He launched his tokens with the slogan, 'The gift is mine, the choice is thine'.

In that same year, the record company His Master's Voice introduced its Christmas gift certificate. This was a type of cheque which HMV dealers filled out for whatever amount the customer wished. About 20 years later, it developed into the **record token**. By the end of the 1980s, more than 10 million record tokens were being sold each year, with the figure rising 20 per cent annually.

Record tokens are now produced by EMI Token Services, and are not only 'currency' but also serve as advertising incentives, persuading people to buy certain breakfast cereals and encouraging young people to open building society and bank accounts.

## ENOUGH IS ENOUGH?

In his *Popular Fallacies* Charles Lamb had this to say about the expression *Enough is as good as a feast*: 'Not a man, woman or child in ten miles round Guildhall, who really believes this saying. The inventor of it did not believe it himself. Morally interpreted, it belongs to a class of proverbs which have a tendency to make us undervalue *money*.

'Of this cast are those notable observations, that money is not health; riches cannot purchase everything; the metaphor which makes gold to be mere muck. This we verily believe to have been the invention of some cunning borrower, who had designs on the purse of his wealthier neighbour, which he could only hope to carry by force of these verbal jugglings. Goodly shoulders of mutton, books, pictures, the opportunity of seeing foreign countries, independence, heart's ease, a man's own time to himself, are not *muck*—however we may be pleased to scandalize with that appellation the faithful metal that provides them for us.'

### THE INVERTED PRINCIPLE OF THE GIFT TOKEN

The growing popularity of vouchers of all kinds is a paradox, since it is the exact opposite of the credit system. Instead of 'buy now, pay later', as the implicit slogan behind the credit card, the gift token involves a procedure of 'pay now, buy later'. In this sense, vouchers are almost a second currency, rivalling the 'real' currency of coins and notes.

Apart from Book Tokens and record tokens, many stores operate a token system, from Marks & Spencer to Mothercare. In 1989 the gift voucher market was worth £375 million a year, of which an estimated £80 million to £100 million is tied up in Marks & Spencer alone.

Although many people do not give vouchers as presents because they regard the idea as being unimaginative or a 'cop-out' for choosing a proper present, market analysts have established that

## TO NO AVAIL

The word 'avail' is connected etymologically with 'value'. We still avail ourselves of something when we make use of it, but we no longer use the word 'vail' as it was frequently used in the 17th and 18th centuries. During that time vails (usually in that form) was the tip which a house-guest gave to a servant when he left the house where he had been staying. Such vails were very important to the servants, making up a large part of their annual income. Jonathan Swift therefore wrote, in 1729: 'I advise you of the servants . . . who expect vails, always to stand rank and file when a stranger is taking his leave.'

The custom of giving vails to servants died out to some extent by the end of the 18th century, though a visitor to Ireland in 1805 referred to 'the vale, or parting token, which the menial servants still in many houses expect'. A. Clarke, writing in 1823, refers to vails as 'that sovereign disgrace to their masters', presumably because employers paid low wages and forced servants to depend on gratuities.

many people do like receiving them. To this end, a London businessman opened the first of a chain of 'Voucher Shops' in 1989, selling nothing but gift-wrapped vouchers of almost 100 different kinds.

As well as prizes and presents, **vouchers** are also widely used as incentives, whether given by a firm to its employees or a manufacturer to potential customers. The latter is the familiar '10p off coupon' found in magazines. The theory is that one buys the product at the stated reduced price and returns to buy it again at the normal retail price. The principle is that of a bait to a fish: you're 'hooked'!

## LUNCHEON VOUCHERS

The most widely used voucher of all, however, is probably the Luncheon Voucher (LV). LVs were introduced in 1955 and were soon adopted by employers to give as a 'perk' to their employees. they have the added advantage (to the employer) of being exempt from National Insurance. Today LVs involve a turnover of £62 million a year, and can be used in 30 000 restaurants, wine bars, pubs, cafés, bistros, supermarkets and the like.

Luncheon Vouchers Ltd, who organize LVs, are now branching out into other types of vouchers, such as child care vouchers (used by working parents to pay a childminder) and elderly care vouchers (for company employees who have to look after elderly relatives).

No doubt when Britain enters the full European Common Market in 1992 it will be possible to use European vouchers to obtain goods or services anywhere in the EEC.

## FREEBIES

The term 'cashless society' tends to reinforce the popular notion that *everything* we get or need can only be obtained either by paying direct for it or by using one of the many substitute 'cashless' methods mentioned. In other words, that 'everything has its price', or that one cannot get 'something for nothing'.

But one can, of course, and it is possible to obtain many things quite free, without the use of money or its substitute at all.

Cynics say that the only free material thing one can get is air to breathe. (Perhaps they have misunderstood the phrase 'free as air'!) Realists know, however, that there is some truth in the old saying 'The best things in life are free'.

The best things in life that are truly free are not material or tangible at all. They involve abstract qualities such as love, loyalty, friendship and peace of mind. They have the greatest value of all, but it is not one which can be expressed in terms of money.

# BIBLIOGRAPHY

Button, Henry and Lampert, Andrew, *The Guinness Book of the Business World*, Guinness Superlatives, Enfield, 1976

Chamberlain, C. C., *The World of Coins: A Dictionary of Numismatics*, revised by Arthur Blair, Hodder & Stoughton, London, 1976

Cribb, Joe, ed, *Money: from Cowrie Shells to Credit Cards*, British Museum Publications, London, 1986

Cribb, Joe, Cook, Barrie and Carradice, Ian. *The Coin Atlas: The world of coinage from its origins to the present day*, Macdonald, London, 1990

Crowther, Geoffrey, *An Outline of Money*, Nelson, London & Edinburgh, rev ed, 1948

Fengler, Heinz, Gierow, Gerhard and Unger, Willy, *Lexikon der Numismatik*, Transpress, Berlin, 3rd rev and enl ed, 1982

Hewitt, V. H. and Keyworth, J. M., *As Good as Gold: 300 Years of British Bank Note Design*, British Museum Publications in association with the Bank of England, London, 1987

Junge, Ewald, *World Coin Encyclopedia*, Barrie & Jenkins, London, 1984

Packard, Vance, *The Ultra Rich*, Little, Brown, Boston, 1989

Pennant-Rea, Rupert and Emmott, Bill, *The Pocket Economist*, Basil Blackwell/The Economist, 1983

Room, Adrian, *Dictionary of Coin Names*, Routledge & Kegan Paul, London, 1987

Sampson, Anthony, *The Midas Touch*, Hodder & Stoughton/BBC Books, London, 1989

Walter, Ingo, *Secret Money: The Shadowy World of Tax Evasion, Capital Flight and Fraud*, Unwin Hyman, London, 2nd ed, 1989

# INDEX